THE MEANING AND ROLE OF ORGANIZATIONAL ADVOCACY

Responsibility and
Accountability in the Workplace

Jane Galloway Seiling

QUORUM BOOKS
Westport, Connecticut • London

Library of Congress Cataloging-in-Publication Data

Seiling, Jane Galloway, 1940–
    The meaning and role of organizational advocacy : responsibility and accountability in
    the workplace / Jane Galloway Seiling.
        p.   cm.
        Includes index.
        ISBN 1–56720–371–X (alk. paper)
        1. Communication in organizations. 2. Interpersonal communication. 3. Responsibility.
    4. Leadership. I. Title.
    HD30.3.S453   2001
    658.4′092—dc21   00–062774

British Library Cataloguing in Publication Data is available.

Library of Congress Catalog Card Number: 00–062774
ISBN: 1–56720–371–X

First published in 2001

Quorum Books, 88 Post Road West, Westport, CT 06881
An imprint of Greenwood Publishing Group, Inc.
www.quorumbooks.com

Printed in the United States of America

The paper used in this book complies with the
Permanent Paper Standard issued by the National
Information Standards Organization (Z39.48–1984).

10   9   8   7   6   5   4   3   2   1

To Irene Dibert Galloway
Whose wisdom, love, courage, and unfaltering faith
have guided so many.

To William Walter Seiling
A person who loves and understands more
than one can reasonably expect.

Contents

Preface

This book was written by one who is an advocate for the advocates located *everywhere* in our organizations. It is written for formal and informal leaders, the academy, and the students of organization management, those aspiring to be members and those who are already members who seek to make meaningful contributions to the achievements of their organizations—wherever they are located in the black and white spaces of the organizational chart. *Organizational advocacy®* calls for an emphasis on a segment of participation that has not been seen as important enough to emphasize in the past.

This book is a contribution to the growing number of voices inviting the understanding that leadership is everyone's role, that personal responsibility is a choice that decides the amount of effort put into our work, and that constructive accountability matters at every level of our companies. To discount even one person as not being important to accomplishment both now and in the future is to lessen future potential for not only that person but for the group and organization. To discount energy, ideas, and potential innovation of individuals or whole groups is a *promise* of lowered organizational performance, causing potential disaster. People want to contribute and they want to do meaningful work in organizations they can be proud of. They want to learn and serve in places where they can be advocates for themselves, their groups, and their organizations.

Organizational advocacy calls for recognition that responsibility and accountability as well as leadership at the personal level are where organizational effectiveness becomes real. Some will struggle with being open to advocacy as part of organizational "reality." It is, after all, raising the bar for verbal and task performance for all organizational members. What was in the past noted as extra-role behavior becomes part of normal ways to work. For the few, there will be a recognition that their advocacy activities started long ago and they only have to recognize their activities as organizational advocacy in action.

Decades ago, Gibb (1978) noted that persons and organizations seem to do best when members

1. Are trusted;
2. Have confidence in their own capacities to make choices, solve problems, perform tasks;
3. Have freedom to succeed or fail;
4. Are *with* others in deeply significant ways; and
5. See each other as resources, friends, allies—rather than as enemies, competitors, threats. (p. 65, italics orig.)

Gibb's list suggests being involved in the design of the organization, interdependence, and community building. He says, "With you, I co-author our shared experiences. None of us exists by and to ourselves" (p. 132). It is courageous to every day purposely work as a "co-author" in an organization that is not inviting coauthorship; one that does not honor the efforts and contributions of those beyond the top group. It takes courage under these circumstances to continue to act and work with integrity.

Of course, to expect to do so all the time, even in the best of companies, is expecting perfection—the unachievable. There will be *many* failures and many tests. As I saw on the wall of a hotel outside of Raleigh, North Carolina, "There are refining moments in life when we are faced with giving up or going on." Forgiving ourselves and others for lapses in integrity often are defining moments, requiring the courage of recognition of our current state and the determination to "be" and "do," (as noted in Chapter 5) in ways that contribute to coconstructing a better place to work in the future.

We all know that the workplace is calling for new approaches, even new definitions of participation, contribution, obedience, and loyalty. So far these redefinitions have not been made in definitive ways. I invite you to consider the following definitions of how meaningful participation and contribution happens. People who behave in these ways are described as organizational advocates, and their tactics contribute to the welfare of the organization— and themselves. Organizational advocacy enhances opportunities to do well on the job for themselves, those they work with, and their organization. Their efforts, as described, include verbal and task performance contributions in ways that are meaningful to personal and organizational accomplishment.

ADVOCACY ISSUES IN THE WORKPLACE

Organizational Advocacy

Organizational advocacy is the spontaneous, value-added activities of workplace members that are significant to expanded achievement and furthering the well-being of themselves, their comembers, and the collective workplace community.

Advocacy participation influences the performance and achievement of the organization and the accomplishments of the contributing individual and his or her group. Being willingly responsible and accountable for one's own workplace performance is significant to performing as an organizational advocate. Organizational advocacy includes the following issues.

Self Advocacy: Actions of workplace members who appropriately promote themselves and their comembers as capable, productive members of the group and organization.

Leader Advocacy: Member actions and activities that promote organizational leaders as competent, desirable leaders whose actions are beneficial to organizational achievement. Leader advocates also encourage and support the learning of those leaders who have much to learn about leading.

Member Advocacy: Leader actions that promote individual and group members to others as beneficial performers, leading to expanded opportunities to contribute to organizational achievement.

Customer Advocacy: Member actions of positively representing the company to the customer and the customer to the company. These actions are linked to performance with both internal and external customers.

Community Advocacy: Includes member actions that promote the existence of an inclusive, integrative, and flexible internal workplace community while encouraging their organization to respond to the needs of the outside community.

Inclusion Advocacy: The responsibility and accountability of the individual, whatever his or her role, and the organization in the quest to include and respect the worldviews of all members in the expansion of individual and organizational potential.

BIBLIOGRAPHY

Gibb, Jack R. (1978). *Trust: A New View of Personal and Organizational Development*. Los Angeles, Calif.: The Guild of Tutors Press.

Acknowledgments

As with all work, one cannot put one's beliefs on paper without the help and support of others. The list could be lengthy, but I want to especially recognize my husband, Bill Seiling, for his patience and his willingness to bring home dinner and be out of the way when the thinking and doing was happening. To my children, Terri, Michael, and Stacy, and my grandchildren, Maggie, Sam, and Tucker, who thought it would never get to "done," I promise to take my life back and share it with you again.

Marge Schiller, as my coauthor for Chapter 10, contributed greatly while so very busy with her own work. *Thank you*. It was more than I should have asked for at this busy time. It is a *big* debt I owe you.

Patrecia West became a friend and colleague during the writing. She is a dedicated and fascinating person regarding diversity, inclusion, and professional development. May our long conversations continue.

There is also special recognition for the people who encouraged me. My sisters—Janet McCormick (my twin who is always there when I need her), Jackie Muter, and Kay Boley—and my friend and mother, Irene Galloway. Her wisdom continues to guide and surprise us. Penny Groscost's calls, Leatra Harper's e-mails, and Sheila McNamee's conversations were what kept me going. Amy Mullen gets special notice. As my closest friend and advocate, she has been wondering if this would ever get done and we can have a real conversation again. It is out, Aim, let's have lunch.

Finally, Eric Valentine, my publisher at Quorum Books, has been more than patient. Toward the end, his e-mails were asking "Is it in the mail yet?" and justifiably so. His tolerance has been much appreciated and far beyond the call of duty.

1

Introduction

Each of us "decides" how successful we will be on the job (and off the job). We do it every day by what we think, say, and do—and what we appreciate. Ultimately, the smallest actions of individuals and the people they work well with decide, even design, the success of their organizations. One thing done really well or differently by one or several people can determine a company's future opportunities.

This book is meant to "start rumors," to increase awareness of how each of us as contributors determines what can and what cannot be accomplished in our organizations. Each of us determines the amount of energy that we will commit to doing our jobs. Whatever our role, we each are accountable for our own level of achievement, as well as that of our organizations. For this reason, the following is offered as the premise of personal responsibility and accountability in this book:

> What we do, how we act;
> what we praise and what we ridicule;
> what we see as consequential and what we see as inconsequential;
> what we appreciate and what we do not appreciate; and how
> we support the appropriateness of the actions of our
> comembers and our collective organization
> demonstrate our message of encouragement or our "wish" for failure
> of our comembers, customers, and our organization.

No one, one would say, wishes failure on our comembers, customers, and organization. After all, our jobs and our security, our opportunities and our well-being, would be in jeopardy if people acted on these wishes. And yet every day we work with people who appear to be ungrateful and uncaring, frustrated and angry, even deceitful and unethical. The suggestion that they are "wishing for failure" is scary. It also seems strange that we are asking the question, Could it be that, according to the premise, we are each responsible and accountable for how we work and that there are potential consequences beyond the moment if we are not putting energy into doing our work well?

There are contributors in the workplace who "demonstrate messages of encouragement." These are the ones, whatever their roles in their organizations, who want to be considered thinking adults rather than dependent children. They want to be involved in assuring that they are working hard at the right things. They know that working hard for activity's sake alone is no longer a virtuous, achieving activity. These contributors actively take a stance to make things happen. When blocked, they also express their concern and discontent. These actions may at times make them appear disrespectful to each other and to their supervisors. Are they being disrespectful when they are advocates for accomplishment by saying what may be controversial and what needs to be said, appropriately, and doing what needs to be done—even causing conflict? The scholars and new leaders are regularly saying that "conflict is good," but do they really mean it? It doesn't appear so on the job.

The internal environments of our organizations are beginning to reflect the desire of workplace members to be more involved. And yet there are still barriers to it happening. Could it be the people requesting more involvement are also putting up barriers for their own expanded involvement?

Many members are no longer feeling "captive" in their jobs. For various reasons, they sense there will be another, better job—and in some cases, rightly so. For some, if or when they choose to leave for another organization, the knowledge that walks out the door with them may be irreplaceable. For the same various reasons, when they are unhappy, they are more likely than in the past to watch for other opportunities.

Like it or not, the American workday and workweek have gotten longer instead of shorter—far different than a European country that reduced the working week to thirty-five hours, with annual vacation time in amounts Americans only dream of. Adding to the frustration, there are fewer people doing the work. The increased expectations of customers, who are now global in many cases, have also impacted the internal environments of our organizations. Whatever the reason, uncertainty and unpredictability in the workplace has increased concern about the future at all levels. There is a heightened necessity for leaders to listen to those previously ignored and expected to do what they were told. There is a stronger need than ever to listen to all the voices that care about the growth, durability, and long-term survivability of our organizations.

This book is not about anger and frustration. It is about how each person, in every job, every day, consciously or unconsciously contributes to the growth, stagnation, or demise of his or her organization. It is about personal responsibility and the role each person has in contributing to the success of the organization. It is also about the organization's role in making it possible for each person to choose to be responsible and accountable. It is about our own and our organization's role—wherever we work in our organization—in the causes for discontent and unconstructive disruption. It is about a new, more workable workplace. As noted by Jan Krieger, a communications specialist in a midwestern manufacturing company, "In order to create a new, more successful organization each one of us has to be in charge of making it happen. Each person must nurture, be part of, and actively 'construct' instead of 'obstruct' a new way to work together."

Some would say this is a futile effort, that the workplace will always be a two-way street of abusive behaviors, that "best practices"—or at least the most prevalent practices—will always include managers and supervisors who command and control and employees who respond accordingly. Yet many known and unknown organizations, small and large, are striving to prove this assumption wrong.

ASSIGNING A MEANINGFUL MEANING

It is the goal of this book to assign a meaningful definition and to encourage meaning-making for the term "organizational advocacy." The definition used will be as follows: Spontaneous value-added activities of workplace members that are significant to expanded achievement and furthering the well-being of themselves, their comembers, and the collective workplace community. It is said that a new term cannot be so new that it cannot be understood. Yet a new term does require a "border," a meaning, so it can be separated from other terms, such as, in this case, "corporate advocacy" (Albert 1998, 5).

The term "meaning-making" goes deeper than a definition. Meaning-making is evolutionary; it takes time to decide what a meaningful meaning really is—and then it continues to change. In the past meaning-making in organizations was solely the role of leaders. In doing so, they set the sails of the organization in a direction. Then they kept their eyes on it, because there were times when the wind would turn in an unintended direction. And then they would bring it back or make adjustments when the new direction appeared to be rewarding. Now, since organizations are recently understood to be dynamic instead of mechanistic, meaning-making falls to everyone. Members are continuously sense-making about what is or what could be. Each person, whatever his or her role, is involved in seeing whether the sail for the organization is set to take the organization where it needs to go. It may be that there is only one person willing to ask the fool's hard questions that call everyone else to the need to change direction. This person is the organizational advocate and change agent of the moment, the one who chooses in some small or large way to be personally responsible and accountable for organizational achievement. As meaning-makers, advocates are coconstructing with others the organization's reality, something that is impossible to do alone. As noted by Edgar Schein (1980, p. 251), "Good leadership and good membership . . . blend into each other in an effective organization. It is just as much the task of a member to help the group reach its goals as it is the task of the formal leader."

Why Should Organization Leaders Be Interested in Organizational Advocacy?

Leaders are beginning to understand that (1) each person makes choices about how contributive and involved he or she will be; (2) individual choices make a difference in the success of the organization; (3) what members think, say, and do signals their choices; (4) actions and attitudes chosen by individuals are often contagious, eventually being reflected in the actions and attitudes of others; and (5) it is more vital than ever that leaders lead in inclusive ways, yet it is the role of everyone to make a company successful. Otherwise, why are they there? Productivity is enhanced, even magnified, when an individual makes a choice to be highly committed and contributive and works well with their group. With these realizations come reasons for organizational advocacy to become part of the language and actions of the workplace community. These reasons include the following:

1. Organizations are now realizing that encouraging both personal power and shared power can be very effective. We are living and working in a "both–and" world. Individualism has in the past typically been thought to insinuate competitiveness or strong self-interest. It is now seen that valuing the contributions of both individuals and the teams and groups they work in or belong to is important. The individual is expected to cooperate and collaborate with those worked with and learned from. Our customers benefit from this new way to work because they have opportunities to become part of this process also—and to show their appreciation of what they are experiencing by becoming advocates for the company and the people they appreciate.

2. New sets of skills are needed more and more to locate, organize, and retain or change information. Members not previously exposed to routinely working with others now need to do so. The casual use of technology is part of this process. Achievement of goals and new competencies make it possible to personally and organizationally evolve and expand learning and serving opportunities. Group and one-on-one interaction is essential to getting the best results.

3. The issue of retention is addressed through organizational advocacy. Mimi Wallace, president of FasTrak Personnel in Washington, D.C., is very concerned about the retention rate in the Washington, D.C., region: "The cost per hire here averages $8,500 and the regional retention rate is 18%. Technical people are moving every 18–24

months because of the surge in the telecommunications industry and the willingness to pay high wages," says Wallace. With all the hype that Generation X is looking for a more balanced life and places to work where it is great to work, companies are looking for ways to more fully incorporate them and their knowledge into the workplace making retention more possible. This means working hard to change some of the old ways of working together. Organizations are seeking to be more inclusive—creating a place where people want to stay.

4. As human beings and members of organizations we make choices about what our "total behavior" means to ourselves and others. This text suggests that personal responsibility and distributed, constructive accountability are part of being effective. William Glasser (1984) says, *"I have almost complete ability to change what I do, and some ability to change what I think, regardless of how I am choosing to feel"* (p. 51; italics orig.). This statement places accountability for our actions on ourselves. This will be difficult for some to accept. This premise is not difficult for people who desire to contribute their best. Organizational advocates are more likely to reflect the total behavior of top performance.

5. The reputations of our companies are vitally important to the opportunity to grow and profit. Whether the information is fact or fiction, companies thrive or die on what their reputations are saying about them. Reputation is an outcome of the actions of the company regarding its products, treatment of its people, its service delivery, its commitment to the external community (including the company's choices around social responsibility), and the list goes on. Organizational advocacy, when practiced by members who value their work and their company, can serve as early warning systems regarding potential missteps in these areas. A good organizational reputation:

   • Is easy to destroy and tough to restore

   • Separates high performing organizations from others (differentiation)

   • Reinforces member pride in his or her work

   • Attracts high performing personnel and contributes to retention

   • Supports customer reasoning for using products and services

   • Encourages customers to try new products

   • Enhances growth and profitability

   • Is essential to gain involvement of financial markets

   • Contributes to gaining the support of the surrounding community

   • Supports retention of customers during difficult times

6. Finally, and most significantly, the most important reason organizations focus on organizational advocacy issues is that to do so will provide the most powerful advantages an organization can and must have, now and in the future. Every mind is encouraged to contribute to the fullest; every available energy used, whether human or technological; every process is as effective and efficient as possible; and every customer experiences differentiating service to their own advantage. It is beneficial when each person knows these advantages are real and he or she is willing to take part in making his or her company beneficially different from all the others that appear to be the same.

Are Actions of Organizational Advocacy New to the Workplace?

Organizational advocacy has always been present but has not been emphasized—perhaps even recognized. As members of organizations, our obligation has always been to contribute to the welfare of our organizations—and to do so willingly and voluntarily. Examination of the term looks at the level of physical effort (actions), the psychological involvement (outlook) of the person, and the emotional involvement (feelings) that contribute to efforts of advocacy participation in the workplace.[1] Van Dyne, Graham, and Dienesch (1994, 783) identified advocacy participation, along with loyalty, functional participation, and social participation, as part of "organizational citizenship behavior."

Organizational citizenship behavior (OCB)—willingly doing more than is required—is more likely to occur when people are emotionally connected to their organization and when organizational support is perceived to be present. When one feels supported, fairly treated, and "connected" with those one is working with, whatever their role, there is an impact on workplace relationships. Morrison and Phelps (1999) noted that research on OCB "has concentrated almost enrirely on what Organ (1988: 6) referred to as modest, some would even say trivial, behaviors that sustain status quo" (p. 403). When positive advocacy actions and behavior are occasional and noticeable because of being out of the norm for that person, one would agree to label it organizational citizenship behavior. When it becomes the norm of the performer—and many others—it raises the bar of performance, becoming "advocacy participation." Advocacy participation is seen as including innovation, maintaining high standards, challenging (questioning), and making suggestions for change. It includes a willingness to be controversial, often including the "behaviors typical of an internal change agent" (Van Dyne, Graham, and Dienesch 1994, 780–783). Morrison and Phelps refer to this type of behavior as "taking charge: voluntary and constructive efforts, by individual employees to effect organizationally functional change with respect to how work is executed within the contexts of their jobs, work units, or organizations" (p. 408). My choice of terminology is "advocacy participation" in an effort to emphasize that it is an ongoing spontaneous activity of contribution and advocacy, not an occasional effort to take charge.

Whether consciously choosing to be or not, members are advocates for (or against) their organization both on and off the job. Each organizational member is their organization's representative. As such, each one is individually responsible—even accountable—for what he or she thinks, says, and does—as well as what he or she is seen as appreciating or not appreciating about the organization.

- What we *think* is framed by our interpretations of what we pay attention to.
- What we *say* (and the words we use to say it) symbolizes our thoughts and intentions.
- What we *do* suggests the outcomes we desire.

- What we value is known by what we *appreciate.*

These positive or negative organizational advocacy activities are understood by others through their perceptions of what is observed and experienced. These actions impact, even mold, how employees, customers, and observers experience and perceive the organization. (It is not what happens, it is how it is interpreted.)

Organizational advocacy activities "design" positive contributions to organizational success. Besides being verbal, they include actions and activities that are significant to representing the meaning of the word "advocacy" (an act of pleading for, supporting, and recommending) and that "inquiry" is included as part of advocacy. Peter Senge (1990) and Chris Argyris (1985) note there must be a balancing of inquiry and advocacy, suggesting that "pure advocacy" (inflexible, challenging behavior) does not include inquiry. Senge states, "The most productive learning usually occurs when managers combine skills in advocacy and inquiry," and "When operating in pure advocacy, the goal is to win the argument. When inquiry and advocacy are combined, the goal is no longer 'to win the argument' but to 'find the best argument,' making it possible to together reach the best outcome" (p. 199).

This text also recognizes inquiry as a central part of the advocacy exchange, that effective advocacy participation is inquiry centered—agreeing that advocacy is only effective when inquiry is naturally incorporated into it. Weick (1995, 136) says that the way to enhance the quality of information is to challenge the information of others, and, "we should see orderly interaction around *arguing*" (p. 143, italics orig.). Hot debates that are carried on just for the sake of debating (shutting down the exchange) are not appropriate to advocacy participation. This suggests that the word "participation" is significant to the term being used for activities of spontaneous advocacy. In a truly participative environment, people, as they participate daily in the design and construction of their organizations, have the opportunity to offer opinions, express concerns, demonstrate beliefs, and take action when action is called for within their realms of accountability (whatever their roles are in the organization) and includes opportunities to offer impressions and suggestion inside and outside their realm of accountability, even to improvise in conversations about future organizationwide possibilities. Unfortunately, it is not always going to be easy and it is not always going to be pretty.

What Does Organizational Advocacy Look Like?

In an organization that provides a "holding environment" that invites or even seeks member involvement in deeper participation, high-level advocacy can happen. It would include the following:

People put contributions of energy and investment of their knowledge into what they believe deserves their attention. An organizational advocate takes a constructive, contributive, learning stance and stands up for (or against) something perceived as beneficial (or not beneficial) to organizational accomplishment. The work gets done. When someone feels strongly about something and does not take action, one questions that person's position. One's high energy, commitment, and partnering relationships make advocacy activities possible—even probable.

Those who feel strongly about a position may make strong statements and use challenging questions, seeking explanations for what is or is not happening. They want justification for the way things are or reasons why it cannot be another way. They attempt to influence others toward a way of thinking. The organizational advocate is open to examining his or her own thinking and to consideration of the thoughts of others in order to reach the best, most productive outcome. Positive organizational advocacy activities occur constantly, both on and off the job.

Organizational advocates seek support for and invite others to participate in whatever they are promoting. Harsh, divisive status and departmental lines on the organizational chart are barriers to advocacy. These lines make it difficult to directly share ideas, thoughts, or concerns. The advocate, when he or she is truly seeking support, also seeks to have the opportunity and the ability to influence others without regard for status and title. Leadership support promotes the belief that they will be heard and values their participation in open discussion.

Organizational advocacy indicates a willingness to consider the purpose behind what is being discussed and to communicate thoughts and interpretations of that purpose. The combination of consideration and advocacy participation indicates that standards of silence are not beneficial to the advocate or to others who need to be learned from to spread knowledge and skills.

Reaching an understanding of new concepts may require the use of new language and actions to make sense of what is being advocated. Confusion happens when new approaches and activities are introduced. This requires patience and repetition in ways understandable to learners.

The organizational advocate is open to learning from others and contributing to the learning of others. An organization where active advocacy happens provides an environment where spontaneous learning occurs on a regular basis. Informal exchanges of ideas create opportunities for growth of all individuals and groups, and the organization as a whole. Asking questions and giving explanations provides opportunities to promote ideas and consider the opinions of others. The advocate's hope is to participate as a partner with others in forming and framing new ideas and actions; to be an agent for change and profitability. The organizational advocate wants to make a difference in what is going on around him or her.

Organizational advocates want to be part of good interpersonal relationships, which make it possible to work with others in contributing to the welfare of the organizational group as well as to the welfare of the individual and the company. Effective short-term and long-term partnerships are the outcome of an informal environment of effective exchange.

Advocacy happens only where there is an opportunity to exercise free will to perform as an advocate. The choice to be an advocate cannot be mandated. Advocacy occurs when trust and respect are valued and exchanged. People guard the dignity of others while addressing issues of concern in an environment where advocacy participation flourishes.

Advocates speak and act with authenticity and acceptance. They openly express in inclusive ways a viewpoint, cause, or learning. They listen, soak in, and consider the acceptance and adaptation of the views and ideas of others. Their authenticity is observable. Their actions verify what is being said as believable, whatever the status or title of the organizational advocate. Eventually a decision to accept or reject what is being advocated is made by all involved.

An advocate is identified as a committed organizational learner. And there are times when a change agent of the moment is the role most needed. There will be occasions and circumstances when it is uncomfortable, even very uncomfortable. These incidents, hopefully, will provide learning opportunities to participate in the direction or redirection of whatever is under consideration.

The actions of the organizational advocate include the following:

- A free will, a choice, to be an organizational advocate.
- Contributions of physical energy and investment of their knowledge toward the work/product/issue being promoted—when they believe in it.
- Strong statements and challenging questions to find reasons for something that may appear questionable to the advocate—while remaining flexible and responsive to the input of others.
- Seeking and providing support for what or who is being promoted.
- A willingness to consider the purpose behind whatever is being offered.
- The use of new language and actions to make sense of what is being advocated.
- Contributions to the learning of others while also being open to learning from others.
- Seeking and maintaining beneficial interpersonal relationships.
- Speaking and acting with authenticity and acceptance to a viewpoint, issue, or learning.
- Identifying the advocate as a committed organizational learner and agent for change in partnership with others.

It is all about communicating the benefits of contributing to the success of our organization and each other.

Is There a Need for a New Definition of "Obedience"?

Successful leaders encourage and train those around them to also be leaders. To do so, a new understanding of "constructive disobedience" is to be considered. In Western organizations, the work ethic of the past demanded full obedience, generally based on fear. Thus, the "organization man" of decades ago was blindly obedient. Many leaders prefer this same behavior today. Rules of obedience, as enforced in highly bureaucratic, controlling organizations, suggest feelings of fear based on the following:

- A fundamental threat of unemployment.
- A lowered sense of contribution.
- Feeling undervalued or devalued.
- The possibility of gaining a reputation for being a "troublemaker."
- Penalties for taking risks or disagreement.
- Threats to enrollment in groups.
- "Being seen as irrational" and in disagreement with those in charge.
- Having few opportunities for interesting work.

Acting from fear, according to Helena Flam (1993, 67), "causes a profound loss of self-respect." Yet people are forced to "play act" at work as if they are loyal and very connected to strong abusive cultures. The organization that does not make it possible to take risks, be innovative, seek unusual partnerships, make mistakes, and at times be constructively disobedient may be taken in by the play actions of enthusiastic, highly loyal, dependent obedience. Constructive disobedience is invaluable to an innovative, competent, and future-oriented organization. It is to ask questions, raise concerns, and make needs known; it is to be an advocate for change when it may not be called for; it is to step up to be a leader and change agent when one sees a need.

Constructive disobedience in the workplace includes (1) when the advocate disagrees with a decision or process he or she suggests or advocates for an alternative to be considered; (2) not being satisfied with the status quo (seeking new ways of doing things and new opportunities—to be innovative); (3) actively seeking and participating in new and unique partnerships that are beneficial to achievement (competence and relationships are the basis of accomplishment—without one, the other is diminished); and (4) being nonparticipative (if an ethical issue is involved, participation is out of the question). In a rigid, status quo organization, these activities may cause problems for advocates or for the people around them. In these organizations, it will be courageous to be an organizational advocate who occasionally practices constructive disobedience.

Can the Advocacy Issues Be Separated?

There are multiple advocacy issues in the workplace described in the following pages. One should be reminded that no activity in an organization can be separated from other activities. Organizations are systems of (1) competencies and accountabilities; (2) roles, rules, and relationships; (3) processes that are used to design, produce, and distribute products or services; and (4) advocacy participation activities that impact all three. These active systems ripple, react, and respond at both micro and macro levels. For this reason, it is impossible to separate one advocacy issue from multiple others. Every advocacy issue in Part II has a multiplier effect, intensifying its impact on other systemic activities.

What Is Coming

To introduce organizational advocacy and the practices of advocacy participation, this book looks at organizational advocacy and six components of organizational advocacy. The book is broken down into three parts. Part I (Chapters 2–4) introduces the concept of organizational advocacy and defines advocacy participation as it happens in the workplace.

Chapter 2, "What Is Organizational Advocacy," defines and describes the borders around organizational advocacy and its relationship to corporate advocacy. The actions of the advocate describe the activities of performance as an achieving advocate. It requires advocacy thinking.

Chapter 3, "How to Be an Organizational Advocate," describes a "positive holding environment," further describes advocacy participation, and looks at barriers to advocacy participation. The chapter also redefines responsibility and accountability and examines cynicism in the workplace.

Chapter 4 addresses questions, concerns, and barriers to organizational advocacy and advocacy participation and some of the implications and dilemmas that may become apparent while reading the chapters that follow.

Part II (Chapters 5–10) provides a chapter on each of the six advocacy issues in the workplace. Chapter 5, "Self Advocacy," validates the process of promoting yourself and those around you as capable, contributing members of the organization. Peggy Holman's (1999) model of *The Model of the World I Want to Live In* is translated to *The Model of the World I Want to Work In.* The Model discusses the connection that is essential between the individual and the workplace community.

Chapter 6, "Leader Advocacy," discusses activities of those members who add to or detract from the success of their leaders, themselves, and their group by what they think and say openly or covertly about their leaders. This chapter also includes messages for leaders about their role in making it possible for organizational advocacy to occur.

Chapter 7, "Member Advocacy," describes actions of leaders in promoting those they work with as effective, capable members of the group; these activities enhance individual and collective pride in organizational membership, and the willingness to put more energy into work performance. Member advocacy also notes that, when a union exists, it is the role of both leadership groups to work in partnership to make success possible in the long term—for both the organization and the union.

Chapter 8, "Customer Advocacy," emphasizes that all members are representatives of their organizations, both on and off the job. Current customers and potential customers "see" the organization through the eyes of the members they come in contact with. This chapter describes the role of the customer advocate—the position of being a representative of the customer to the company and of the company to the customer.

Chapter 9, "Community Advocacy," notes there are two "communities" to be concerned with in the workplace: the internal, workplace community, and the external, home community, which provides customers and the workforce for the organization.

Chapter 10, "Inclusion Advocacy," suggests that members who think, act, and appreciate different ideas and ways of working contribute to organizational achievement. The monumental social, demographic, and political changes that are taking place all around the world have brought into focus the need to utilize the full workforce in order to gain competitive and cooperative advantage. Organizational leaders are recognizing that this requires all members to contribute their best, calling for development of the full workforce, including previously unheard voices. The dawning of this new realization is bringing new opportunities and new learnings—and more profits. Inclusion is a part of the new workplace community.

Part III includes Chapter 11. The last chapter looks at movement toward recognizing the benefits of organizational advocacy and the need for organizational reinvention, with the ups and downs that inevitably occur. The three common desires of members inside organizations are discussed, emphasizing the role of all members in coconstructing the reinvention of the organization.

In carrying the message about organizational advocacy, this book (1) emphasizes the importance of personal responsibility and accountability at all levels, (2) looks at the organization's role in providing a workplace environment where extra-role or organizational citizenship behavior becomes the norm and people are willing to become organizational advocates, (3) emphasizes that everyone automatically influences the outcomes of their organizations and the existence or nonexistence of pride in the work and their organizations, and (4) brings into view the advocacy issues that already exist in our organizations.

QUESTIONS YOU MIGHT ASK YOURSELF

In an effort to guide the reader toward understanding and application of this concept, the author offers the following questions you might ask yourself in the following chapters while considering the implications of organizational advocacy. These questions are the basis for consideration of any initiative to be considered in our organizations:

1. Can the concepts be tied to the vision, mission, purpose, and goals of my organization? (Meaningfulness)
2. How many issues can the concept address in the workplace? (Usefulness)
3. Are the concepts of advocacy understandable and transferable? (Simplicity)

4. Does it enhance human coherence in the workplace? (Connection)
5. What is the potential of it bringing or nurturing change? (Impact)
6. Is the potential outcome worth the effort? (Worthwhileness)
7. Will these activities impact the bottom lines of my organization? (Achievement)
8. Can these concepts be sustained over time? (Sustainability)

NOTE

1. The author acknowledges the writings of Linn Van Dyne, Michigan State University, and her colleagues as supporting the process of thinking through the introduction of organizational advocacy in this book.

BIBLIOGRAPHY

Albert, Stuart. (1998). The Definition and Metadefinition of Identity. In *Identity in Organizations: Building Theory Through Conversations*, edited by David A. Whetten and Paul C. Godfrey. Thousand Oaks, Calif.: Sage.

Argyris, Chris. (1985). *Strategy, Change, and Defensive Routines*. Boston: Pitman.

Flam, Helena. (1993). Fear, Loyalty and Greedy Organizations. In *Emotion in Organizations*, edited by Stephen Fineman. Thousand Oaks, Calif.: Sage.

Glasser, William. (1984). *Control Theory: A New Explanation of How We Control Our Lives*. New York: Harper & Row.

Holman, Peggy. (1999). Unlocking the Mystery of Effective Large-Scale Change. In *At Work*, edited by Alise Valencia. San Francisco: Berrett-Koehler Communications.

Leonard, Bill. (2000). Employee Loyalty Continues to Wane. *HR Magazine* 45 (1): 21–22.

Morrison, Elizabeth Wolfe, and Corey C. Phelps. (1999). Taking Charge at Work: Extrarole Efforts to Initiate Workplace Change. *Academy of Management Journal* 42 (4): 403–419.

Organ, D. W. (1988). *Organizational Citizenship Behavior: The Good Soldier Syndrome*. Lexington, Mass.: Lexington Books.

Seiling, Jane. (1997). *The Membership Organization: Achieving Top Performance in the New Workplace Community*. Palo Alto, Calif.: Davies-Black.

Senge, Peter. (1990). *The Fifth Discipline: The Art and Practice of the Learning Organization*. New York: Doubleday.

Van Dyne, Linn, and Jeffrey A. LePine. (1998). Helping and Voice Extra-Role Behaviors: Evidence of Construct and Predictive Validity. *Academy of Management Journal* 41 (1): 108–119.

Weick, Karl E. (1995). *Sensemaking in Organizations*. Thousand Oaks, Calif.: Sage.

CONVERSATIONS AND INTERVIEWS

Jan Kreiger, communications specialist.
Mimi Wallace, FasTrack Personnel.

PART **I** ⎯⎯⎯⎯⎯⎯⎯⎯⎯⎯⎯⎯⎯⎯⎯⎯

INTRODUCING AND DEFINING ORGANIZATIONAL ADVOCACY

Change is not about understanding new things or having new ideas; it's about seeing old things with new eyes—from different perspectives. Change is not about reorganizing, reengineering, reinvesting, recapitalizing. It's about reconceiving! When you reconceive something—a thought, a situation, a corporation, a product—you create a whole new order.

Dee Hock, Founder and CEO Emeritus, Visa International

2

What Is Organizational Advocacy?

ORGANIZATIONAL ADVOCACY

Every day we react for things we see as beneficial and against those we see as not beneficial. We advocate in an attempt to adjust the world to fit our personal assumptions of what should and should not be taking place. At work, in order to reach personal and organizational goals, we try to influence how things should or should not be done. Both at home and at work we promote activities and behaviors we believe will make it easier to get along. When dealing with friends we agree to do things that are fun or pleasant and refuse to do things that we anticipate will be unpleasant or drudgery—or we go along reluctantly and look forward to it coming to an end. Life is a process of advocating what we do and do not want—all day, every day, in every moment.

When we perceive something as good or if something bothers us, it is human to relate it to the nearest person. This person may be someone whom we think needs to hear "the facts," someone we are recruiting for agreement and/ or action, or someone we want to influence to see the world as we see it. In all instances, whether it is done consciously or unconsciously, we are, through our words and actions, promoting our case and attempting to persuade to our viewpoint. This is advocacy in action.

"Telling it like it is" has always been an American trait for influencing others; we often use it in an attempt to bring people to see things our way. In some instances, bluntness, like a slap in the face, works. In others, subtle insinuations or suggestions are used to guide our "target" to a shared understanding of what we are advocating.

Influence, as with power, is without meaning in the absence of individuals making valuations, decisions, and comparisons. Through these actions we "see" the future, even imagine what the future might be. If we then decide we can influence the future, we are willing to make decisions, act on the decisions, and be accountable for the results. When we purposely do and say things to influence, we are an advocate for what is being promoted.

Organizational advocacy was introduced in the book *The Membership Organization: Achieving Top Performance Through the New Workplace Community* (Seiling 1997, 168) as an important element of the consultative (relationship) role of all organizational members. Advocacy is defined in *Webster's Dictionary* as an act of pleading for, supporting, or recommending. It is a natural activity for the human endeavor to intervene on behalf of ourselves and others. An attorney, someone representing others in a court of law, is an advocate. Everyone, every day, promotes people, products, organizations, and ideas to others, whether formally, as an assigned task (corporate advocacy), or spontaneously, during everyday activities and discussions (organizational advocacy).

In this text, organizational advocacy is defined as spontaneous value-added activities of workplace members that are significant to expanded achievement and furthering the well-being of themselves, their comembers, and the collective workplace community (see page 5). Performing as a workplace advocate suggests being a positive contributor—having the intent to improve a situation (LePine and Van Dyne 1998, 1). "Advocacy participation," a term introduced by Van Dyne, Graham, and Dienesch (1994, 783), suggests the actions of an organizational advocate go beyond the normally observed activities of workplace. Like extra-role behavior, it is positive and discretionary. It is not planned, it is a spontaneous personal choice. It is also not directly recognized by formal reward systems, nor is it something that usually results in punitive consequences (Van Dyne and LePine 1998, 108). These performers choose to make extra, unasked-for contributions. As noted by Van Dyne, Cummings, and McLean Parks (1995, 256), these behaviors include challenging/promotive behaviors that are constructive; there is an intent to improve, rather than to criticize.

Successful advocacy participation identifies the advocate as an agent for change in service to others, to their organization, and, directly or indirectly, to the customers being served. Organizational advocacy also promotes, even delivers, hope, even when hope is not recognized as necessary or possible. Advocacy participation influences and expands the performance and achievement of the individual, the workplace community, and the organization's role in the home (external) community.

An advocate is willing to communicate in ways that make it possible for others to hear what is being advocated. Interpersonal connection is vital to doing so. The willingness to be a change agent, to contribute to the creation of new visions by people who are not always willing to listen, is essential.

Advocacy participation is not always invited or encouraged by leaders or coworkers, and therefore advocacy participation can be risky. Rejection and degradation can occur. An advocate contributes meaningfully by having the courage to act when action is called for but not requested.

AN ATTEMPT TO REMOVE AMBIGUITY

Our workplaces are full of confusion, disconnection, and lack of energy. Gestures of advocacy participation around issues and beliefs are attempts to remove ambiguity and to still—or lessen—the chaos around us. Ambiguity occurs as a consequence of lack of clarity or detail, and/or inappropriate or confusing communication. Ambiguity is challenged and addressed by advocacy words and actions that seek to clarify.

Unintentional ambiguity or lack of attention occurs when an issue or activity is not emphasized. A supervisor discovers too late that he or she has not been clear about a report and the deadline looms. A full section of the vital report is missing; those who must redo the report will have to work the weekend. The supervisor should have been clearer the first time and those doing the report should have asked more questions. It takes both activities—an exchange—to get it done right the first time and on time.

Ambiguity is often accidental and unintentional. It includes (1) being misunderstood (understanding others can be nearly impossible), (2) words and conversations are in "another language" (the participants are hearing different meanings; how often do we hear an instruction and walk away like it is clear when we are still in confusion?), (3) intentional misunderstanding to avoid involvement, or (4) perceiving something as unimportant, resulting in lack of attention or a misunderstood time frame. The advocate always assumes ambiguity and clarifies, clarifies, clarifies.

We Are Our Organization

People are representatives of their organizations, both on and off the job. Each individual is their organization in the eyes of others. In 1992 David Drennan noted that, although the figures vary from year to year, company members are routinely shown to have the greatest impact on organizational favorability scores. An organization's advertising lifted the favorability score by +2, reading about the organization improved favorability by +5, seeing a company's name on buildings and vehicles brought a +7 increase, and using the products or experiencing service jumped the favorability to +12. The largest increase was +30, based on knowing someone who works or worked there who believed in the organization.

It matters that members act as positive representatives and ambassadors (advocates) of their workplace community, both on and off the job. Obviously, a company's best advertising is done by its own ambassadors, its own people. Therefore, organizations would be best to actively seek to create a workplace where members experience the desire to contribute to their company's welfare. This makes it possible for them to feel their contributions add value, encouraging them to influence the customers, both inside and outside the organization. Member pride is built by openly providing trustworthy information, making decisions based on that information, and providing the opportunity to influence others and their workplaces. Our sense of ownership and contribution expands through being entrusted with the opportunity to knowledgeably share and discuss valued information. The feeling we can influence the viewpoints of others is important; we want them to see our contributions as worthwhile.

Being "Scrutinized"

Companies are constantly under the scrutiny of outsiders as well as their own members. Insiders check with others whether this is the place they want to come to every day. They may do it consciously, but it is largely an unconscious evaluation. The comments of family, friends, customers, and strangers impact their own impressions of their company. Hearing a friend say, "Why do you work there anyway? I hear they treat you people awful," will force an instant mental evaluation. A customer stating, "This thing is junk," will focus the listener on the product as never before. The worker may ask themselves questions:

- Is this company/product/service something I can be proud of?
- Is it respected by others? If so, why? If not, why not?

Such scrutiny may result in further reflection. The progression is natural. Consciously or unconsciously, they ask themselves deeper questions:

- What is the "character" of my company?
- Does it treat everyone with dignity and respect or just the chosen few?
- What is the collective attitude of the leadership?
- Do I have a sense of security and stability here? Or, do I feel threatened?
- Does my organization focus on the welfare of its people and the customer?
- Do the leaders and the collective organization acknowledge and appreciate my efforts?
- Am I respected as part of this organization?
- Is this thing junk?

We are seen as representatives and agents of our companies on and off the job. "Agent pride" in the organization and its products or services gives out a message. The evaluation we go through whenever a comment is made calls for verification and an expression of agreement, disagreement, or a disclaimer.

Our response (or our lack of response) impacts the perceptions of the person who has expressed the opinion. What is said or done by the agent-representative matters to their own sense of identity to their organization.

Organizational Advocacy as an Influencing Tool

Advocacy participation requires a safe workplace environment. In a safe workplace environment members are able to comfortably make decisions, challenge the status quo, try new ideas, and feel good about their workplace community. A safe environment welcomes constructive input and supports the feeling that members can influence what is happening. Advocacy of known or different diverse alternatives (and people) adds to knowledge and wisdom while recognizing that there is no one way to "get it done" (if "done" is ever achievable). Essential to advocacy participation is an environment where members are open to listening, taking risks, being flexible, experimenting, and considering different viewpoints. In such an environment members acknowledge that approval and disapproval are both appropriate ways to provide and receive information. A caveat here: "Appropriate ways" means that attacking is not an effective approach and that exchanging information constructively requires respectful, honest, and open conversations connected to the situation while avoiding personal vendettas. Appropriateness does not suggest that constructive conflict is out of bounds; on the contrary, it adds to and requires input shared with conviction and energy while honoring the offered influence and information of others.

The knowledgeable, credible person discusses, examines, and challenges what is happening when he or she is in an open, flexible workplace community. He or she contributes to decisions, bringing more balance to the discussion and consideration of additional alternatives. Knowledge, skill, and attitude contribute to or detract from credibility. Knowledge is *what to*, skill is *how to*, and attitude is *why to* and *want to*. The person who is willing to participate in healthy, even potentially conflictive discussions of what could be (or not be) done supports the process of considering how to take action. He or she contributes to identifying decisions most beneficial to the organization, its members, and its customers or clients. Open participation, as a positive influencing gesture, encourages the consideration of people and community needs in decisioning, expanding reasoning beyond the immediate economic or financial impact on the organization.

ADVOCACY THINKING

An advocate sees the glass as half-full instead of half-empty. The advocate seeks reasons why to accept and reasons why to reject. He or she collaborates, cooperates, and looks for reasons something is contributive or disruptive. He or she reframes, innovates, and redesigns.

Although it seems that one ought not need to be reminded, responsible behavior includes authentic appreciative behavior. Appreciative behavior includes positive acknowledgment and advocacy of others; that is, sincere, respectful, and valuing of the dignity of others, having commitment to mutual accomplishment, and being vulnerable yet challenging in the right way. Appreciative behavior demonstrates positive beliefs that influence the behaviors and contributions of others. These are all behaviors of the responsible organizational advocate.

Influencing positively does not include enhancing controversy. Richard Carlson (1997) believes that "blaming thinking" has become common in our culture. They don't want a solution. "Could it be," asks Glen Shull, an organizational consultant in Findlay, Ohio, "executives and internal customers alike want to know whose throat to grab?" The outcome is adversarial instead of appreciative. This allows the participant to not be completely responsible for his or her own actions, problems, or happiness on a personal level. He or she may be responsible for "this" and not responsible for "that." In addition, it is a matter of degree: He or she may be highly responsible (do it really well) in doing a report he or she enjoys doing and not so responsible (a bit sloppy) for a report he or she dislikes doing.

Personal responsibility for doing something is removed when it is pushed away by blaming and shaming others. Lack of personal responsibility also makes it possible to be fully convinced of being a helpless, powerless victim rather than a powerful advocate. Unhappiness grows with feelings of helplessness and frustration, anger, depression, and stress. Helpless and hopeless people also are likely to choose not to take responsibility for their own reactions to what is occurring.

It is *their* fault. Carlson (1997) notes, "When something doesn't meet our expectations many of us operate with the assumption, 'When in doubt, it must be someone else's fault'" (p. 194). This is the basis for the "devil-made-me-do-it" syndrome. Helplessness encourages victims to choose to be negatively reactive rather than positively proactive. They refuse to hold themselves accountable for their own actions or lack of action. Through their reactions, they demonstrate negative advocacy participation. They consciously or unconsciously promote failure, distrust, and discontent. They can no longer impact what is happening in ways that matter. They, and others around them who join in their thinking, are stalling or stuck. Progress slows or stalls.

The people who take action in organizations often move ahead without the approval of the people around them or above them. Alan Frohman (1997, 42) studied 100 people who had been identified as "movers and shakers" in their companies. It was discovered that often people knew they were doing "something" but others didn't especially approve of it. After all, this group was changing things. The results of the study indicated the following:

1. People who brought about the changes were easily identified.

2. They were often not on the company's "high-potential" list.
3. They were directed by organization needs to go beyond their jobs.
4. Their learning focused on meeting the organization's needs.
5. They were driven internally to make a difference.
6. They were action oriented.
7. They focused on results more than teamwork.

Often these change agents are easily identified by their leaders. They know who they are and yet they don't make it easy for them because it "upsets things." As noted, these people are not always on the high-potential list. When they go ahead and do things out of the norm they stir things up. Their actions, although they seem to be driven by the desire to meet an identified organizational need, indicate a bent toward nonconformity. They want to make a difference, so they are not content with mediocrity when something can be improved and it positively impacts the financial bottom line or makes things easier. One of their inner needs is for their company to be better. They make waves, they are creative thinkers, and they are not afraid to behave and take action differently. Their comembers don't always like it. Advocates for change make things uncomfortable.

Effective members at all levels seek opportunities to take action in their areas of accountability, allowing them to anticipate success. They want to be provided with the tools and information to think through what needs to be decided or done. The desire to put energy into a task is thwarted or expanded by the availability of the knowledge and influence they need to perform, as well as the availability of resources to successfully do the task in question. Without these, members are more apt to dwell on the formidable aspects of the process or project, exert insufficient effort, and, as a result, be less than successful or fail.

Our thinking creates not only our emotions but also the actions that we take. If we are upset, we have upset ourselves. We are what we think. If we decide someone is incompetent, somehow we will discover something that proves that incompetence. If we markedly change what we pay attention to and how we frame it, we cannot avoid changing the thinking, feeling, and physiological components of what we do. If we force ourselves to act a certain way, the outcome is often new thinking.

Discouraged and disappointed people can choose to reframe their thinking by reexamining the event and evaluating what was done that was right, what was accomplished, and what was learned that could be beneficial. Discouraged thinking includes self-fulfilling prophesies; more disappointment and discouragement are likely to follow. Reframing our discouraged thinking to learning thinking promotes contributive action, part of advocacy participation. The individual makes the choice to reframe and reexamine—or do nothing.

Coconstruction

No matter what the task or responsibility you have in your organization, what is said, done, and appreciated (or not appreciated) contributes to the "design" of the organization. Every day, individuals act as architects and builders of the coconstructed organization. People at all levels actively participate as partners in this design process. Ongoing, recognized or unrecognized, positive or negative gestures of advocacy are the normal, everyday, spontaneous, and purposeful activities of the workplace participant. Everyone has the potential to participate as significant, difference-making, value-producing, choice-making members of his or her workplace community.

In 1978, Jack Gibb wrote, "With you, I co-author our shared experiences. None of us exists by and to ourselves" (p. 132). This statement is a calling for each of us to expand our connections and accountability to those around us. We affect them and our organization, every day.

The energy of each member, in large or small ways, every day, contributes to what the organization becomes. What individuals and the collective organization pay attention to, ignore, and legitimize or delegitimitize identifies where energy will be focused, where urgency and importance pushes for action to be taken. These actions identify and construct the workplace partnerships that will happen. It has been said, "We create ourselves by how we invest . . . energy. Memories, thoughts, and feelings are all shaped by how we invest this energy" (Csikszentmihalyi 1990, 33). The possibility of success for each of us is improved or diminished by the energies each applies and the way we focus our attention. We coconstruct the potential of our current and future organization.

Leaders in an inclusive, top-performance organization invite and include everyone in the process of growth and success. Leaders and change agents exist across the organization. Without everyone's purposeful yet spontaneous participation, growth will be limited.

Community Membership

Inclusion, participation, and connection are central to this new organizational philosophy. Workplace community implies an organization that is interconnected, productive, and beneficial. It is integrative and inclusive. People work well together because they are interdependent *and* autonomous. Together they create an atmosphere where members want to contribute with high levels of responsibility, activities of partnering, and collaboration. The goal is to impact the survival and growth of the members and the overall organization.

The Foundation for Community Encouragement in Seattle, Washington, defines "community" as "a safe atmosphere that enables us to transcend our protective identities and learn, through increased personal responsibility, risk, and communication, to create an environment where self-discovery and shared understanding can flourish" (personal communication). Ann A. Hoewing, an organizational consultant associated with the foundation, states, "A workplace community is any organization that is interested in designing an organization where it is possible to work together around the concepts of community to accomplish the goals and purpose of the organization." Both the individual and the collective organization are responsible for making this community environment possible. It also suggests images of belonging and pride, a place that is moral and respectful and that treats everyone as responsible agents of the organization and each person as a member instead of an employee.

The term "member" suggests voluntariness, a place where each person works by choice and is willing to work to the benefit of his or her comembers, customers, and the workplace community as well as himself or herself. As "volunteers," we serve others while we also learn from them:

- We are there because we believe in the purpose of the organization.
- We make positive choices about the amount of energy we will put into the endeavor.
- We appreciate the opportunity to serve.
- We are willing to make sacrifices so we can serve effectively.
- We seek a common bond.
- We offer skills and learn new skills.
- We learn from the experience of others.
- We are depended on—the work would not get done without us.
- We believe we can make a difference.
- We feel needed and valued.
- We have our own internal reward for the sacrifices made to serve our organization in meaningful ways.

People at all levels in a community- and membership-oriented organization are members. This use of language and meaning removes the divisiveness of the term "employee." Everyone—CEO, professional, secretary, executive, machine operator—is a member and is personally responsible and accountable for their own work and the success of their workplace community. But whether you call them members, shareholders, or associates, the point is that all participants, as responsible agents of their organization, feel and act like partners in contributing to and adding value to their company. And they do it to the best of their abilities.

The language of membership creates images that impact the perceptions and actions of people working in a "circle of inclusion." A circle of inclusion is an organizational structure where leaders have purposely blurred the lines of power and status (see Figure 2.1). The blurred boundaries of the leader circle spread effectively to the edge of the circle, inviting all members into leadership roles, as needed. Responsibility springs to and from the individual.

Figure 2.1
The Circle of Inclusion

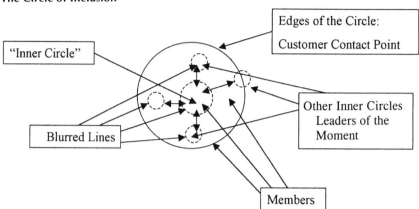

Accountability flows to the edges and is located with the persons doing the work. Everyone is accountable for organizational performance (this also means that rewards are equitably shared). The realization of community as an inclusive, membership-oriented organization

1. Is enhanced by intertwining partnerships that enrich the involvement of the individual and the whole group.
2. Is a never-ending initiative and is sustained by an ever-expanding commitment of effort, resources, and the achievement of personal, group, and workplace community goals.
3. Requires an individual and collective sense of urgency, investment of energy, and commitment of time, and an expanding voluntary enrollment in the purpose and vision of the organization.
4. Involves matching and meshing individual and collective values that "fit," while sustaining beneficial differences in ways of thinking and contributing.
5. Includes physical energy, emotional determination, and self-alignment of mutually understood values, resulting in a collective energy.

Self-management, self-accountability, and involvement in the achievement of organizational goals is initiated by the desire (attitude) of the participant to contribute to the greater good of the larger group, and knowing that individual contribution includes the role of the organizational advocate.

Reflections on Connection

Working together is not easy. The inclusive, respect-filled organization that is working well is not a utopia. It requires hard work that is dependent on positive attitudes and contributive performance of all members of the community. In the home (external) community, connection is enhanced by sidewalks, porches, and houses with adjoining yards. In the workplace community, connection is sustained through interaction in corridors, meetingplaces, clusters of offices, and spontaneity that comes from caring about your work. These connections make it possible for people to talk, discuss, relax, constructively argue, and build comradery. There is a buzz of voices and energy—and laughter while the work gets done. An organization where doors are kept tightly closed to the hallways is in all probability not a connected community.

An atmosphere of naturalness, openness, and connection encouraging workplace interaction makes it possible to create meaningful partnerships that are usual and unusual. To accomplish this, there is a willingness to respect others, share information, challenge assumptions, and learn from one's own experiences and the experiences of others. Other regarding and service-offering activities focus on known and understood coconstructed goals.

Learning and serving relationships require constant vigilance in negotiating how to work in successful partnerships. Opportunities are created to negotiate how to manage and develop shared tasks, roles, and understanding. These negotiations occur as an extension of the organization's recognition of the need to nurture an atmosphere where partnerships have an opportunity to work well. It is the function of organizations and institutions to diligently provide a holding environment or culture that feels safe and valuing. Members at all levels participate in the creation of these qualities through the design and negotiation of a coconstructed culture. The underlying values, characteristics, or assumptions about the organization reflect the outcome of those negotiations over time.

It is through the coconstruction of this holding environment that anxieties are minimized. A more casual atmosphere occurs where development, informality, comfort, and real, meaningful work are possible. Briefly, this membership organization (an organization where people want to be)

- Requires all to think and do, both independently and together.
- Is open and relational.
- Recognizes that difference, diversity, and sameness add to accomplishment.
- Utilizes connected, empowered partnerships across the circle.
- Will include constructive conflict across blurred lines of status, title, and departments.
- Addresses issues of control and power.
- May take more time while achieving better decisions.
- Adds to and detracts from leadership activities.
- Increases personal responsibility and accountability.
- Diversifies the locations of decisioning activities.

Now more than ever, members desire to work where they can feel valued and respected by those around them. Although we may be capable of surviving in the most repressed of circumstances, we no longer think we must do so.

This sensemaking brings us to reflect on and evaluate the organizations and situations we go to every day. In doing so, some see a place that is threatening and stressful, a place where learning is limited and the desire to risk vulnerability by partnering with and serving others is anticipated as potentially dangerous. Being responsible is not encouraged here. Accountability is a "find and punish" excuse-generating activity. People "withdraw from active participation in operations and workplace relationships by physically and emotionally distancing themselves" (Alcorn and Diamond 1997, 34).

ADVOCACY LEARNING AND SERVING

If the history of our work environment has been command and control, the transition to being a learning and serving member and organization will not be easy. Learning and serving is an outcome of experiencing fair treatment, pleasant partnerships, and comfortable, enlivening exchanges. We have learned well how to work in a telling, blaming and shaming, punishment, and do-as-I-say-not-what-I-do work environment. The involvement of everyone requires creating new conditions of being and ways of doing that are facilitated by credible, energetic, and determined formal and informal leaders throughout the organization. (Needless to say, if there is a union, it must be a central part of an organizational transition.)

Learning

An intentional organizational message of a learning philosophy is be developed and delivered (see Appendix A for an example). The message is this: Learning at the individual level is the foundation of organizational capability, and each individual is responsible for activating and sustaining their own employability. For this reason, the definition of organizational learning used here is as follows: integrated, ongoing learning processes at the individual, group, and organizational level that support the coconstruction of a successful organization. Ideally, the leader group is committed to a holding environment that promotes learning, purposely taking this message of expectation to all members, providing them with opportunities for continuous updating of skills. It is an invigorating, lively climate for learning.

Individual

Learning is not always intentional; an individual often is not aware of its occurrence. Monika Aring and Betsy Brand define informal workplace learning as learning in which the learning process is not determined by the organization (1998, 19). In most cases, learning is somewhat automatic, spontaneous, unintentional, serendipitous, and uncontrollable. We learn things that are later seen as significant. It does not always happen in a training room or educational environment—the workplace itself is a classroom. A part of informal learning is being open and vulnerable to new thoughts, the input of others, and exchanges of perceptions and impressions. The willingness to ask questions, listen, and add to exchanges and discussions also contributes to learning. Such learning simultaneously expands knowledge and strengthens connections within groups; without the willingness to learn from each other, individuals, groups, and organizations falter.

Learning Is Contagious in the Right Environment

Opportunities to learn expand with the benefits and experience of pleasing connections within and across groups. Positive consequences of learning are passed on, supporting, encouraging, and transferring learned information. A sense that something has been or is being learned and accomplished adds energy. Added energy creates opportunities to express, question, and/or redirect and redesign ideas. Meaningful learning exchanges increase mutual respect while acknowledging the capabilities of participants.

Informal learning activities include scanning the actions and responses of others; people constantly appraise expressions, behaviors, and gestures of others. They unconsciously ask themselves, "What does that mean?" When something is out of sync, it is noticed. Distraction occurs. For example, when a tone of voice does not fit the words being expressed, the mind says, "Be alert," and asks, "What's wrong with this picture?"

A more structured form of informal learning is peer training or "peer mentoring." Comembers support the learning of a colleague they have been asked (either formally or informally) to coach or train. In an environment where peer mentoring is supported, the orientation process can be a thoughtfully organized sharing of information and skills. It includes learning encounters with peer trainers who have learned peer mentoring techniques. Steve Trautman, while with Microsoft, developed a program for improving the skills and motivation of peer mentors. He recognized that employees were already relying on their peers to gather information and develop job skills, and built a program to make them more effective communicators. The program, called Technical Peer Mentoring, teaches peer mentors how to set expectations for the relationship, organize their thoughts, prioritize and deliver content, and then assess understanding and give feedback.

For most of the 1990s, Microsoft supported peer mentoring by providing this training for those who wished to build skills. The result is a growing culture of communication in their active, fast-moving environment. As new employees, contractors, or interns join the company, managers are encouraged to assign a trained peer mentor to help with the transition. Fundamentally, peer mentors explain how things get done. According to Trautman, now president of Solution Strategies (www.peermentoring.com), another reason it is important at Microsoft is to understand and learn to thrive in the corporate culture. It is extremely helpful to receive practical advice on how best to become productive. Peer mentoring of new members serves that purpose, making it more likely the new member will do well while at Microsoft and be comfortable while doing so. Trautman, in his work with Technical Peer Mentoring, suggests, "On the job training is already the most common way for people to share information. Expert peer mentoring simply makes it more efficient, and more fun."

Where formal training for a peer mentoring responsibility is not available, one-on-one peer mentoring has less structure. The learner may be assigned as an apprentice for a length of time, or shadow the mentor/trainer on the job. In this atmosphere, the trainer has not learned peer mentoring techniques. The mentor is passing on what he or she has previously learned or experienced. These techniques may or may not be beneficial.

We all get peer mentoring. It is part of the socialization process. The Aring and Brand study (1998) tells us that 70 percent of our learning in the workplace takes place through casual observation and communication exchanges. The most casual peer mentoring is secondhand, passing on the habits and attitudes of others. Based on the definition of advocacy activities used in this book and that of Van Dyne, Graham, and Dienesch (1994), advocacy participation and peer mentoring, when purposeful and beneficial, are acts of member advocacy.

Collective

Organizations, when attempting to introduce and sustain new learning, offer formal group training. Sustaining such learning requires immediate application, verification by leaders, accountability, and recognition and acknowledgment of the resulting changes. The leader group regularly examines and evaluates collective performance as it relates to the overarching design (vision, mission, goald, values) and the three bottom lines (human, social, financial). Sharing this information openly with the membership makes it possible for all to learn from and contribute to sustaining progress or call for redirection in areas of concern. Recent efforts to redefine members as businesspeople requires education and the open distribution of information previously reserved for the eyes of top executives.

Collective learning also occurs through observing the example of leaders. It is through "teaching by example" and regularly carrying messages regarding learning and serving that members sense leader commitment to becoming a learning organization. Harley-Davidson leaders teach a course on the values of H-D to their direct reports, stakeholders, dealers, and suppliers. Through Harley-Davidson University the values are represented around "what you do and what you say." These efforts place even more accountability for doing what they say on the shoulders of the leaders. It also provides the foundation for spreading accountability for organizational values across the organization. Seiling (1999) writes,

The Harley-Davidson workplace is now a more informal, value reflective, connected place in which inclusiveness, distributed authority, and partnerships prevail. It is where members are willing to work on providing quality products and services to their internal and external customers. At Harley-Davidson, after a successful turnaround in 1988, the company purposely started emphasizing five values, which they call its Business Process: (1) Tell the truth; (2) Be fair; (3) Keep your promises; (4) Respect the individual; and (5) Encourage intellectual curiosity.

H-D's Business Process influences union–management relations by making it important for both management and labor to live the Business Process together. And a partnership between the two unions and the management of Harley-Davidson, which is supported by such values, has brought important input by members at all levels of the organizational community. (p. 19)

Aring and Brand (1998) found that there is a synergy to learning: "Formal learning and informal learning occur simultaneously and exist along a continuum." And add that "there must be opportunities for learneres to test and try out their knowledge in informal settings and ways: through interaction with peers, reflection or exploration" (56). If members find that learning can improve their opportunities to achieve personal, group, and organization goals at the same time, all will benefit from the convergence of informal and formal learning that has been tested and moved into the daily activities of the learners.

Serving

Serving is a mind-set. It also involves serving attitudes. It goes beyond gestures of customer service, which for many is the tokenism of "just keep them happy." On the job, real service is part of working together in positive ways. Internal members work together with the added energy of pride in their organization and in their coworkers. Benjamin Schneider (1990) says,

To become more service oriented . . . will be more difficult than it first seems, for two reasons. First, service is more than a smile and a handshake; this calls for many issues to be attended to if change is to become a reality. Second, while there are many reasons why change is difficult in any organization, the primary reason is that it requires the people in the organization to change. They must change what they think about, how they think about it, how they spend their time and effort, what they reward and support, and so forth. (p. 127)

The difficulty of this undertaking cannot be underestimated. It would require a revolution in some organizations to demonstrate a mind-set of service and for members to see themselves as essential to their organization's achievement. Change would be required from top to bottom. In some cases punishment for good service would have to cease. New service attitudes would have to be recognized as beneficial, even essential to growth and accomplishment.

The *law of effect* states that behaviors having pleasant, positive consequences are more likely to be repeated; conversely, behaviors that have unpleasant or negative consequences are less likely to be repeated. This appears to be a no-brainer: We do what "feels good" and is "fitting." One would assume that this means that working well together would be automatic—people would just keep trying to get to community until they found it. Yet every day people go to work where negative conflict is rampant. In these organizations it is a struggle to get through the eight to ten hours of each workday experiencing all the "stuff." People are routinely punished for thinking differently, checking new ways of doing things, or questioning the unquestionable. Under these circumstances, advocacy behaviors eventually disappear, if they ever happen at all. As the saying goes, "No good deed goes unpunished."

Questions hang in the air: Why would we become organizational advocates? How do we become willing advocates for our comembers and organizations? Where do we begin? Organizational advocacy begins with organizational leaders. The human bottom line expands or retracts through the serving behaviors of people in the workplace, including the behaviors of formal leaders. The leadership style of "working for" or "under" (superiority) changes to "working with" (partnering and collaboration). Partnerships, where all workplace participants are encouraged and expected to think and do together, expand the human bottom line. Yet all across organizations many participants feel ignored, disconnected, discounted, and not listened to. The outcome, based on the law of effect, is withdrawal, disconnection, disinterest, and lowered energy. How can we expect loyalty and commitment from this disenfranchised many?

Advocacy as an Appreciative Gesture

People build a chain of optimism and enthusiasm, are neutral and lifeless, or display levels of negativity and pessimism. The organization is represented to comembers and customers through gestures of appreciation. Appreciation includes being authentic and credible; when someone or something is not viewed as credible, it will not be taken seriously. What we do take seriously usually includes the dynamics of appreciation. People make decisions based on what is heard and signaled by others regarding a specific subject.

Judgments (deciding what is to be appreciated) according to a 1995 study, cannot be made without efforts to merge the combination of three things: (1) what is reality (judgments of fact about the state of things), (2) judging what is of value (deciding what ought or ought not be—what is significant), and (3) making instrumental judgments (deciding how to reduce the mismatch between what is and what ought to be. Information is an incomplete concept: it tells us nothing about the understanding and perceptions of the recipient. What is appreciated (judged as right) designs what has been communicated.

Thus, our individual appreciative judgments decide what we will promote and participate in. Without appreciation, identification of our own understanding of what ought to be and can be done, we could have no hope for the future. Decisions (judgment) occur only when appreciation is present—one has used the three components of appreciative judgment to decide what is possible. A lack of appreciation slowly creates disaster by the elimination of the identification of what or who is significant, what is of value in the information received, and what is to be constructively done.

Hopeful and appreciative people who practice advocacy participation bring an aliveness to their interactions with others. They believe that things can be made to happen. Through shared hope, conversations, and partnering ways of working together, appreciative movement toward change can happen. Our methods of advocating (the way we work; the energy we put into it; what we think, do, say; and what we appreciate) designs new perspectives of hopefulness. With appreciation we discover new understandings of personal responsibility and worth.

Yet it is absurd to believe that an appreciative stance (including contributive judgments) can be held at all times. It is impossible because we are human and because "stuff happens." It is imperative, therefore, to ask ourselves: Why did this happen? and forgive our deficiencies when personal actions of nonadvocacy and lack of appreciation occur. Often we learn much about advocacy participation from our mistakes—when we strive to learn from those mistakes.

TWO ADVOCACY STANCES

There are two advocacy stances in the workplace: corporate advocacy and organizational advocacy. Corporate advocacy will be visited briefly before turning to organizational advocacy, the focus of this book.

The following is a simple comparison of the two advocacy stances:

Corporate Advocacy	*Organizational Advocacy*
Assigned task (not a choice)	Voluntary (chosen)
Planned project	Spontaneous, ongoing
Short term	Long term
Selling the message	Living the message

Corporate Advocacy

Corporate advocacy is not to be mistaken for organizational advocacy. The defining difference is that corporate advocacy is performed by designated, assigned persons who are responsible for carrying out a plan of influence. It is a corporate activity. Organizational advocacy is spontaneous, belief-based gestures in words and actions performed by members throughout the organization. The verbal gestures are performed both on and off the job.

Corporate advocacy includes focused and planned activities around a specific issue. Corporate advocates (1) are authorized and designated by the company, (2) have appropriate knowledge and job credentials, and (3) are often in departments or divisions called marketing, advertising, public relations, or issues management. The primary focus is on the external audience, outside the organization, in attempts to persuade toward a defined sense or understanding about a designated issue.

Corporate advocacy efforts attempt to impact and align the beliefs and/or behaviors of the target audience with the organization's needs—to maintain or adjust a corporate reputation. According to Rindova and Fombrun (1998), "Corporate reputations are a mechanism through which outsiders externalize their expectations by signaling satisfaction or dissatisfaction with organizational actions and identity" (p. 64). Corporate advocacy efforts attempt to move an understanding toward a desired position. When executives decide to commit resources to external communication, they often have some form of public communication in mind. Public communication may include newsletters, video programs, television and radio ads, posters, and so forth meant to influence groups, not individuals.

The response of Johnson & Johnson during the Tylenol tampering incident of 1983 is an example of efforts to impact the perceptions of current and potential customers about a crisis issue, product, or incident. The company's effective and aggressive response was to pull back the over-the-counter medication. This was done against the advice of Wall Street, which suggested the company would be irreparably damaged. As people watched television and read their newspapers about the incident, they were influenced by the humanness and genuineness of James Burke, the CEO of Johnson & Johnson, who served as the designated corporate agent (advocate) in enrolling the listening and reading audience in their cause.

Johnson & Johnson changed the corporate world's response to disaster. They turned a disaster into a marketing opportunity through corporate advocacy. Although hit with immediate losses, the company experienced increased sales and market share over the next months and years.

A more recent, less effective response to a recall situation was Firestone, subsidiary of Bridgestone Corp., and a tire producer with a long reputation of reliability. When faced in early 2000 with an investigation regarding 119 deaths when tire treads separated from their tires, there were excuses offered to the public and consumers. When called on to consider additional recalls, there were denials and refusals to do so by Yoichiro Kaizaki, president of Bridgestone. Ford Motor Company, who used Firestone tires on Ford Explorers, ultimately shut down two plants with full pay for employees to provide tires for the recall. Local dealerships calmed fears of buying tires from Firestone by saying that all new Ford Explorers were using other brands of tires. It was soon predicted that Firestone would become a "secondary tier provider of tires." In November 2000, the company estimated recall costs to reach $450 million. Consumers became wary of the excuses and the lack of an early, definitive response by the Nashville-based company. Late in the year, sales were off 40 percent. It appears the future of the organization is threatened by a poor response to customer concerns (AP Wire Services Tokyo 2000).

Thinking corporations actively design and maintain a plan for crisis management, an immediate response to be used when they are forced to defend or apologize for negative effects of products, practices, or services. It is in the direct interest of organizations (and stakeholders) to be alert to corporate practices that may result in potential failures. When incidents occur companies must hit the ground running, knowing who to contact and who is responsible for what needs to be done. They are ready for action. Successful companies are prepared for the unthinkable.

Corporate advocacy also includes usually short-term planned efforts to support internal stakeholder groups in "making sense" of what is going on, and with good reason. In 1996 the Conference Board surveyed human resource executives and affirmed that a company's reputation has a "great deal" (61%) of impact on whether a company is a potential employee's employer of choice. Reputation ranked third of twenty-one choices, with only career development (68%) and compensation (65%) ranked higher (p. 4).

Newsletters, team training, cultural training, skills training (problem solving, etc.) are planned ways used to impact assumptions and "what we know." The goal is to "sell" a new viewpoint. Strategies around these efforts are planned and replanned in order to implement and achieve the purpose of the effort.

Organizational Advocacy

Organizational advocacy requires that organizations provide opportunities for members to choose to be positive advocates for their organization and to support them in doing so. Advocacy cannot be forced. It is a choice made by the individual member to heighten involvement and put energy into personal contributions. For advocacy participation to occur, an encouraging atmosphere is required to support the conscious and unconscious actions of members who are connected with the organization they represent, both on and off the job.

As Weick (1995, 51–52) says, "noticing must happen" (activities of filtering, classifying, and comparing) in order to consider actions of advocacy as contributive. Then sensemaking (interpretation and determining what things mean) is essential to seeing as important those things that need to be considered or done. People must see the significance of the concepts, behaviors, and justifications around advocacy in order for individuals and groups to see the benefits of advocacy participation.

The benefits of organizational advocacy are that it

- increases hope, freedom, and effectiveness.
- is a choice of the individual.
- is an indication of loyalty and commitment.
- includes actions of learning and serving, reflection, and inquiry.
- nurtures partnerships all across the circle.
- deemphasizes differences.
- creates a stronger sense of urgency.
- is an outcome of working in a respect-based organization.
- more directly connects the organization and its members to the overarching design of the organization.

PARTING THOUGHTS

There are often changes to be made in the collective organization in order to make new ways of working possible. Individual awareness of the benefits and responsibilities of what is being advocated is important. Change happens at the speed of the understandings and acceptance of members, releasing their learning and serving energies. Organization leaders who demonstrate a solid conviction and long-term commitment to development of this new mind-set of learning and serving will enhance member involvement. Actions of organizational advocacy and profitability are not mutually exclusive; they enhance one another, over time adding to the expansion and sustainability of the organization.

NOTE

The author acknowledges the writings of Linn Van Dyne, Michigan State University, and her colleagues as supporting the process of thinking through the introduction of organizational advocacy in this book.

BIBLIOGRAPHY

Allcorn, Seth, and Michael A. Diamond. (1997). *Managing People During Stressful Times: The Psychologically Defensive Workplace.* Westport, Conn.:Quorum Books.

Aring, Monika, and Betsy Brand. (1998). *The Teaching Firm: Where Productive WOrk and Learning Converge.* Newton, Mass.: Center for Workplace Development, Education Development Center, Inc. <http://www,edu,org>.

AP Wire Services Tokyo. (2000). Bridgestone Chief Says Sales Off 40%. *The Lima News*, 11 November, B4.

Carlson, Richard. (1997). *Don't Sweat the Small Stuff . . . and It's All Small Stuff.* New York: Hyperion.

Conference Board. (1996). *H.R. Executive Review: Competing as an Employer of Choice.* New York: Conference Board.

Csikszentmihalyi, Mihaly. (1990). *Flow: The Psychology of Optimal Experience.* New York: Harper & Row.

Drennan, David. (1992). *Transforming Company Culture: Getting Your Company from Where You Are Now to Where You Want It to Be.* New York: McGraw-Hill.

Frohman, Alan L. (1997). Igniting Organizational Change from Below: The Power of Personal Initiative. *Organizational Dynamics* 25 (3): 39–53.

Gibb, Jack R. (1978). *Trust: A New View of Personal and Organizational Development.* Los Angeles: Guild of Tutors Press.

Glasser, William. (1985). *Control Theory: A New Explanation of How We Control Our Lives.* New York: Harper & Row.

Manning, George, Kent Curtis, and Steve McMillen. (1996). *Building Community: The Human Side of Work.* Cincinnati: Thomson Executive Press.

Pearson, Christine M., Lynne M. Andersson, and Christine Porath. (1999). Workplace Incivility: The Target's Eye View. Manuscript under consideration.

Peck, M. Scott. (1993). *A World Waiting to Be Born.* New York: Bantam Books.

Rindova, Violina P., and Charles J. Fombrun. (1998). The Eye of the Beholder: The Role of Corporate Reputation in Defining Organizational Identity. In *Identity in Organizations: Building Theory Through Conversations*, edited by David A. Whetten and Paul C. Godfrey. Thousand Oaks, Calif.: Sage.

Schneider, Benjamin. (1990). Alternative Strategies for Creating Service-Oriented Organization. In *Serve Management Effectiveness*, edited by David E. Bowen, Richard B. Chase, and Thomas G. Cummings. San Francisco: Jossey-Bass.

Seiling, Jane Galloway. (1997). *The Membership Organization: Achieving Top Performance Through the New Workplace Community.* Palo Alto, Calif.: Davies-Black.

Seiling, Jane Galloway. (1999). Reaping the Rewards of Rewarding Work. *Journal for Quality and Participation* 22 (2): 16–20.

Snyder, C. R. (1994). *The Psychology of Hope.* New York: Free Press.

Van Dyne, Linn, L. L. Cummings, and Judi McLean Parks. (1995). Extra-Role Behaviors: In Pursuit of Construct and Definitional Clarity (A Bridge Over Muddied Waters). In *Research in Organizational Behavior.* Greenwich, Conn.: JAI Press.

Van Dyne, Linn, Jill W. Graham, and Richard M. Dienesch. (1994). Organizational Citizenship Behavior: Construct Redefinition, Measurement, and Validation. *Academy of Management Journal* 37 (4): 765–802.

Van Dyne, Linn, and Jeffrey A. LePine. (1998). Helping and Voice Extra-Role Behaviors: Evidence of Construct and Predictive Validity. *Academy of Management Journal* 41 (1): 108–119.

Weick, Karl E. (1995). *Sensemaking in Organizations.* Thousand Oaks, Calif.: Sage.

CONVERSATIONS AND INTERVIEWS

Ann Hoewing, Foundation for Community Encouragement.

Glen Shull, organization consultant.

Steve Trentman, Solution Strategies.

3

How to Be an
Organizational Advocate

> No matter how great an organization's potential, no matter how good its products or services, it is the influencing abilities of members at all levels that determine its success.
>
> Jane Galloway Seiling (1997)

> As humans, the only world we can have is the one we also create together through our language and interactions. . . . This very knowledge compels us to see that our world, our communities, our organizations will change only if *we* change.
>
> Joseph Jaworski (1996)

The ability to impact or influence the future in a way we can feel good about is possible when we successfully influence those around us. A lack of power and the inability to influence others limits both individual and organizational achievement. To influence others requires us to know what advocacy participation is about, present our ideas well, be open to the influence of others, and seek partners who can and will do the same. This is true at all levels of the organization, but is especially so for formal and informal leaders.

Informal leaders often become so because they communicate well. Whatever their status or title, each member can become a leader and/or change agent at any given moment when leadership is called for. To receive approval suggests that leadership activities of the not-as-usual leader or change agent are culturally based and culturally biased. A workplace that lacks the awareness and appreciation of change agents is unlikely to include advocacy-promoting activities as part of the workplace culture.

As noted earlier, to share stories, information, and provide impressions is human. But is it ethical to perform as an advocate, to promote our own and our company's beliefs, values, and assumptions as appropriate, beneficial, and the right standard or choice? To do so with the intention to contribute to the welfare of the organization is ethical, even essential to the maintenance of contributive energy. It serves as validation of why the member is actively involved and committed. Part of doing so involves communication of our needs, knowledge, and curiosity. Advocating for a decision or activity creates and/or sustains impressions, viewpoints, and actions and activities.

People either ignore, reject, question, or accept what is brought to their attention by others. The information is acted on or stored away for consideration at a later time, when new information is available. When questioned, it forces the advocate to dig deeper to justify, even question, his or her own position. Questions stimulate internal questioning: Should I believe this way? Why so or why not? Being questioned by others adds to or detracts from a person's stance and the energy being put into it. Listening carefully brings attention to other alternatives or verifies and clarifies the advocate's current position, idea, or objective, forcing us to dig deeper into our own considerations.

Digging deeper forces us to pay closer attention to what is being questioned or advocated. Paying attention helps us to "select relevant bits of information from the potential millions of bits of information" (Csikszentmihalyi 1990, 31). We retrieve needed information from memory making it possible to evaluate. We then choose what is to be done. In addition, attention, whether for, neutral, or against whatever is observed at that moment, helps to focus on comparison of past and new information. Paying attention makes it possible to more clearly remember, think, feel, reflect, and decide.

MAKING ADVOCACY POSSIBLE

Organizational advocacy is an outcome, a signal, or an indication of an organization that (1) makes possible member actions of advocacy through facilitation of a meaningful holding environment for people to work in; (2) hires willing and competent members who want to develop positive, highly functional relationships (partnerships) that actively promote the welfare of the organization; and (3) provides training, education, and rewards that encourage and sustain high performance.

Advocacy participation does not "just happen." Certain behaviors, activities, and levels of participation indicate the learning and serving energy of an individual and the collective organization. The holding environment impacts the probability of advocacy activities happening. The participant decides whether acceptable performance includes advocacy participation in this organization and if it is beneficial.

Barrett (1995) describes high-performing organizations as containers in which "people can explore the assumptions that inform their actions" (p. 46). Learning is part of high performance, requiring an atmosphere that deliberately notices and increases individual and group potential. Barrett describes this atmosphere as "appreciative learning cultures" that

- create arenas of accessibility in which members are included in the evolution of policies and strategies;
- hold a disrespect for [bureaucratic] hierarchy and other boundaries to inclusion and involvement;
- deliberately create access to decision-making forums by fostering norms that legitimize members' right to question and provide answers at all levels of organizational activity;
- encourage members to think creatively, question commonly accepted definitions and go beyond previous conceptions;
- create multiple forms of responsiveness, remain accessible and open to the emergence of new voices and perspectives and are willing to have their thinking interrupted; and
- create contexts in which members have a sustained presence and are free to respectfully vocalize perspectives without restraint or fear of reprimand or censure. (p. 46)

People sense where they stand with others and make choices that impact how they will perform now and in the future. This information influences the level of interest and the energy one will apply to a task. The outcome is a choice to act or respond in certain ways.

Respect, dignity, and personal growth expand in appreciative environments. Advocacy participation is more likely to happen in a respectful organization, an organization where people at all levels respect the knowledge, contributions, future possibilities, and applied energy of others. Of course, respect is earned and is also a significant point in establishing exchanges of trust.

The activities of advocacy participation are assumed as happening normally within relationships in the workplace. After all, people are being paid to work. One would assume they would be appreciative and contributive, even enthusiastic about their work, their comembers, and their organization. One would also assume that they would act like adults and work at designing relationships and work processes to get the work done efficiently, get along, and be advocates for each other.

These are problematic assumptions, especially in a defensive, self-protecting atmosphere that supports entitled attitudes. It has been said that managers see one organization and "those below" experience another. Somewhere there is a chasm of dysfunctional activities. These attitudes prevail when work bonds are flawed and the holding environment or culture is perceived and experienced as different at different levels.

The outcome of a positive holding environment is, it is assumed, an organization with a culture that supports the willingness of members to promote their workplace (and their comembers) as beneficial, constructive, and worthwhile. This environment makes it possible for the covenantal relationship of advocacy participation, characterized by open-ended commitment, mutual trust, and shared values, to happen (Van Dyne, Graham, and Dienesch 1994, 768). A positive holding environment does the following.

Communicates the Overarching Design

The holding environment communicates an anticipated future tied to an overarching design (vision, mission, values, and goals), making it possible to anchor all activities to the organization's purpose and goals. A positive holding environment supports and encourages advocacy participation. The contributive advocate tells positive stories that increase personal efforts to perform. It is more likely that members will anticipate a positive outcome, prepare (learn) to contribute more, and do what is necessary to contribute to accomplishment of the organization's vision.

Increases Awareness

Reliable information is a vital ingredient to making sound decisions and judgments in the workplace. In an atmosphere where people are aware, they are more willing to seek and give input as partners in workplace transactions. Information flows more freely. The organization and the individual benefits.

Frames and Interprets Experiences and Expectations Accordingly

In a positive holding environment advocacy participation helps organization members understand what is seen and experienced. Knowing what we are accountable for and the behaviors that are expected makes it possible to know boundaries—and where they can be stretched to include innovative practices. New levels of involvement and understood expectations expand opportunities for personal achievement. (The organization with employees who are unwilling to risk or to be proactive will have limited success over time.)

When there is a shared interpretation of the vision and purpose of the organization and how to meaningfully contribute, it is possible to tie our work to the overarching design. There is a natural response to interpret what is happening through a sense of hope, expanded personal power, and a sense that contributing with energy will lead to improved outcomes.

Brings Attention to Contribution

Acknowledgment, rewards, and recognition bring attention to the significance of individual and group contributions. The members are more responsible and accountable for their work and seek to nurture partnerships that are beneficial to performance.

Expands the Members' Sense of Pride

As a response to a positive holding environment, organizational connection initiates and increases actions of advocacy. Member pride is increased by focusing on issues not before seen or reflected on as beneficial. Acting as if something is good actually focuses the member on the fact that it *is* good, making possible new enlightenment around an issue or concern. The positive holding environment makes it possible to see and experience what is good about our workplace. This creates a sense of appreciation, increasing while member pride in membership enhances a sense of community.

Increases Appreciation by the Customer

Who would know more about an organization than those who work there? When a member is seen as putting effort into his or her work and expresses pride in the product or service, those who listen hear about an organization worthy of their admiration and business. Of course, when hearing words of discomfort and disconnection, suspicions are raised or verified. I observed a customer's discussion with a server named Maria Maya in Las Vegas, Nevada. His comments invited her to criticize the hotel she worked in. She chuckled and responded, "I've been in this town for 24 years and I've worked in a lot of places. This is the best. I've worked here 10 years and don't ever intend to leave." She was practicing organizational advocacy.

Increases Connection

People want to "connect" and establish healthy relationships that make it possible to interact both pleasantly and productively. Organizations, through their holding environment, make it possible or impossible for members to see positive possibilities for the future. Understanding what is possible and what is required to get to goal accomplishment is spread to the edges of the circle through emphasis on and connection to the overarching design. Having the opportunity to hear this information increases feelings of being valued by those in the inner circle. Still, the choice to be more deeply involved remains with the individual.

To summarize, a positive holding environment does the following:

- Communicates the overarching design.
- Increases awareness.
- Frames and interprets experiences and expectations accordingly.
- Brings attention to contribution as a personal choice.
- Expands the members' sense of pride.
- Increases appreciation by the customer.
- Increases connection.

BEING AN ORGANIZATIONAL ADVOCATE

In the not far distant past, duty dictated loyalty and commitment and included "talking nice" about where we worked—when certain people were listening. But even if they weren't listening, we were usually civil to each other. Our expectations were lower regarding our own treatment but higher around how we treated others. Status and title mattered, often including unspoken permission to those in management roles to use and abuse those who were "less than" those with higher ranks (the "more thans"). When people outside the company asked "How are things at work?" the automatic response was an unenthusiastic yet civil, "Fine—it's okay." If these words did not reflect true feelings, the speaker often felt it was their own fault—that they were the cause of problems and if they just applied themselves more, things would be better. Management thought "our people" should be grateful for their jobs and they should submit to being a tool for getting work done. As a tool, they were not seen as a source of creativity, innovation, and accomplishment. Eventually, the tools would ask themselves, "Why bother?" and the spiral continued its downward descent.

The descent toward being a dispirited organization occurs over time. It may be unnoticed or undetected. Early on the connected, spirited organization included people who cared about themselves, others, and the organization. At some point there may have been concerns that were dismissed as insignificant and unimportant, or a leader demonstrated "more than" and "less than" attitudes. When not addressed, frustration and anger brought incivility. Cynicism may have resulted when cynical personalities were hired. Their abusive and punishing behaviors were not addressed, spreading to the actions of others. Eventually the outcome was lack of energy for doing, elimination of thinking, and silent or vocal disregard (see Figure 3.1).

A positive holding environment is essential. All members must also realize that each person participates in constructing this holding environment and culture. It cannot be designed by the leaders alone—everyone's impacts are what it becomes.Contributions include being a value-added representative and performance-based advocate. To become a contributing advocate, people seek to do the following:

Figure 3.1
Becoming a Dispirited Organization

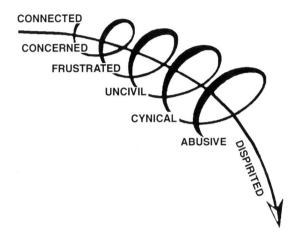

Identify and Act on Their Roles in Contributing to the Welfare of Themselves, Their Group, and Their Organization

Most important, if members are not in roles that are personally acceptable and beneficial to their own top performance, they take responsibility to identify their qualifications, develop capabilities, and seek opportunities for change. If a change to another position is not possible, a member is forced to make a choice to be positively patient and keep his or her leader aware of the need for a change, or leave the organization for other more fitting work.

Create a Good "Trail"

Each day we create our own trail that follows us as we proceed through our working career. What we do or say today *always* has ramifications in the future. For that reason, listening for the good and responding based on reflection and inquiry (tools of advocacy) make it possible to create trails of experience and relationships that are beneficial and productive. Of course, to suggest that relationships are always stable and predictable is to deny our humanness. Our responses to different people and different situations is often spontaneous and undeniably unpredictable. In *Leadership and the New Science*, Wheatley (1992) says, "None of us exists independent of our relationships with others. Different settings and people evoke some qualities from us and leave others dormant. In each of these relationships, we are different, new in some way" (p. 34).

Consistently Behave Responsibly Toward Others

Workplace performance is emergent. Each day we add to and/or detract from a future we cannot see. Since we are also the future of our organization, our gestures of learning and serving, thinking and doing, are also vital to the success of those around us and our collective organization. For this reason, we are accountable for our own performance.

Operate with a Positive Approach

We decide what our worldview will be: Attitudes are a choice. Although our background and current situation affect our ability to be openly positive about our work, our demonstrated "good" feelings about our work and our organization are seen by others as verification of connection or disconnection from the organization. Participants display the workplace culture's definition of "acceptable ownership" through practicing what is seen as a positive approach, including actions of advocacy participation.

Put Energy into Their Work

The success of an organization is an outcome of (1) the amount of effort we choose to exert in performance of our work, (2) systems that make it possible for us to do so, and (3) the learning and serving perspectives we have that impact 1 and 2. As stated by Carlene Reinhart (2000), president of CLR Associates, "An organization may redesign, reconfigure, and reorganize for the greatest efficiency and productivity, and yet it is the performance of people every day on their jobs that cause an organization to run well, only adequately, or not at all" (p. 20). Innovations, creativity, top performance, and all those other breakthrough words only happen when the people doing the work decide to uncap their energy and knowledge to use the resources at their disposal in the best way possible.

Seek Change When Change Is Needed

Status quo is deadly. The contributive member (and advocate) seeks to notice and take action when there is a sense that "something isn't right." Advocates carry the role of change agent with them, making it possible to see the unseeable and question the usual. The willingness to risk discomfort, to be seen as different, and to stand up for right when wrong is the action of the day is also part of the scenario.

Partner with Others

Producing results usually requires exchanges of information and utilizing the talents of more than one person. Expanding the potential of an organization is based on the proliferation of productive partnerships across groups, status levels, and even physical facilities. Multiple voices of different and similar people working in different areas and circumstances challenge themselves and others to reach agreed-upon results. These partnerships expand the possibilities of the organization's future (as well as their own).

Be Credible

Gaining and maintaining credibility requires advocates to perform as moral agents (consciences) of their organization. According to Driscoll and Hoffman of The Center for Business Ethics, "Every individual . . . has a shared responsibility to be a moral leader" (1997, 140). Organizational success is expanded through each participant being responsible ethical agents, both inside and outside of the group. People who are known for keeping their word and actively working for the welfare of the organization over time are seen as credible. They are trustworthy and respectworthy representatives of the company.

In summary, advocacy participation includes the following:

- Identifying your own personal role in contributing to the welfare of yourself, the group, and the organization.
- Creating a good "trail."
- Consistently behaving responsibly.
- Operating with a positive approach.
- Putting energy into your work.
- Seeking change when change is needed.
- Partnering with others.
- Being credible.

Advocates demonstrate commitment to their organization, its mission, and the goals and aims laid out for the future. Is it realistic to strive to gain member commitment to the cause of the organization? Not only is it realistic, it is essential. If it is not done, achievement of potential will not happen. Instead of cooperation, competition and mediocrity can prevail. Instead of thinking, doing, and appreciative judgments, people do only what they are told to do or find excuses for not doing it at all. Instead of innovation and creativity, status quo guards the doors. Instead of growth, stagnation occurs. Member actions that reflect commitment are imperative to personal and organizational growth.

Business Partners

Organizational advocates are business partners and, as coconstructors of their organization, strive to contribute to the accomplishment of its strategic priorities and goals. As partners, they want the knowledge to contribute to high-performing partnerships inside their organization and to positively represent their workplace community outside of the organization. To do so, they need the business understanding, technical understanding, interpersonal skills, and intellectual skills to serve well as business partners (Seiling 1997, 48–52). Being an effective business partner is especially difficult when misguided decisions are made because of lack of information and there are no opportunities to challenge the validity of the decisions of others.

To not serve as a conscience and business partner is to only be a mouthpiece or strong back. Controlling environments do not make it possible to be consultative advocacy-oriented members, a role of the organizational advocate. This is not a wise approach. The "consultative approach" of sharing ideas, information, and concerns is the role of every member–business partner. When doing so they are serving as an internal consultant of the moment. Consultative members add value. They communicate effectively, giving input and adding energy to the partnerships in which they participate. They share their knowledge while expanding their skills. They exercise power and authority beyond their status and title, and they are willing to risk chastisement in order to do so. In today's workplace, consultative members want thinking and doing to be part of the job. No longer can anyone be considered a pair of hands. Consultative members are not necessarily in the leader role. Everyone is a consultant about their own work and how it is best to be accomplished.

Consultative members are the following:

- Business partners.
- Learning and serving effectively.
- Credible in their work and their relationships.
- Able to communicate needs, expectations, and expertise clearly.
- Willing to take risks by exercising power and authority beyond their status and title.
- Working with members all across the organization.

Mihaly Csikszentmihalyi's (1990) description of "flow" is an example of where consultative contributions occur. It is in this place between the feelings of anxiety and boredom where top performance happens (Figure 3.2). Anxiety and boredom are part of the human condition. Without anxiety, the willingness to stretch would disappear. Without boredom, the human desire to reexamine and challenge our world would suffer. An overabundance of either state lessens responsibility and accountability and reinstates status quo and do-as-they-say as the way to work. Consultancy, where flow happens, is part of advocacy participation (further discussion of consultancy can be found in Chapter 7).

The model also suggests the need for members to be aware of the "normal" response to anxiety and ambiguity. Robert Cialdini (1993) says, "In general, when we are unsure of ourselves, when the situation is unclear or ambiguous,

Figure 3.2
Flow Model

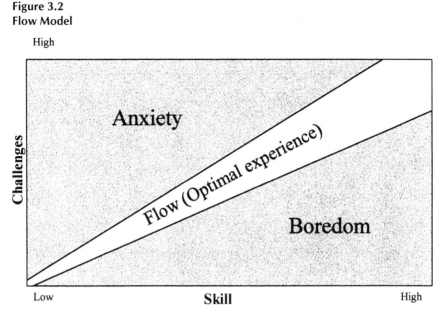

Source: Ed Hamson, ed., *After Atlantis* (New York: Butterworth-Heinemann, 1998). Used with permission.

when uncertainty reigns, we are most likely to look to and accept the actions of others as correct" (p. 129). It is easy to assume someone else knows what needs to be done. We get lazy or we are unsure of our own information and don't check for facts and fallacies. When unsure, we may assume there is superior knowledge in the mind of another; we ignore the opportunity to consult with others to consider alternatives and potential outcomes. The advocate, even though uncertain, recognizes the need to clearly identify alternatives through shared information.

CONSTRUCTIVE ACCOUNTABILITY

Accountability, as practiced in most organizations, is a find-and-punish cycle of dealing with members who are seen as a "problem." It means (1) sit them down and tell them this won't be tolerated, (2) punish them for doing it, and (3) tell them what will happen if it is repeated. Although punishing accountability insists the person give technical (what/method), system (how/process), or people (who) failures as "excuses," there is no place to examine the possibility of the accountability issue being a feelings (why) issue. Ignoring feelings tells the target, "We won't tolerate this soft stuff here." According to Putnam and Mumby (1993), "non-scientific" and feminine values of emotionality, empathy, and subjectivity are marginalized and considered noncontributive behaviors (p. 48). This forces people to be in control at all times, an emotional impossibility, denying the presence of stress and ambiguity. It means never show emotion, never get out of control, and certainly, as the saying goes, "never let them see you sweat." It means be an adult, while being treated like a child.

Being treated like a child does not allow for constructive accountability. Being treated like a child suggests one-way communication, sit and listen, one person is right, and there is going to be a not-so-good outcome. Constructive accountability is, of necessity, a consultative opportunity for the participants. To do otherwise raises barriers to learning, causes distrust and disconnection, and heightens the possibility of hostility. As noted previously, consultative members are business partners, are credible, are able to communicate needs, expectations, and expertise, and they work with people of all levels and status. To suggest a member is not to be treated with dignity and respect is to delegitimize their work. The message is: Your work is not valued and it definitely does not contribute to the success of this organization. Do better.

Accountability, Used Constructively, Is an Exchange of Information

Constructive accountability provides opportunities to set benchmarks; it clarifies and provides learning and serving opportunities for future performance. It supports partnering efforts. All members involved are responsible for being willing to talk, listen, and be flexible. Without effective consultative exchange as part of accountability, all parties are in the anxiety state of the flow model, threatening the possibility of getting to "productive flow." When not acting responsibly during these times, each participant senses the threat and seeks to convince and control. It is through learning exchanges of accountability that new levels of learning and achievement occur.

Constructive Accountability Sustains Member Credibility

Credibility is orchestrated and sustained through the expectation and exchange of constructive conversations of accountability. These conversations encourage heightened responsibility and effective individual performance and provides vital performance parameters. Constructive accountability also includes opportunities to provide information and stories about successes, enhancing credibility. Sharing what has worked well provides opportunities for members to learn from the advocate. Why did it work so well? What would be changed next time to further what has already worked well? How can others use what has been learned? Accountability, coupled with authenticity, blocks unethical, irresponsible, or simply thoughtless action (Lipman-Blumen 1996, 19).

Constructive Accountability Requires Listening to Learn

People tend to quit listening or participating in discussions about controversial topics. For this reason, the communicator's history of influencing others, as well as the environment and circumstances of message delivery, contributes to the willingness of participants to not shut down. Successful exchanges of accountability over time are significant to introducing and sustaining improvement. For this reason, communication should be for the purpose of questioning and expressing, not for impressing those one hopes are listening.

Constructive Accountability Provides Opportunities to Gain Support

Accountability that includes beneficial achievements as well as needed learnings provides opportunities for giving and getting support. The goal is for all participants to learn from each other, not to focus on the wrongdoings of one person or a group of people. Is it possible that the word "kindness" could be part of constructive accountability? Why must the participants be angry, sad, or unkind, or even uncivil?

Constructive Accountability Includes the Potential of Separation

Creating a place where advocacy participation is part of how people work together involves coconstructing an organization where people all across the organization *want* to be members and advocates of their organization. For many organizations this will be a struggle; it would take major surgery—even changing management—to make it possible. It may also force the dismissal of people throughout the organization bent on sabotage or destruction of the new way to work together. Being willing to address conflictive behavior is tough. There are legal, social, contractual, and procedural reasons why organizations don't do it. It is hard work, but it must be done. Leaders ask themselves the question, "What can be done for the benefit of all parties?" when considering this dilemma. The answer is critical to making the changes needed to become a positive, highly productive workplace community.

To summarize, constructive accountability does the following:

- Is an exchange of information.
- Sustains member credibility.
- Requires listening to learn.
- Provides opportunities to gain support.
- Includes the potential of separation.

Conscience

Advocacy participation includes a sense of feeling a moral obligation to the company and its members, the absence of which may be uncorrectable in persons without it (Brion 1995, 1190). The availability of valid information is significant to performing as a moral conscience, yet the people who "do protest too much" are often kept out of the loop for information, especially regarding the "undiscussables" that may raise concern. One would agree that there is a benefit to having a member who is willing to stand up and be counted, to advocate for what is right or protest against what is seen as wrong. But in the workplace this can be an uncomfortable place. In some organizations, having different perspectives can bring scrutiny, even punishment. To have a different view is to appear to be an "intruder," one who doesn't go along to get along. When one intrudes on progress by inquiring and challenging the validity of what is being done, it slows things down, causes confusion, and destabilizes.

These distractions and interruptions can be disturbing and irritating to others. It can be a moral issue (subjective) or a performance issue (objective). John Brion (1995) states, "*Moral autonomy* is the capacity to make moral decisions regardless of peer pressure or the dictates of higher authority, thus a capacity for pro-social non-compliance on unacceptable social rules" (p. 1189; italics added). The willingness to question and speak your own thoughts (in a constructive way) may bring refocus and rethinking. It may even bring others to question what is being done or foster innovation. To do without the questioner, the person some call "the devil's advocate," is to be open to disaster. In an organization with blurred lines there is more likelihood that an organizational advocate will call attention to concerns before a disaster occurs. When there are signals that inquiry and challenge is appropriate and acceptable, the advocate takes the information to those needing it on a timely basis—before full commitment to a process or procedure is not alterable.

Leaders must ask themselves, What if a member on the edge of the circle stands up and says "no" when others with more power are saying "yes"? Will that voice be listened to and be given consideration? Or will it be ignored, teaching the member and observers that what they say is unimportant, unappreciated, and problematic? Dawn-Marie Driscoll and W. Michal Hoffman of The Center for Business Ethics at Bentley College in Waltham, Massachusetts, note that "ethical leadership isn't reserved only for those at the top, rather it's a quality held by individuals and organizations with the moral courage and dillegence [*sic*] to talk and walk ethical values" (p. 136). If leaders cannot ask themselves the sticky questions, how can they expect it to be done by others?

Competence

There are connections between feeling capable, feeling appreciated, and whether we see our workplace as a great place to work. To strive for new levels of competence and employability, effective leaders identify, appreciate, encourage, and validate learning and serving behaviors as part of being competent. They also openly acknowledge, reward, and recognize these differentiating behaviors as vital to organizational achievement.

We make sense of our world through what we experience. We notice how people respond to us and how they acknowledge our efforts (Weick 1995, 52). If there is no acknowledgment or a lack of appreciation, we fill the void with assumptions. We assume a personal level of performance and competence based on nonverbal feedback that may or may not be valid. We may assume top performance and competence when we are a mediocre, less-than-effective performer. Or we may judge our performance wrongly as less than adequate, increasing anxiety when in actuality we are exceeding expectations.

Our outlook is colored by our ability to perform. There are core competencies in all jobs that the performer must be able to do well or have the ability and willingness to learn. Of course, there is a dynamic nature between performing our tasks, the feelings we have regarding the work we do, and our relationships with our colleagues. These and other factors impact the choices we make to be advocacy participants.

High performers and contributors are those with the will to achieve. In some organizations "getting ahead" requires conformity and compliance. In others it means deep participation and innovation. Achievers, as defined by the members and the culture of the organization, are presumably rewarded with advancement, status, and/or titles. When they experience boundaries they cannot surpass without danger, they double their efforts and strive even harder for accomplishment, or their efforts wane and they become complacent.

Competence, according to Spencer and Spencer (1993, 15), can be divided into two categories: threshold and differentiating. When working at threshold competency we are minimally effective—only working to the level necessary to remain in the position—and out of trouble. This is where mediocrity occurs. Differentiating competency separates superior and mediocre performers. The contributions at this level usually include the motivation to impact and influence what is happening in a positive way. Inclusion, flexibility, and integration of ideas are practiced in the differentiating category.

To be competent in the workplace, members (1) know what their roles are; (2) know and understand what competencies are embedded in the differentiating category of top performance; (3) understand that what they think, say, do, and appreciate contributes to individual and organizational achievement; (4) regularly and realistically assess their own competence; (5) consciously determine where their attention is best focused; (6) identify what coaching and development assistance is available—and go after those resources; and (7) purposely seek competency development. It is through these steps that members identify what steps are possible to move from where they are to a desired level of performance and competence.

Differentiating competency requires formal training, informal peer mentoring, coaching, constructive accountability, and other competency development activities essential to making it happen. These consultative activities stimulate and sustain the desire to become organizational advocates. Pride in our role in our organization is expanded when we contribute to the learning process of others.

Hopefulness

Advocacy participation is an outcome of having hope. Many of our organizations are realizing that to generate hope and to expand interest in complex and disillusioned organizations requires the organization's vision to be anchored in concrete information that is understood by the members about where the company came from, where it is now, and where it is going. Increased hope and interest expands advocacy participation of members in moving toward the hoped-for future.

Members who previously have been treated badly will be reluctant to believe in the possibility of a new culture. Their interest will be low; they will guard themselves against future disappointment. Convincing these members that a new workplace community can happen—and that they are part of the construction of that organization—involves acknowledging the past. Hope is based in past experiences that have been explained and future visions seen as possible. Hope involves the perception that goals can be met and that those involved are interested in and willing to commit to making what is hoped for possible for the long term.

Magic happens with the emergence of a workplace atmosphere where hope and advocacy participation occurs spontaneously. It leads to the verbalization of feelings of ownership and energy. A hopeful holding environment is where (1) leaders believe their role is to lead and partner with their fellow members, (2) shared knowledge and intentional action becomes possible, (3) all members at all levels make choices to become more tolerant and dedicated—and act on those choices, and (4) people at all levels are accountable for making it possible for every member, and the organization, to achieve.

SPREADING ADVOCACY

How do the activities of organizational advocates become part of the way to work for many in an organization? Spreading advocacy participation requires members at all levels to influence those around them. Once the few understand and believe in the concept and it becomes their way of working, it is their role to encourage the same behaviors in others. They rehearse, recruit, reinvent, reward, revisit, and renew. Only through authentic, believable advocacy participation can one, and eventually many, change an organization. It is a movement toward advocacy participation.

Rehearse

Learning new behaviors is not automatic. Those who believe in the deeper participation of the advocate become aware of what the role is; they practice or rehearse how to do it. No one will be perfect; it will be a continuous process of learning for themselves and serving; it will mean caring for the achievement of others, their organization, and performing accordingly. Often, it takes courage to display new behaviors. To do so requires the willingness to do the following:

- Rethink what personal responsibility and accountability is in his or her daily life.
- Say no (or yes) and stand behind it.
- Be open to new relationships (partnerships).
- Be willing to be imperfect.

It is likely that people learning new contributive behaviors and activities will struggle in areas they do not understand—or may not fully believe in. Having a goal gives one direction and purpose, but it doesn't necessarily make life easier. Rehearsing leader advocacy (Chapter 7) may be easy; self advocacy (Chapter 5) may be tough. Rehearsing new partnerships may work well; customer advocacy (Chapter 9) may not be possible in the culture of the organization at this time. But one has to start somewhere and rehearse constantly: Stick to it, try new ways of doing things, and experience the advantages and disadvantages of doing so.

For the lone advocate, making personal behaviors more open and inclusive can cause all sorts of complications. When we change, it confuses those around us, causing efforts by others to force the advocate back into alignment. It may not be pleasant. Sooner or later the advocate will step beyond where he or she would have gone in the past. Someone will question it; someone may protest—loudly: "You can't do that." "Who told you that is part of your job?" "We've never done it that way and we're not going to start it now." When the trouble starts it is easy to retreat to past behaviors. It is a less risky place to be. The advocate will wonder why they have started this new path. It takes determination to work differently and a resolve to address inner conflict and doubts that inevitably go along with making a personal movement to change.

Recruit

The likelihood would be that rehearsal of advocacy participation would occur while working with peers. Others verify what we think about certain things through their responses when we make personal changes. It is logical that, in whatever is done, the advocate would want the support of comembers, especially when experiencing the stress of trying new things. People want to be connected to those around them.

Enthusiasm tells us we can convince others of the benefits of organizational advocacy. The advocate can influence and encourage, but he or she cannot enroll others. Recruiting advocacy partners requires advocates to stay focused on their own journey, stay committed to their own higher involvement, and relax. The advocates actions and contributions will invite stronger, more connected partnerships that can convince others to fall in step beside him or her. The better approach is to remain steadfast and let others come to their own choice.

- Be enrolled yourself. It is folly to attempt to enroll others unless you are committed yourself. People are watching. One cannot convince others of the benefits of organizational advocacy when the promoter is not demonstrating advocacy participation.
- Be on the level. Describing the benefits of advocacy participation without the disadvantages is being less than honest. There are challenges (and rewards) in taking participation and commitment to another level.
- Let the other person choose. Pushing to convince turns people off. The willingness to try out new performance activities is self-initiated. It is far better to have the person be convinced by the impressions and successes of the advocate who influences through his or her own actions.

Commitment is essential to being highly participative. Senge (1990) says, "Traditional organizations did not care about enrollment and commitment. The command and control hierarchy required only compliance . . . there is nothing you can do to get another person to enroll or commit" (pp. 222–223). Even in the best environment possible, enrollment and commitment are the outcome of personal choice.

New levels of performance and stronger interpersonal connections strengthen relationships, providing even more opportunities to contribute. Top performers become models for others. Good models for performance are those who routinely demonstrate "orderliness" in how their work is done. The work to be done is likely to become even more complex when one signals the desire to be more involved. With a heightened willingness to contribute, expanded choices and challenges are more likely to occur. This person gets beyond how things ought to be and is willing to see how things are. He or she is willing to move to taking a larger part in reshaping how things can be.

Reinvent

To reinvent suggests there is a need to come up with something else that better meets current needs as well as those seen as necessary in the future. Reinvention of ourselves, our capabilities, our relationships with others, and how we personally contribute on the job requires determination. To reinvent ourselves is to purposely change past practices, to take the things that worked before and reexamine how to do them better, to learn new serving ways, and to show a willingness to expand beyond what was seen as expertise in the past.

Reinvention of the work-self only happens when one is strongly convinced there are benefits to being highly responsible for what happens on the job all day every day. The member (1) wants to change for the better how he or she experiences work each day, (2) wants to change past personal outcomes so there are stronger feelings of worthwhileness, (3) realizes that what one accomplishes and how one treats others on the job carries over off the job, and (4) knows that if one does not change, feelings of personal confidence, pride, and value will continue on a downward cycle.

Realistically, personal dedication to reinvention requires having a new vision of what success can be on the job and requires practicing self-regulation in order to maintain change efforts. The desire to reinvent happens because one is not benefitting from current activities and/or it is painful to continue in the same path. Self-reinvention is not a one-day, one-month, one-year activity. It goes on forever.

Reward

Will there be a reward for being more responsible and accountable for our personal workplace performance, for investing ourselves at a higher place in what we do all day? The message here is that doing it because there will be a direct financial reward will be disappointing. There is a possibility that, because the member was performing adequately before the commitment to change (surely the company weeds out the noncontributors), the only person who knows there is a change may be the member himself or herself.

There are rewards experienced for consistently going beyond the norm. Increased pride and a sense of contributing to the welfare of self, others, and the organization is not measurable. Being more contributive and having stronger relationships with others are personally rewarding. Eventually, there may even be a financial reward.

Revisit

Consideration of "why I am doing this" makes it possible to stop and start over. People tend to justify what is being done instead of evaluating with the intention of possibly taking a new direction. We tend to put energy into maintaining the status quo. It is easy to ignore signals and just keep doing what is being done and not take on the pain of a changed direction. In order for the efforts of an individual or group to remain effective (or to become effective), regular visits to evaluate the goals, structure, processes, procedures, and my personal involvement are made, with the intention to look at what needs to be changed.

Renewal

Renewal follows the revisit and evaluation. Renewal and revitalization follows constructive accountability. Long-term success for the individual and the organization, we are finally learning, requires renewal of energies and revitalization of learning efforts. What is being done every day becomes boringly routine. With routines come habits that should also be regularly revisited.

Renewal and revitalization occurs differently for each person. But we must take action to do so. To stay committed to our purpose and to be continually alert to improvement requires us to renew and revitalize.

Several years ago, Carter T. Funk, Jr., COO and vice president of a natural gas utility and a talented, caring leader who believes in the capabilities of the people who work with him, made the comment, "Somehow we must hear and understand that if each one of us would commit to working better just 10% of the time, it would make a huge difference, not only for that person, but also for the company." Considering that U.S. workers are working at 65-percent capacity, even a small increase would change everything.

BARRIERS TO ADVOCACY PARTICIPATION

Often barriers to advocacy participation occur when the person attempting to be an advocate is seen as not doing it for the right reason. Judgment starts with observation, negative evaluation, and the assignment of a selfish motive by the observer. It may include a determination that the member has a hidden agenda or that what he or she is promoting is not beneficial to others, or the person's motives are open and obvious and don't agree with what is seen as appropriate by observers.

Turn-Off Behaviors

There are personal behaviors that influence the acceptance or nonacceptance of advocacy gestures. The participant may seek to be a positive advocate, but their own behaviors prevent them from doing so. "Turn-off" behaviors will be barriers to advocacy participation. Turn-off behaviors include cynicism, intolerance, defensiveness, and disillusionment.

Cynicism, it is said, is everywhere. A cynic is defined in the *Oxford English Dictionary* as "one who shows a disposition to disbelieve in the sincerity or goodness of human motives and actions, and is wont to express this by sneers and sarcasm; a sneering fault-finder." Unfortunately, we see and experience cynical behavior everywhere. An advocate cannot be effective if perceived as a cynic. Being perceived as having a positive, contributive organizational view and attitude is essential. Questions to ask yourself: Are you angry more than half the time you spend at work? Do you feel powerless to change things? Do you often bad-mouth the boss and "them"? Do you think people purposely pick on you? If so, you may be a cynic.

It should be noted that even the advocate occasionally slips into turn-off behaviors. Nothing and no one is perfect, especially in the workplace. All of us experience temporary disillusionment with circumstances. The difference is that organizational advocates seek reasons to restore themselves to positive organizational advocacy. They want to see their workplace as a good place to be.

Unmet expectations of society, institutions, or other authorities are based on unrealistically high expectations of ourselves and others. These unmet expectations greatly influence how the cynic sees things and how others see the cynic. In 1989 Kanter and Mirvis found that 43 percent of the American populace fit the profile of the cynic (p. 10). They found that (1) cynics believe that the average person is unconcerned with the problems of other people, (2) they believe that it is not possible to really understand the feelings of other people, and (3) they have a self-sealing and self-reinforcing view of the world. Cynics, they note, ingeniously twist the meaning of events to fit their own outlooks, especially when it comes to their dealings with other people (pp. 23–24). In the workplace, these perceptions cause disconnections that may reinforce cynical attitudes and behaviors.

Based on the desire to shame and blame others, cynical behavior can be seen in temporary disillusionment with circumstances, but this cynic is seeking reasons to restore to a stance where positive advocacy can occur. If not temporary, cynics often do the following:

- think their workplace should be "perfect."
- have a personal bent for a cynical attitude before being hired and he or she slips through the cracks.
- are underperformers, who, in the past, were top performers.
- have a desire for retaliation, whether deserved or undeserved.
- use it as a method of getting attention.
- use it as a tool for demonstrating disrespect.
- have feelings of hopelessness, helplessness, or haplessness that may be real or unreal.
- use it as a covert method of dealing with discomfort.
- lack a desire or ability to directly or constructively deal with issues.
- have real or unreal perceptions of unfairness.
- have a desire to create excitement or lessen anxiety.
- see themselves as experiencing a lack of respect and being undervalued, whether real or unreal.
- work in a job in which they are not competent or bored.
- are often isolated and ostracized by their immediate group or supervisor.
- may display bullying behaviors.

As negative advocates, cynical employees also recruit, rehearse, and reinvent, but it is done in subversive ways in order to retaliate. They don't evaluate their own cynical behaviors or make attempts at renewal. Their stories become convincing by reframing them, bending them, and fitting them to reflect the cynical message they want to spread. They rehearse their biased stories by sharing them over and over in order to convince themselves and others that they are right. They busily go from person to person to recruit others to their cause. (As victims, they do not like to be the only victim.) They go from group to group, person to person, playing the "ain't-it-awful" game, seeking those who can be recruited to the cause of their own victimization. They also retaliate through advertising victimhood and perceptions of unfairness. They want others to care about them, to be loyal to them, and to chastise their target. They want to shape an attitude that impacts the effectiveness of their target. This becomes a ritual of displaying negativity, dislike, and disconnection. These are unhappy people, and the likelihood of finding a workplace where they can find perfection and be happy is limited.

The cynic is often a bully. Their cynical behaviors may include shouting (they yell so loud, we can't hear them); complaining (they complain so much, we don't hear their valid concerns); constant "squeaking" (as in the "squeaky wheel" seeking to get oiled first—only the wrong wheel gets the oil), or repeating (they remind everyone that something was done wrong sixteen years ago—and "I was the victim"—over and over).

It is normal to react to the cynical person by not listening, but it is not the best response. Not listening verifies his or her suspicion that "no one ever listens to me around here." It may also result in his or her one idea or concern that could make a difference not being heard. We must force ourselves to listen—really listen—to what cynics have to say, and invite them to participate in orchestrating a solution. Helping them to see why they are not being listened to by others, when done with caring accountability, is also important. Genuine sincerity in carrying this message to the cynic may get the message across to them that how they act and what and how they talk impacts their opportunities to be heard. We at least have to try.

No one is inferring cynics are not intelligent. In fact, it may be just the opposite. Intelligent, productive people who are bored or not listened to may become cynical. They may be past top performers who feel let down and no one noticed or cared. They may feel victimized by an aggressive supervisor or comember. They are using inappropriate tactics to say, "Listen to me, just this once, listen to me." They may be a long-term member who is tired of fighting the system. Or there may be outside influences of personal concern that are affecting their workplace activities. The member who is experiencing a difficult divorce, sick children, or many other issues that cause an otherwise productive member to see things differently can be temporarily cynical.

It is sad to say that many of our organizations have historically ignored actively cynical employees, allowing them to recruit, rehearse, reinvent, and retaliate. Cynicism is contagious and, as a result, whole organizations can, over time, become cynical. In these organizations, rebellion has replaced co-operation, mediocrity has crowded out productivity, and responsibility and accountability have been replaced with competition and cynicism. Then these organizations wonder why low productivity and possible failure looms.

Early on, leaders must take steps individually to address cynical behaviors through inquiry, support, coaching, and follow-through. Asking questions about how things are going and how something was accomplished may get a surprised response, but it helps and you may get information that will surprise you. Or it can validate that coaching and support won't help. Waiting to deal with problem people validates the cynic's negative advocacy behaviors as acceptable, even appropriate behavior. Eventually, other members and the organization become the victims of the victim.

New research has provided some information to pay attention to: Being cynical does not automatically mean one distrusts the organization. Recently, Whitener, Brodt, Korsgaard, and Werner (1998) reported two studies designed to investigate if cynicism and trust are distinct concepts and can coexist. In other words, could one be cynical and still have high trust? The results confirmed cynicism and trust as separate concepts. Whitener, Brodt, Korsgaard, and Werner (1998) stated, "Indeed, approximately half the respondents reported both high cynicism and high trust" (p. 13). It should also be noted that leader behavior had a significant relationship with achieving member trust: the demonstration of concern (p. 12). If a leader shows empathy and concern, the level of cynicism is potentially lowered.

McAllister (1995) also studied the dynamics of distrust in organizations. He states, "Cynicism functions to reduce complexity by positioning undesired events and outcomes as certain rather than uncertain (p. 6). McAllister also found that "As it pertains to both coworker relations and the organization, trust and cynicism appear to be distinct constructs" (p. 9).

Much time and energy has been spent on the study of trust, yet the study of cynicism is still in its infancy. Cynicism is the one that appears to be contagious and trust is not. McAllister also noted, "It appears that varying degrees of trust (things to be hoped for) and cynicism (things to be feared) are present in virtually all working relationships" (p. 11).

Intolerance is an indication of being closed minded, negatively judgmental, and resistant. Successful advocacy participants are more open and tolerant. Closed-minded people see those around them, especially their leaders, as guilty. To do so is a self-protecting device and, as noted earlier, results in the unending search for what or who is not guilty (perfect). The outcome is a futile quest for someone or something that will not fail them.

Richard Carlson (1997, 93) suggests we should "look for the innocence" of those around us who are bothering us. We must learn to be "less bothered." We respond badly to bothering. Looking for the innocence requires us to do the inhuman: We must "look beyond behavior." This is often a difficult process of stepping back and reframing our perspective about what is occurring. When someone regularly discounts what we offer as input or ignores the work we do, it is hard to look beyond these behaviors. Could it be cynical behavior is an effort to preserve their own sense of contribution? In looking for the innocence, we do the following:

1. Look for the grain of truth in what a person is saying.
2. Consider that truth.
3. Look for the innocence of what the person is saying or doing.
4. If these behaviors are a pattern, challenge (question) the person in an empathetic way regarding his or her actions and give feedback about how you feel when he or she repeatedly uses destructive, reaction-seeking behaviors.

Get comfortable. Practice this behavior as part of your way of working. Getting the message across takes awhile. It takes two people being intolerant for tempers to flair. By assuming the existence of and searching for the innocence of the actions of others, the resulting tolerance creates opportunities for high-performance partnerships to occur that would probably otherwise be missed.

Defensiveness occurs when there is a lack of trust. People make quick assessments of whether other people take into account their interests and needs. The assessor decides if he or she will or will not be willing to be vulnerable to the actions of another person.

Defensiveness is an influencing tactic. It is used to repair, justify, or account for something that has gone wrong. It delivers the message, "You should agree with me, even if you don't." Retribution, embarrassment, or bullying may cause otherwise high-performing members to step into defensive tactics. Relationship quality, a sense of low status, unfairness, the lack of opportunities to be heard, and past successful use of this tactic can also initiate defensiveness. The tactic is meant to force others to give up for the sake of peace and unity.

Attempts at dealing with conflict are initiated more toward fixing the individual and less toward fixing underlying, subtle, and pervasive dysfunction around the conflict that is occurring. Participants routinely step into highly defensive activities that make it difficult, even impossible, to get to agreement. Defensive activities may include the following:

1. Defending what is wrong as right.
2. Going along to get along (having no opinion).
3. Reshaping the same solution.
4. Ignoring unacceptable behavior in order to not embarrass the performer.
5. Competitive actions which cause conflict.
6. Ignoring solutions that may make uncomfortable changes.
7. Diverting attention to other problems.

By not being willing to identify and use constructive conflict techniques, individuals of high ability with good ideas frequently feel punished and discounted, and ultimately they are underutilized.

Research has told us that disappointment and disillusionment are often underlying causes of cynicism in those who, at one time, were the most optimistic, successful contributors. "Optimists are always prey to disappointment," says Charles Handy (1998), "but life without hope is dismal" (www.mgeneral.com).

But disillusionment happens. We are human and our organizations are an extension of our humanness. It is difficult, if not impossible, to have others, whether comembers, family, or friends, consistently meet our expectations over time. What we expect of them constantly slides on a spectrum between unrealistic to realistic. Where we are at a given moment and how we respond to occasional disillusionment and disappointment creates our healthy or unhealthy responses.

Staying Positive

It is impossible to always be a positive organizational advocate. We are human and our expectations of ourselves, others, and our organizations are often too high. We want to be proud of the organization we work for. But we cannot stay on top of that hill all the time. So how do we deal with those nagging suspicions of organizational incompetence? How do we deal with times of disappointment and frustration? The possibility of becoming a silent or loud unappreciative employee is always there. Expecting ourselves and/or our companies to be perfect is not a place of comfort. According to an employee of the Boeing Company, Seattle, Washington, "I've been with Boeing for twenty years and they have been good to me. But I've been cynical, too—I've been there and back. I don't know that I can even tell you why it happened. Now I just remind myself that *things happen*, that this is a good company and I want to be part of making it better. I just make adjustments and move on."

These statements describe the challenges of advocacy participation well. To become beneficial organizational advocates, we have to start with dealing with ourselves. To do so makes it possible for us to positively influence others. It requires

- the awareness of what advocacy participation is and what it can achieve.
- the opportunity to be an advocate.
- the desire and willingness to stop and reflect on our own roles in success for ourselves, others, and our organization.
- being willing to influence and support the activities of our comembers and our organization.
- being in an organization we are proud to represent, both on and off the job, every day.
- allowing ourselves, others, and our organization to occasionally misstep.

As stated earlier, things happen. People make big and little mistakes. When people have the opportunity to make decisions and participate at a higher level, people will make wrong assumptions and mistaken decisions, just as those making these same kinds of decisions before them made mistakes. The challenge is to rethink and deal with the consequences of the misguided decision, learn from it, and, as stated earlier, move on.

PARTING THOUGHTS

No matter what our job is, there are few things that impact our lives as much as our work and our situation at work. Organizational advocacy participation, as performed by individual members and groups, can be positive, neutral, or negative (the neutral advocate is "just there"). It is an outcome of the beliefs of members, the environment, and every day, ongoing member feelings of being valued or not valued in their organizational situations.

BIBLIOGRAPHY

Barrett, Frank J. (1995). Creating Appreciative Learning Cultures. *Organizational Dynamics* 24 (1): 36–49.

Brion, John M. (1995). *Leadership of Organizations: The Executive's Complete Handbook*. Greenwich, Conn.: JAI Press.

Carlson, Richard. (1997). *Don't Sweat the Small Stuff . . . and It's All Small Stuff.* New York: Hyperion.

Cialdini, Robert B. (1993). *Influence: The Psychology of Persuasion*. New York: William Morrow.

Csikszentmihalyi, Mihaly. (1990). *Flow: The Psychology of Optimal Experience*. New York: Harper & Row.

Dricsoll, Dawn-Marie, and W. Michal Hoffman. (1997). Spot the Red Flags in Your Organization. *Workforce* (June): 139–140.

Dulebohn, James H., and Gerald R. Ferris. (1999). The Role of Influence Tactics in Perceptions of Performance Evaluations. *Academy of Management Journal* 42 (3): 288–303.

Field, Jim. (1996). *Bully in Sight*. Oxford, U.K.: Success Unlimited. Available <http://www. successunlimited.co.uk>.

Fineman, Stephen. (1993). Organizations as Emotional Arenas. In *Emotion in Organizations*, edited by Stephen Fineman. Thousand Oaks, Calif.: Sage.

Handy, Charles. (1998). Feed the Spirit! *LeaderLines*. Available <http://www. mgeneral. com>.

Jaworski, Joseph. (1996). *Synchronicity: The Inner Path of Leadership*. San Francisco: Berrett-Koehler.

Kanter, Donald L., and Philip H. Mirvis. (1989). *The Cynical Americans: Living and Working in an Age of Discontent and Disillusionment*. San Francisco: Jossey-Bass.

Lipman-Bluman, Jean. (1996). *The Connective Edge*. San Francisco: Jossey-Bass.

McAllister, Daniel J. (1995). Affect- and Cognition-Based Trust as Foundations for Interpersonal Cooperation in Organizations. *Academy of Management Journal* 38 (1): 152–172.

O'Reilly, Charles A., and Jennifer A. Chatman. (1996). Culture as Social Control: Corporations, Cults, and Commitment. In *Research in Organizational Behavior* 18-57-200, edited by Barry M. Staw and L. L. Cummings. Greenwich, Conn.: JAI Press.

Pfeffer, Jeffrey, and John F. Veiga. (1999). Putting People First for Organizational Success. *Academy of Management Executive* 13 (2): 37–48.

Putman, Linda L., and Dennis K. Mumby. (1993). Organizations, Emotion and the Myth of Rationality. In *Emotions in Organizations*, edited by Stephen Fineman. London: Sage.

Reinhart, Carlene. (2000). How to Leap Over Barriers to Performance. *Training and Development Magazine* 54 (1): 20–24.

Seiling, Jane Galloway. (1997). *The Membership Organization: Achieving Top Performance Through the New Workplace Community.* Palo Alto, Calif.: Davies-Black.

Senge, Peter M. (1990). *The Fifth Discipline: The Art and Practice of the Learning Organization.* New York: Doubleday Currency.

Spencer, Lyle M., Jr., and Signe M. Spencer. (1993). *Competence at Work: Models for Superior Performance.* New York: John Wiley & Sons.

Van Dyne, Linn, Jill W. Graham, and Richard M. Dienesch. (1994). Organizational Citizenship Behavior: Construct Redefinition, Measurement, and Validation. *Academy of Management Journal* 37 (4): 765–802.

Weick, Karl E. (1995). *Sensemaking in Organizations.* Thousand Oaks, Calif.: Sage.

Wheatley, Margaret. (1992). *Leadership and the New Science.* San Francisco: Berrett-Koehler.

Whitener, Ellen M., Susan E. Brodt, Audrey M. Korsgaard, and Jon M. Werner. (1998). Manager as Initiators of Trust: An Exchange Relationship Framework for Understanding Managerial Trustworthy Behavior. *Academy of Management Review* 23 (3): 513–530.

CONVERSATIONS AND INTERVIEWS

Jim Field, author, *Bully in Sight.*
Carter T. Funk, Jr., CKS Enterprises.
Maria Maya, Las Vegas Server.
Carlene Reinhart, CLR Associates.

Questions, Concerns, and Barriers to Organizational Advocacy

> The assumption of personal responsibility is necessary for individual and organizational learning and development, and for what is, at times, maintaining the thin veneer of civilization.
>
> Seth Allcorn and Michael A. Diamond (1997)

> People will hurt others, double-deal, cheat, or do worse, if the company ethos support such behaviors, *and* the cost of not doing so seems too great. Some will act with a cynical shrug; others will feel ashamed, but still conform. We also know that many corporate actors will do things at work that they would not contemplate doing outside of the organizational setting.
>
> Stephen Fineman (1993)

> It is about overcoming boredom and fear and anger. It is about a capacity for new ways of knowing. . . . It is about the principle that there is more to life than eating or fighting or power. It is about visualization, the process of imagining ourselves as a part of our ultimate dream—feeling it, touching it in our minds. It is about overcoming the fear of learning and the fear of seeing the godlike in ourselves.
>
> Joseph Jaworski (1996)

Although management groups of successful organizations have long known the benefits of participative management, enlisting member participation in decisions has been a struggle. Outdated management styles of authoritarian leaders and the expansion of bureaucracy continues to thrive in many U.S. businesses. "Deep" participation by members remains remote. Cynicism and distrust are increasing instead of decreasing. Under these circumstances, spontaneous value-added actions of advocacy participation remain foreign to many organizations. This chapter addresses some of the questions (attempting to make sense), concerns (things seen by many as "certainties"), and barriers (things seen as blocks and limitations) limiting the possibility of advocacy gestures becoming a part of organizational sustainability.

QUESTIONS

As humans, we are assumed to be rational beings. Humans take facts, or what are assumed to be facts, as reasons for behaving one way rather than another. We base our decisions on whether things will fit our needs, plans, and hopes. We care what happens to *us*. All this reasoning requires asking questions and getting answers that we use to refine our assumptions and make decisions regarding situations or problems.

This section addresses questions we may have about how organizational advocacy can become meaningful in our organizations. Without addressing these questions, we are limited in our willingness to consider what can or cannot be changed in ourselves and our organizations. It helps us use the "law of proportion": Is it important enough? Is it worth the effort?

What Are These Words, "Organizational Advocacy"?

The words "organizational advocacy" and "advocacy participation" are difficult for some people. I hear, "I prefer ambassador. I see advocate as something I associate with lobbying at the state or federal level. For me, not a good connotation." Or, "Advocate is such a legalistic term. It tells me I am arguing in court for something but other people really are in control." It's a language thing.

Organizational advocacy is about clarifying and participating in defining what our organizations are and what they are going to become. We care about the organizations we work in and the people we work with. We want our organizations to be honorable, professional, and profitable. As Barry Oshry (1977) notes in his writings about tops, bottoms, and middles, we know that whatever position we are in we shape the systems around us that make up the organization, and they shape us. "We may think of ourselves as independent individuals, oblivious to the processes by which system membership shapes our consciousness, yet these influences are there; and we may be unaware of the consequences our actions have for these systems, yet these consequences are also there" (p. 2). These are not mutually exclusive happenings. Our actions are reflected throughout the systems around us. Each one of us contributes to what the organization is now and what it will be in the future.

Organizational advocacy occurs when one serves as a voice (possibly even a conscience) for what he or she believes as good and important. Advocates participate openly in forming (coconstructing) their organizations and their groups. Advocates hold themselves, others, and their organizations accountable, in appropriate ways, for being value-added, productive, task-driven members of the internal and external community. It is when one activates and participates in what is contributive, potentially at a cost. It is not always an easy place to be in organizations.

Finally, organizational advocacy is not about always being nice or agreeable. It is about consistently affirming what one believes. It is about learning from and listening to others while openly sharing your own ideas and contributions. It is about working effectively with others. It is about contributing to the organization in ways that are meaningful, not meaningless. It is about what each person—and each group—thinks, says, does, and appreciates about his or her own performance and the performance of others and his or her organization.

Is Organizational Advocacy Relevant?

Organizations need innovative and creative ideas more than ever before. Organizational advocacy forces people to be more open to questioning of past practices and the existence of status quo protection. Advocacy participation is especially relevant to organizations with dynamic environments. Change and innovation is important for timely and speedy adaptation and success.

Advocacy participation creates, sustains, or changes impressions, viewpoints, and actions. People either accept, question, reject, or ignore what is heard. The word "participation" is significant. It suggests action, involvement, doing, and getting your hands dirty; people who work with others to show them what can be done, and how. Verbal advocacy activities may encourage the listener to dig deeper to test his or her own position. It may add to or detract from a stance, change a direction, bring attention to another alternative. Verbal advocacy, whether questioning, suggesting, or agreeing, also verifies or clarifies current positions, ideas, or objectives of participants. For sure, members are positive or negative advocates because they feel strongly one way or the other about issues. Certainly, being an organizational advocate cannot be an act.

To create an atmosphere where advocacy participation is possible, new centers of power and new awakenings about what occurs in an organization are designed with the involvement of people at all levels. It happens spontaneously and positively or through well-thought-out change processes.

Constructing new standards of work and behavior takes time. Requiring authenticity and member understanding of why it should happen, these shifts are not made quickly. Over time, members will try the experience of connection and commitment across blurred lines of the organizational circle. Leaders and change agents emerge everywhere, making a difference in themselves and their organizations.

Is This What We Ought to Do?

When we look at reasons to do certain things, we are constructing a concept of "ought." "Ought," as what is right, appropriate, or necessary, is based on collected impressions, perceptions, and beliefs. It is what we think we are supposed to do. People consciously and unconsciously think things through and make decisions about the potential consequences of their behaviors. From the viewpoint of the person taking action, what is done at the time is realistic. As an example, an organizational community making inconsistent decisions (e.g., treating people differently because of status, title, race, or gender, etc.) is an offense against morality because it is an offense against what is seen as reasonable (Rachels 1995, 91). If we consistently look at the strengths of one race or gender and focus on the weaknesses of another race or gender, there are inconsistencies in our actions. It is not what we ought to do.

People and organizations make choices to be rational or irrational. They choose to do right because they have rationally decided to do so. Some choose to do wrong, even though they know it is wrong. Or a person does wrong because he or she does not know it is wrong. A person of good moral worth, with the right information, will routinely choose to do what is right—what ought to be done. They do so even if it is painful, or they feel guilty.

Our choices often design how we are treated by others. What we give out, we often get back. We also adjust our treatment of others to match how they have treated us. We reward some for being nice and hold grudges against those who treat us badly. They become "deserving" of the treatment given them. It can become an exchange of mistreatment.

The outcome is that even though we ought to treat each person in a right way, we make decisions based on past relationships and viewpoints that in our minds justify doing or not doing what we ought to do (Rachels 1995, 91). It is at this point that questions of fairness, justice, and deservedness arise.

To be a responsible agent of our organization, one displays a dependable and ethical value system and a reasonable desire to make a constructive contribution to the welfare of the organization. Striving to be a responsible agent highlights dependability and validates the constructive contributions being made.

In many organizations, this is a courageous path. Courage requires us to strive on solid ground and to use an honorable wisdom. This kind of wisdom is learned from questioning (including the unquestionable) and doing the right thing (ethical behavior) because you value and appreciate your organization and the people you work with. Wisdom, uncommon sense, ethical and appreciative judgment, and a willingness to collaborate and work well together comes with both clear and unclear answers to questions we (ought to) ask with courage.

CONCERNS

It is human to be concerned. And it is also beneficial. To lack concern is to not be attentive to what is going on around us. Lack of concern lessens our opportunities to address issues and to make improvements. Lack of concern is to be vulnerable and not take action. This section will address some of the concerns that may occur when considering the benefits of being an advocate.

Am I Vulnerable?

In the workplace, many feel personally vulnerable, organizationally vulnerable, or both. Being alert to our vulnerability is normal, especially in times of downsizing, outsourcing, or movement of jobs out of the country. It is a self-protective device, and a result of the fight-or-flight response is part of the human condition. Being vulnerable implies that there is something of importance to be lost. The question is, How vulnerable am I?

As workers, many work every day with people who are uncivil and leaders who push them to the limit. Not only do many people face victimization by management (excessive overtime; dirty, unpleasant work environments; and hapless supervisors), but these same managers don't care enough to even notice the impact of the victimization. They are taking their people for granted. A 1995 survey (Giacalone and Greenberg 1997, 51) of 300 responding senior-line and human resource executives by Towers Perrin placed people-related issues at the bottom of a list of organizational priorities. The top three priorities were customer satisfaction, financial performance, and competition. It appears many are taking for granted the people who make the success of these top three elements possible. Not much has changed since then.

The unrelenting focus on the financial bottom line by management without regard for the human bottom line is noted by workplace members. People watch for cues of impending doom. When noted, there are rumors and gossip of possible actions to be taken to remain competitive, often at the expense of the human and social bottom lines. For those feeling most vulnerable, there is a corresponding shift in motivation and/or attention to their daily tasks. Incidences that normally would be ignored cause increased concern and lowered productivity. George and Brief (1996) note, "Feelings of vulnerability are likely to be prevalent in organizations facing decline or imminent demise" (p. 187). These same member vulnerabilities exist in organizations making high profits. Time and again people have watched others become victims of closing plants, and the rhetoric of "being more competitive" while the financial bottom line is still flush and growing.

Bulletin boards give signals of feelings of vulnerability. As rumors persist of cutbacks in overtime or, worse, potential layoffs, the bulletin boards become crowded with boats, cars, motorcycles—luxuries purchased when money was flowing. It is hard to remain optimistic and positive when you are giving up your toys.

Does Organizational Advocacy Really Matter?

Will the things an organizational advocate does matter to accomplish change? As noted, successful organizations seek the willing ongoing input of all members in positive change. Their involvement is vital to change happening. Beneficial exchanges and contributions support the establishment of an environment and culture where advocacy participation can become part of the way people work together. Change works when the people are the ones making it possible. The signals come from consistent, repeated, positive leadership activities of individuals. Leaders' new inclusive activities cause members to "notice" positive discrepancies between past negative, punishing management and newly occurring membership behaviors. Eventually these discrepancies and revised expectations establish new habits and behaviors. Organizations do not change without people changing. Consistent, insistent, and relevant personal and organizational change eventually causes people to revise their expectations and their activities.

Education and training is most effective when it is consistent with the changes being made, when it is tied to the message of the overarching design, and when it includes cues of relevance from organizational leaders. Change efforts that do not lead to positive performance and voices and actions of advocacy about what is occurring limit the "stickiness" of the change. Eventually, after the heat is off, the old ways of working together are likely to reemerge.

Is It True That Familiarity Breeds Contempt?

A functional organization is constructed through establishing good, effective, long-term internal and external relationships. The results of both individual and organizational success are based on the willingness to collaborate and cooperate to accomplish together. Positive relationships are important to the individuals involved and the outcomes they produce. According to Egan (1994), "In an excellent relationship both parties are competent, both have a positive personal style, both appreciate these factors in the other, and this entire package helps them interact in such a way as to improve both business productivity and the quality of work life" (p. 169). But can positive relationships be sustained over time?

Commitment to relationships is important because disconnection and ineffectiveness delays or sabotages the thinking and doing processes needed to reach decisions and take action. It is best to assume that in working relationships, sacrifices are required. Letting go of past and preferred personal choices may be necessary. Implementation of decisions can be delayed when partnerships struggle. Familiarity and attachment are important to long-run cooperation and effectiveness. When trust is not established, familiarity and attachment are likely to eventually bring feelings of disappointment and disconnection.

Participants are not always prepared for the ups and downs caused by continual exposure to one another. The increased expectations of friendship and partnering are tested over time. As relationships strengthen, boundaries are established and tolerances are pushed. Sensitivity, increased expectations, and the normal aggravation of routine exposure opens one's eyes to the real person. Frustration occurs if humanness, fallibility, the opportunity to have a voice in decisioning, and forgiveness are not part of relationships.

Realistic people recognize that problems will exist in relationships. Working partnerships will always be faced with this reality. To lessen issues that may cause controversy, organizations actively prepare, educate, and train around relational issues, and expect civil behavior. To do so makes it possible to agree to performance expectations and ground rules up front in how to address issues of concern. Ground rules set up reference points and tools for mediation to lessen the possibility of antagonism and group disconnection. Agreed-to achievable goals and performance expectations lessen the likelihood of stress-producing issues occurring later on. Discussion and awareness early on of potential problems that stretch patience provide opportunities to talk them out and clarify partnering needs. Ignoring the existence of potential problems leads to disruption, even failure for the partnership or group. Lack of pride, productivity, and determination on the part of individuals affects the welfare of other members. To not address issues increases the possibility of trust being lowered and distrust occurring in relationships. There is no doubt that contempt breeds distrust. Distrust and anger can destroy partnership opportunities quickly.

Of course, advocacy participation is more likely to occur in positive relationships located inside positive environments. In the last decade much has happened to heighten the recognition that intentional orchestration of a positive holding environment leads to new opportunities for cooperation. Organizations have increased expectations of positive interaction between members.

Unrealistic performance expectations in partnerships also destroys relationships. Nonperformance may be a result of (1) no training being provided regarding partnering and effective advocacy performance, (2) members being expected to "always be nice to each other" (expecting perfection), (3) past relationships being touchy, with no attempt at resolution, (4) partners continually pulling along one who is not doing his or her work, and/or (5) supervisors and coworkers ignoring signs of ineffective partnering (including uncivil exchanges). Realistic expectations of performance allow for learning and serving as well as coconstruction of partnerships while expanding the performance of all partners.

Is Instrumentality Part of Advocacy Participation?

Americans have rejected instrumentality (using ourselves and others as instruments for accomplishing goals) as self-serving and manipulative. It is seen as unethically, possibly selfishly, creating personal opportunities where otherwise opportunities would not have existed. We tie it to Machiavelli's advice to the prince (manipulative power). According to Lipman-Blumen (1996), *"Used ethically for the good of the whole community*, instrumental strategies can be extremely effective—particularly in dealing with the political realities that lace an interdependent world. . . . Drained of self-aggrandizing toxins, this type of political behavior is particularly relevant to a complex, interdependent world" (p. 17; italics orig.).

Ethical instrumentality, being interested in and striving for accomplishment in meaningful ways, is a core ingredient of organizational advocacy (see Chapter 5). It answers questions, such as, Who can do what? How are we doing on this project? What can we do better? What resources do we have in our people and customers that can be tapped to move forward? Ethical instrumentality is essential to achieving top performance by the individual and the organization being advocated. Advocacy participation by members in the workplace expands and brings recognition to the abilities, actions, and skills of ourselves and those around us. It supports the identification of what works and what the possibilities are for ourselves, others, and our organizations.

Ethical instrumentality does not include violation of another's rights in order to achieve on our own. It is working with, not running over, the well-being of others. It is promoting the success of others, not promoting their failure. It adds value, it does not detract from the value of others.

Does Advocacy Participation Eliminate Adversarial Activity?

Adversary theory holds that the truth should emerge from the argument. This insinuates that one person holds the truth and that if you stand your ground or attack hard enough you can win the war. Mistrust is the basis for adversarial challenges that require a loser. In the process, mistrust is heightened and bullying, disrespectful, and uncivil behavior occurs. Ultimately, the winner doesn't really win. He or she is just the bigger bully.

Advocacy participation is not an adversarial activity. It is a covenantal relationship, a two-way exchange with the purpose of contribution to the welfare of the people and the organization in a positive way, implying acceptance and commitment, even internalization of organizational values (Van Dyne, Graham, and Dienesch 1994, 768–769). Advocacy participation does not require a loser; it includes collaboration and cooperation and the initiation of meaningful contributions. It is seeing an abundance of resources and using them wisely. When adversarial behavior is occurring, leaders must step back, ask why these activities are happening, and take action.

Adversarial behavior will be part of organizations as long as people have high levels of self-interest that are not kept in check through the attention of comembers (especially those in leadership roles) and practiced self-management by individuals. Turf wars are going on at all levels and are ignored by management. Fear of loss of control of something that is cared about causes people to become defensive. Resources are won through competition or favoritism, instead of sound business judgment. Collaboration is not highly valued space. Mistrust is rampant. The outcome is that self-protection and adversarial activities happen every day on the job.

Adversarial Activities	*Advocacy Participation*
Working for	Working with
Divisive	Inclusive
Resource based	Opportunity based
Weakens	Strengthens
Competition/working against	Cooperation
Diminishes	Enlarges
Nonappreciative	Appreciative
Short-term thinking	Long-term thinking

In abusive, adversarial organizations, people do not learn that what they think, say, and do is vital to achievement. Appreciation and civil behavior are not demonstrated or expected by the leadership group. Energy is wasted in struggles to gain control by those with power and those hoping to gain power. At every level people feel vulnerable.

BARRIERS

Barriers to accomplishment are always present. They can be real or perceived. They can be seen as challenges or blocks to accomplishment. They can create excitement or anxiety. They can cause disruptions or new awakenings. It is our response to and frame around barriers that expands or detracts from abilities and opportunities to address them. Our attention to and persistence in dealing with barriers to performance in the workplace (and our lives) require us not to be reluctant (afraid) to act—and to not give up (resilience) until barriers no longer block achievement. Considering that removing existing barriers brings forward new barriers, it is a long-term activity.

Ignoring the presence of barriers to performance, whether they be in processes, competencies, or relationships, lowers potential future achievement. It doesn't take a genius to see barriers to achievement or to point the finger at others as the cause. Successfully addressing barriers does require the willingness to enroll others in seeing what is happening, share hope in what is possible, design together what needs to be done, and persist in making long-term changes. Together, barriers can be eliminated, lowered, dug under, or walked around, creating new paths. One can accomplish a great deal, and two can create miracles. The remainder of this chapter visits a short list of barriers to organizational advocacy that many are aware of but choose to ignore in the workplace.

Attitudes

The most important influencing gestures are demonstrated through attitudes. Brion (1995) says, "Attitudes are learned predispositions to react consistently in a given way—positively, negatively, or neutrally—toward certain things, people, ideas, or situations" (p. 65). Note the word "consistently." The traditional viewpoint of attitudes has been that they are stable and persistent. This suggests that when asked about something or someone (job, supervisor, a colleague, etc.) an individual opens a "mental file" containing past evaluations and pulls out information that cannot be adjusted easily. In actuality, attitudes are fluid, changing with everyday experiences and observations. To expect attitudes to be stable is unrealistic. Our moods change; our attitudes and perceptions fluctuate with the information we have (George and Brief 1996, 84). Occasionally, even physical ailments and off-the-job realities affect our attitudes at work. For this reason, making changes in how we work together is done through awareness—by changing the mental file from where information is pulled over time.

It is this overall fluid picture of attitude that people see as a person's work behavior every day. For the most part an observer sees the attitude they expect based on past experiences. Therefore, if a member becomes cynical it may not be noticed immediately. But eventually people pay attention and shift what they see as a person's "normal" behavior. Members are seen as positive or negative advocates of their workplace based on the observation of these normal behaviors.

The attitude of positive advocates is one of appreciation and support while encouraging (even expecting) others to be willing contributors with them to enhance the prospects of learning and serving. If their expectations are not met, they check why and tend to overlook or tolerate discrepancies of lesser importance while continuing to set high standards for themselves and others. They take responsibility for their own personal actions and attitudes and expect to be provided opportunities to learn and serve while being held accountable for their work and their contributions. Things will not always go well, but even during the tough times they keep trying to add value to their work, their groups, and their organizations. They know that attitude matters and it is reflected in what they think, say, and do every day.

Contagion

Can the desire to be an advocate be "caught?" Contagion is an emotional activity. We pick up good and bad activities that we see others being rewarded for doing. A broad working definition of "emotional contagion," according to Hatfield, Cacioppo, and Rapson (1994, 47), might be the tendency to "catch" (experience/express/mimic) another person's emotions (his or her emotional appraisals, subjective feelings, expressions, patterned physiological processes, action tendencies, and instrumental behaviors).

Spontaneous reshaping of organizational beliefs and behaviors starts with the actions or words of one person and is passed on to others through cues, actions, interpretations, and emotions. Some researchers say that these activities happen and are accepted and passed on relatively automatically, unintentionally, uncontrollably, and possibly unconsciously. Of course, people, while in conversation, continually mimic, mirror, or synchronize with the person to whom they are talking. Also, we readily repeat words and gestures of respected others. Two people in a conversation in the hall mimic each other as they appear to lean or weave in the same direction. Both smile even though a joke has not been told. Each responds to the other's gestures and both step further down the hall incorporating one another's slow movements. They carry some of this synchronicity with them to the next conversation around a given subject.

There are those who are able to stimulate contagious encounters more than others. It has been suggested that "expressive" people are more likely to create a contagious atmosphere than those who are inexpressive. Some seem to pull others into their beliefs and are able to shape the emotions of those around them, making it more likely for contagion to happen. Tina, a marketing representative for a utility, is bright, innovative, and cheerful. Her customers respond well to her and they are always ready to spend time with her when she calls on them. She is a successful advocate for her customers to her organization and her organization to the customers. They catch her enthusiasm and are willing advocates for her and the company.

Organizational advocacy, this would suggest, can be contagious. The enthusiastic, convincing, thought-provoking actions and discussions of someone who believes in the organization gets the attention of comembers and customers. The potential for influencing others, when done by a respected, responsible representative, is expansive. There is a multiplier effect.

Power Distribution

Effective use of power requires the handing over of decisioning to those most capable of deciding. New and unusual partnerships will disperse power to those unpracticed in being powerful. Members have heard the word "empowerment" before and scoffed at it ever becoming a reality. Even though the word is losing a great deal of its favorability because of these responses, empowerment will more and more become imperative in the faster, more productive, and safer working environments needed in the expanding global community.

Real empowerment will seem strange to those previously watching from outside the leader circle. New decisioners will make even more visible mistakes. Learning includes mistakes and successes. Without distribution of power and shared accountability through empowerment, members will not have the opportunity to exercise personal responsibility and distributed accountability. To not distribute power will limit individual and organizational accomplishment and the availability of new voices and new ideas. For members to be deeply involved requires the opportunity to make decisions.

For those who have difficulty with the new concepts of power distribution, approaches to or from those not previously seen as partners may feel intimidating. They will look for hidden agendas, they will be suspicious of the abilities and talents of partners, and they will be suspicious of reasons why they should partner with someone they see as "not the normal partner." Caring comembers, including leaders, are essential to supporting the learning processes of the uncomfortable partner.

Work is done in the flow of decisions made both alone and with others. This is where people honor each other's contributions or seek to control. Integration of power occurs when members have the authority they need and use it—with honor and respect. They invite others to work with them and, when the time is right, work with them in utilizing the best skills and talents of each participant. Blaine Lee (1997), in discussing principle-centered leadership, says, "When people honor each other, there is a trust established that leads to synergy, interdependence, and deep respect. Both parties make decisions and choices based on what is right, what is best, what is valued most highly" (p. 16). Although this is true in all partnerships, it is especially true in unbalanced partnerships where one has more status power than the other.

Wherever they are located in an organization, members gain a new understanding of the dynamics of empowerment and the new realities about power integration as they seek to establish partnerships. When faced with an issue that requires participative action, they ask themselves these questions about power and integration:

- Who has the real power in this organization around this issue?
- Are they approachable?
- Will they share their expertise?
- Are there others I have not approached before who may have knowledge?
- Would they be willing to partner about this issue?
- Are there those who could learn from the opportunity to participate in this activity?

If we look closely at effective partnerships and power integration, we will see people (1) showing respect and energy, (2) being sensitive to others and the ability to read and understand their needs, (3) being flexible yet willing to question sensibly and stand for what is ethically right for both the organization and the people in it, (4) having the willingness to make decisions and to find and work with those who have the knowledge and ability to lead in the moment, and (5) demonstrating an awareness that the overarching design of the organization is the guiding force for power integration in partnerships across and between groups.

If we assume that most members are willing and wanting to contribute to the best of their ability, power must be distributed to those willing to take action and integrated into how they work with others. Power integration through empowerment is always a work in progress.

Incivility in the Workplace

It is hard to build positive, constructive, trusting relationships when people are not experiencing "civil behavior." Conscious or unconscious retaliation or the withholding of open, connective contact and acceptance is often the response to being on the receiving end of uncivil behavior. (Uncivil behavior can include incidents of rudeness, discounting, harassment, bullying, invalidation, and even intimidation.) These behaviors have long been ignored in our society as "normal playfulness." Only recently has it been addressed in publications. But uncivil behavior is not play; it is demeaning and degrading. And it is spreading unchecked in our workplaces. It is difficult to demonstrate advocacy participation when one is a victim of or a participant in perpetuating incivility in relationships.

M. Scott Peck (1993, 53) suggests that civility is an attitude of humanism, defined as the ethical consciousness of other people, individually and collectively, as precious human beings. He also says that everyday incivility is responsible for a vast amount of misery (p. 44). Everyday civil treatment of those around us gives messages of acceptance or rejection, appreciation or nonappreciation, valuing or devaluing. Acceptance, acknowledgment, and appreciation activates and sustains high-potential working relationships and partnerships. Uncivil behavior will not strengthen working relationships and partnerships or encourage productive service of customers.

In many organizations we experience subtle uncivil behavior every day that is potentially disconcerting and disturbing, making it unlikely that advocacy participation will happen. The boss who rips apart a subordinate over a misstep is uncivil. The loud, demanding coworker who takes advantage of others or denigrates his or her leader is uncivil. The face-to-face customer-contact person who ignores or mistreats customers is uncivil. The leader who makes inappropriate, degrading statements in front of others is uncivil.

According to Adele Lynn (1998), here are ten spirit killers at work:

1. Bosses with celebrity egos. They act as if they know everything and employees know nothing.
2. Blame or shame tactics. It's not recognized that all people make mistakes.
3. Phony techniques. That's when the boss calls you into the office and goes through the motions of coaching and performance appraisal.
4. Insincere gratitude. You can tell it's being given only to get something in return.
5. Incongruent actions. Saying one thing but doing another.

6. Wimpy leaders. Employees want leaders who take a stand, make difficult decisions, address performance problems, and communicate.

7. Expectations that apply to some people but not others. That's especially damaging when these people work side-by-side.

8. Lack of passion. When bosses don't give a darn, how can employees be expected to?

9. Bullying. Bosses who aim to make staff feel bad.

10. No follow through. People who say they will but never do.

Davenport, Schwartz, and Elliott (1999) call it "mobbing." Namie and Namie (1999) call it "bullying." It happens when an individual becomes the target of disrespectful and harmful behavior from one person or many people. They are, as a result, working in a hostile workplace as victims of innuendo, rumors, and even public humiliation. It is the not the same as sexual harassment, so it is often ignored as harmless by management. The victim often experiences emotional, even physical problems from the victimization.

In a recent five-year study involving interviews, workshops, and a questionnaire from a widely diverse organizational population, Pearson, Andersson, and Porath (1999) verified that "civility matters." Civility is formally defined as "courtesy and politeness toward fellow beings." The researchers found, "Civility has less to do with formal rules of etiquette than with demonstrating sensibility of concern and regard, treating others with respect. . . . Within the work context, incivility entails the violation of workplace norms for mutual respect, such that cooperation and motivation may be hindered broadly" (p. 4). In a recent national poll, 90 percent of respondents believed that incivility is a serious problem that contributes to violence and erodes moral values (p. 5). Findings of the study included the following:

- When basic standards of respect are violated, the impact tends to ripple inside and outside the organization, potentially impacting reputation.
- Targets are reluctant to report incidences.
- Leaders are often reluctant to take action when it is reported.
- Diversity, downsizing, budget cuts, increased pressures for productivity.
- The use of part-time workers may lead to increased incivility.
- Instigators are three times as likely to be of higher status than the target.
- Instigators tend to be rude to their peers, disrespectful to their subordinates, and hard to get along with.
- Instigators of incivility are both male (70%) and female (30%).
- Costs of incivility can impact the [human, social, and financial] bottom line[s].

As with other behaviors, expectations of civil behavior are to be clearly defined and modeled by leaders. Steps must be taken when this behavior is reported. Uncivil behavior against one person may likely be met with a response of defensiveness from the victim or another person. A push by Mark in accounting may be paid back by a shove from Martin in sales or possibly by Jennifer, a friend of Martin's in receiving. Messages of unfair treatment will be shared with others and will directly or indirectly be acted on. Eventually whole departments become disconnected and hostile to other departments. Uncivil behavior, left unchecked, becomes a company norm.

In order to maintain dignity and respect in organizations, repeat offenders must face the possibility of being discharged. A leader's willingness or unwillingness to do so gives signals of concern or disregard for the environment people work in. "When uncivil incidents are overlooked, the target suffers, the instigator suffers, and the organization suffers" (Pearson, Andersson, and Porath 1999, 21). A most unsettling statement in the study is that "organizations that condone incivility will attract others who act similarly" (p. 21). Inclusion, organizational advocacy, and forgiveness will be minimal in the uncivil environment.

How people treat each other on the job is significant to the willingness of members to support each other and to take risks in doing so. Lack of support interrupts opportunities to be innovative and creative. Working in a civil environment where people treat each other with regard and consideration facilitates the likelihood of innovation, creativity, expanded participation and productivity, and heightened levels of extra role behavior, the place where advocacy participation begins. Incivility increases tension, withholding of information, and separation—physically and psychologically. According to the Pearson, Andersson, and Porath (1999) study, "In nearly half of the cases, the uncivil treatment caused the target to contemplate changing jobs; in 12% of the cases, the target actually quit" (p. 13). Incivility contributed highly to leaving, but they left without reporting the uncivil behavior to anyone as the reason.

Some victims of this behavior, whether from a supervisor or a peer, call this behavior "bullying." Tim Field, founder of the U.K. National Workplace Bullying Advice Line and author of *Bully in Sight*, suggests this behavior is, unfortunately, not unique or even rare in the workplace. A victim of bullying himself, Field believes bullying behavior is a profile of the "socialized psychopath." Although these are strong words, according to a 1996 study by the International Labor Organization (ILO), it happens all too often (Yandrick 1999, 62). Fifty-three percent of U.K. employees were targets of tormenting behavior and 78 percent witnessed it happening to others.

According to Namie and Namie (1999) of the Campaign Against Workplace Bullying (www.bullybusters.org), a nonprofit headquartered in Benicia, California, "The typical environment where bullying occurs is a cutthroat, competitive workplace with people feeling pressure to perform in a controlling environment and a culture that is fear-based." Namie and Namie define workplace bullying as, "The *deliberate, hurtful and repeated* mistreatment of a Target (the recipient) by a bully (the perpetrator) that is driven by the bully's *desire to control* the Target" (p. 17; italics orig.). Command and control is the way work gets done in many of these organizations. The dignity and self-respect of the individual is at risk.

Why should organizations pay attention to this information? Unknowingly, organizations perpetuate uncivil, abusive behavior by not taking action, often seeing a complainer as weak or whining. Because many times it is subtle and rarely comes to an open confrontation (not done openly in front of "those who matter"), the victim is often seen as the "problem employee." These members may leave for organizations where civility is part of the culture. Unfortunately, bullying behavior is contagious. Sooner or later, all that is left is an uncivil environment where competition and degradation is the way to work together. The impact is so insidious that no one notices top performance is no longer happening. Other reasons are found for lowered productivity. Information is no longer shared and people are no longer open to learning from each other. Quality work slips and no one knows why. A "quality process" is started and there is a struggle to make it work. Possibly, as in one organization, a bully is part of the initiating team, regularly sabotaging the process outside of the meetings while pretending in meetings to be committed. In actuality, in some organizations it has little chance to work: The workforce is too busy blaming and shaming for a successful effort. They outlast the process. It becomes only another program to be joked about over the years. ("Remember when the company tried 'quality?' What a joke. We showed them.")

Bullies do not, for the most part, start out being bullies, and they certainly do not see themselves as being so. The failure of leaders to be advocates for civility to address this uncivil, victimizing behavior has implications on all three bottom lines. The human bottom line will suffer because the best and the brightest will not tolerate this behavior. They will "turn off" or leave. The social bottom line suffers when members become self-protective, no longer desiring to represent their organization in a positive way, inside or outside the organization. The financial bottom line suffers when those who stay are not the best and the brightest, feel captive, or are discounted because they are only hands without contributive minds. There will be no advocacy participation here.

Complacency

Complacency is real and present at every level in organizations. It is a disease representing a different form of cynicism. Complacency is no less destructive and contagious than the cynical saboteur. It is the role of leaders to not ignore complacency, but to continually be aware of the motivational issues essential to contributive performance. To ignore complacency is to bless its existence.

Complacent workers are nonadvocates. They are "just there." Mediocre work symbolizes the complacent worker who seeks invisibility. Mediocre workers do not put energy into learning and serving; they do not challenge through questioning; nor do they care to contribute significantly to the purpose of their organization. Measuring their actions against advocacy participation behaviors indicates they are not positive advocates of their organizations, nor are they negative advocates. They just come to work, do mediocre jobs, and take home the financial resources of the company. Active contribution, even adequacy around earning their pay, is in question. This accountant or factory worker shows up every day applying little energy; he or she does the basic requirements of the job. There is no enthusiasm for doing the minimum of his or her work. There is a signal: I'll do what I am supposed to do, no more. The bank teller who greets customers without eye contact or a smile, or does not offer unsolicited additional information about bank services, is practicing mediocrity and complacency—even laziness. Perhaps there is another position in the bank that would bring more enthusiasm. Or possibly there is another organization this person would be more enthusiastic about.

Silence, quietness, or withdrawal may or may not be part of the equation. Organizations often have members such as Bridgette Hetrick, an accounts receivable clerk. Bridgette's personality is "quiet." She works hard every day, arriving early, often doing unrequested extra work, and is deeply loyal. She is in a back office where few pass by or notice her efforts. Yet often others seek her out for answers to questions and to solve dilemmas. Effective supervisors are alert to these silent contributors. Special effort is needed to notice their work. Bridgette and the many other silent workers, though quiet, are not complacent.

Complacent workers are signalling their lack of interest. They have no interest in serving those around them or the customers they vaguely remember make their jobs possible. The light that creates internal motivation long ago has diminished to dependency. Some are quite happy with this state. Others are frustrated and feel victimized. They are putting out just enough effort to be seen as adequate performers. Mediocrity is a practiced state of working. If someone asks for an opinion, a shrugging of the shoulders while knowing the answer has for many become an art. (It just makes more work if he or she answers.) The questioner is ignored, or receives a glare or gesture of dismissal.

Many however, have not previously been offered opportunities to ask questions or provide suggestions. In these organizations, if approached for input, the questioner would be met with stunned silence, suspicion, or astonishment. They ask themselves, What is going on here? It will take time to get the floodgates open and start to hear these voices. Complacency for some is a symptom of fear, tough lessons learned, lack of acknowledgment when input has been given in the past, or cues heard from leaders indicating, "We are the only thinkers here."

Arrogance

As with complacency, arrogance is identifiable. Actions of arrogance include displays of superiority, being overbearing, entitlement, even pretentiousness, and assumptions of importance and privilege. Entitlement is, on occasion, obvious. Open displays of temper, sarcasm, and impertinence (bullying) push and pull workers to be dependent on and controlled by the arrogant person's whims. Emphatically, these characteristics are not limited to formal leaders. Arrogant members, wherever they are in the workplace, often create an atmosphere of "I know all; you know little." Unfortunately, there are many forms of arrogance. Kathryn Hall, a publicist in Kenwood, California, says, "'Intellectual arrogance' is a trap that cuts off the thinkers from the doers. They align themselves with arrogant act-alikes, putting up higher barriers to connection with the 'normal people' who 'know little.'" In this atmosphere, blurred lines and open communication will not happen. Competition becomes the way to work instead of collaboration and cooperation.

"Status arrogance" separates and divides. Partnerships are not possible when status and title solidifies the lines between people. Cues and exchanges provide signals of the existence of their entitlement around status. The status-arrogant leader occasionally "blesses" the less-thans with his or her presence by visiting the plant. As one person noted, he or she walks the aisles with his or her groupies, somber and disconnected (or attentive and condescending), only talking to those who deserve his or her conversation. Status is the thing.

"Knowledge arrogance" can include an attitude of deservedness. The professional who has spent years in school, passed all the certification tests, and is hired at six figures may not feel he or she has to pay dues on the job. His or her arrogance says, "I know it all," separating him or her from colleagues, and eventually leading to isolation. They see themselves as superior contributors.

"Power arrogance" is demonstrated through the insistence on giving orders. Power and control facilitate separation. "Control is what we do when we don't want to face our fears about our survival and security outcomes, not being accepted by others," writes Linda Whiteside (1994, 28). She adds, "Our own imperfections, ambiguity, and chaos" are part of the energy behind control. New, different, and original ideas from those outside of designated power boundaries are ignored, even scoffed at. They insist on dependent behavior. Many are good at giving "the look" or blaming and shaming in front of others, effectively signaling where ideas originate if they are going to be taken seriously. Control triggers activities of manipulation, negative politics, frustration, competition, even sabotage and revenge. Partnering, interdependent activities, and independent contributions become limited.

"Entitlement arrogance" assumes deservedness. Entitled people do not contribute to the benefit of anyone but themselves, or a limited deserving few. They put in their time every day and count the days (or years) until they collect a paycheck without having to go to work (retirement). They push their work off on those they deem unentitled. Their work is routinely mediocre. When held accountable by supervisors or peers, the entitled employee claims betrayal and attacks the credibility of those holding them accountable. They claim the role of victim, make excuses, and spout negativity. They scream, kick, and puff, while demanding others do something about their being wronged. They know they are always right. After all, "Look what I've done for this company!" Sometimes it is hard to identify what that might have been.

"Customer arrogance" is a new form of entitlement. Customer service is now the difference between success or failure for individuals and organizations. Getting our way as customers is becoming an unrelenting demand. Being reasonable and considering the limitations of others (including organizations) is in many instances the last approach. The first approach is to cry foul and assume we are being taken advantage of. Among many stories of customer arrogance, the tale of a well-known department store paying a customer for "bad" tires when they did not sell tires has contributed to the creation of a monster, whether the story is true or not true. Because of concern for their customer service reputation, some stores allow customers to take advantage of their financial bottom line. As customers, we have gotten good at crying "victim."

Customer arrogance also exists in organization partnerships. Partnering exchanges are stopped or difficult when one organization demands compliance instead of an alliance with another organization. An example is an automotive manufacturing organization that holds meetings regularly with suppliers. Although this sounds like a good idea, it is done in an atmosphere of enforcement rather than an exchange of information and "working with." Formal presentations by a supplier entourage are required, with somber exchanges following each presentation. There is an unspoken threat of disengagement. Suppliers leave "glad that another one is over," hoping they have maintained the blessing of the manufacturer. The cost of preparation is high in personnel hours and stress. If the goal is to create fear of disconnect in the management and professional team of the "partner," it works.

"Oppositional arrogance" is a style of thinking, a habit, a mental model, that often includes negative language and frames by the person. These are the people who, no matter what is said or done, are opposed to it. They are the Monday-morning quarterbacks, who know how it should have been done. They loudly proclaim the faults of what was done, no matter what it was. They grouse around and always find something wrong. These people cannot perform as positive organizational advocates because their judgments are based solely on being on the opposite side of whatever is being represented. They prefer maintaining status quo—but status quo is also threatening to them: Nothing is ever right! These people are a disaster when working directly with customers. They openly demonstrate chronic dissatisfaction with the company and/or the products it makes. These are the people who childishly demand, directly or indirectly, "Do it my way, now, or I won't play." Then, when they get what they want, they are still unhappy.

Subtle oppositionally arrogant people are more dangerous. They "play" with others, pretending to agree and yet never seeming to agree at all. These people will claim to be misunderstood when accountability occurs, if it ever occurs.

"Victim arrogance" involves practicing victim positioning. Victims don't feel appreciated, cared for, or acknowledged. They see messes everywhere and the messes are always caused by other people. They mouth the words or make gestures of seeking involvement, but put up blocks to inclusion. They are engaged and ingrained in victimhood.

Victim positioning is also a potential stance of competitive people who feel they have fallen short of their goals. Often they find someone or a group at which to point the finger of blame: "You did not help me when you should have." "You could do more but you won't." "You are in my way or I could make it." The victim seeks to victimize someone else. Open victim messages cause anger, destroying connections. Hidden subtle signals of "you are in my way" will cause confusion and feelings of frustration by partners. Hope will be shattered for both participants.

Victims are saying, "I've been hurt more than you have." Their focus is on the past, possibly the far distant past. They whine (not always quietly), or they suffer in silence and pout. They have stories to tell and occasionally they find other victims to commiserate with. Because they often have low self-esteem, they usually don't take action to change things that victimize them, even if offered the opportunity. They have become dependent on others feeling sorry for them and learned to like the negative attention victim positioning provides.

Steel yourself. These people are difficult, if not impossible, to change. In many cases they are hard workers, and being a victim is a habit and a way to feel valued. Encouraging them to be more decisive and assigning them tasks that they can accomplish helps increase their self-esteem—if they are willing to do so.

Arrogance has many faces and is not limited to any one place in the organization. It exists at all levels of status and title. Highly arrogant persons are unwilling, even unable, to be top performers unless they are held accountable for their actions while having an accompanying willingness to change. Arrogance is disempowering, both for the arrogant actor and for those victimized by their arrogance. Community is not possible when an organization is rampant with arrogant, disconnecting behaviors.

Fear

Fear is a barrier to the initiation of successful partnerships and workplace participation. According to Judith Bardwick (1993), "You can't have a team psychology when people are preoccupied with protecting themselves" (p. 54). To accomplish, we have to feel we have some control over what is going on around us, making it possible to not always be on the alert as to how to protect ourselves.

If an action is based on fear, it is often an attempt to gain control. A human response is to attempt to take control when there is a sense of loss of control and a lack of understanding of what is happening around the member. Chaos that is threatening brings ambiguity and uncertainty, something, we think, to avoid. According to Linda Whiteside (1994), "Control is what we do when we don't want to face our fears about our survival and security, outcomes, not being accepted by others, our own imperfections, ambiguity and chaos" (p. 28). She goes on to say, "We use control to deny our fears." Kathleen Ryan and Daniel Oestreich (1991, 57–58, 91–96), in their research around fear in the workplace, found that negative feelings and self-protection at every status, title, and rank lead to responses indicating the following:

- Loss of trust or pride (fear of being blamed or shamed).
- Being more political (seeking safety nets) by the use of self-protecting attitudes and avoiding undiscussables.
- Cycles of mistrust that are self-perpetuating.
- Discrediting activities.
- Willingness to undermine the success of those around them and their organization.
- Cynicism (not wanting to be so is seen as naïve).
- Not speaking up becomes the "smart" way to operate.

Fear creates a place where talking to those "above" (those at a psychologically different status level) is limited, and the exchange of information with other departments is avoided ("let them find out for themselves"). In this atmosphere, people are always alert to repercussions for their actions, being disconnected is preferred, and low contribution and collaboration is the norm. In this environment, teaming and partnerships are not the way to work. Personal responsibility is avoided and accountability is painful. Yet people get "moved to other areas where their expertise is needed," rather than working with them to improve their performance.

Nothing Has Changed

Robert E. Cole (1999, 64), a professor at the University of California, Berkeley, suggests that "the new workplace will look a lot like the old workplace with lots of technology." Leaders, organizational philosophers, and consultants are anticipating changes to a more inclusive workplace, but is this even possible?

Although many are suggesting, even claiming, that change is happening, Cole (1999) cites contradictory research by David Levine of the University of California, Berkeley. Levine found "the new employment contact has not resulted in much shorter job tenures, much higher pay flexibility, or much different norms of fair treatment over the last fifteen years." Cole goes on to cite dissertation research by Michael Handel of Harvard University stating that there is "little evidence of flattening organizational hierarchies which supposedly lead to employee participation" (p. 64).

There is no doubt that some companies have been crying "participate!" and "you are empowered!" while not adequately providing the means or knowledge to successfully do so. As a result, the tops and the bottoms of organizations become more divided, frustrated, and alienated. Separation widens. Those in the middle firstline (supervisors) are beaten up by both. Those at the top are telling them, "Tell them to do it." Those at the bottom are shouting, "Tell us how?" and the beat goes on. Collaboration, cooperation, and working with are not the way these status quo organizations work. "Power-over" is still what is happening. Nothing has changed.

For those who want to make a difference, to change things for the better, to know that what they do matters, who seek "power with," and for those who want to appreciate their organization as a great place to work, nothing has changed is a scarey, hope-diminishing thought. These thoughts are validated, for example, by the small number of organizations that shout "teamwork" and actually have it become a reality. This could be an explanation of why a study by the Work in America Institute of Scarsdale, New York, when they surveyed 100 of the most innovative U.S. companies to determine research topics that would have the greatest value for their organization, found teamwork to be a concern by 95 percent of the companies surveyed.

Perhaps nothing has changed and surveyed organizations are sensing it. When a study announces nothing has changed and backs it up with numbers, we wonder, "Are we doing the right things?" and "What is really happening in organizations who are claiming to be changing?"

Dealing with Barriers

Issues around power integration, complacency, arrogance, attitudes, contagion, and fear are real in even the most caring and successful organizations. Sensing that nothing has changed (whether real or unreal) is also a response to sudden awakenings of futility in these same organizations. Every day is not perfect, even though change is moving forward. It is one step forward, two steps back, four steps forward, two steps back, and so on.

Dealing with the barriers and setting expectations tied to the overarching design encourages members to reevaluate their workplace circumstances. People constantly evaluate their work circumstances and experiences on the basis of what might have been under different circumstances and conditions. Dealing with barriers is a group project. Although formal leaders actively address barriers, all members are partners in the process. As partner responsibility for the outcome is heightened and accountability for personal performance becomes constructive, the elimination of barriers becomes possible.

Advocacy participation, like trust, cannot be forced by others. Individuals decide to be advocates based on personal provocation. They may be watching to see if (1) issues are being addressed, (2) there are emerging motives for cooperation because new levels of trust and appreciation are occurring, (3) there is a favorable reason why it is safe to be an active advocate, (4) there will be rewards for doing so, and (5) support for this stance is obvious.

PARTING THOUGHTS

Many members come to work every day with little knowledge of how to individually construct, contribute to, advocate for, or change what is happening around them. They see themselves as just another payroll number doing what is to be done the way they think others want it to be done. Some feel forced to maintain silence while watching the disarray around them. They sense they are participating in the disharmony and frustration. Some have long ago learned not to care. Managers are seen as intimidating and controlling. As in the case of one professional, "To say anything is to put your career in jeopardy. I'll just learn what I can and move on." She was, according to her, helpless to make changes. "It took them years to get this way. There's nothing I can do to change it." She is not aware of the power behind each person's personal performance. The willingness of individuals to sit up, take charge of their own work, and "see" what can be done within their own roles is vital to their own success and the success of those around them. Attending to the questions, concerns, and barriers wherever we are in the organization and the ability to directly and indirectly advocate for a movement toward excellence and change is imperative. Being helpless and hopeless removes individual and organizational potential, limiting future accomplishment by the individual and the organization.

BIBLIOGRAPHY

Allcorn, Seth, and Michael A. Diamond. (1997). *Managing People During Stressful Times: The Psychologically Defensive Workplace.* Westport, Conn.:Quorum Books.

Anderson, Harlene. (1997). *Conversation, Language, and Possibilities: A Postmodern Approach to Therapy.* New York: Basic Books.

Bardwick, Judith. (1993). *Danger in the Comfort Zone: From Boardroom to Mailroom—How to Break the Entitlement Habit That's Killing American Business.* New York: AMACOM.

Brion, John M. (1995). *Leadership of Organizations: The Executive's Complete Handbook.* Greenwich, Conn.: JAI Press.

Cole, Robert E. (1999). The Same Ol', Same Ol'—Only Fancier and Faster. *Journal for Quality and Participation* 22 (2): 64.

Csikszentmihalyi, Mihaly. (1990). *Flow: The Psychology of Optimal Experience.* New York: Harper & Row.

Daniels, Tom D., and Barry K. Spiker. (1994). *Perspectives on Organizational Communication.* 3d ed. Dubuque, Iowa: Brown & Benchmark.

Davenport, Noa, Ruth Distler Schwartz, and Gail Pursell Elliott. (1999). *Mobbing: Emotional Abuse in the American Workplace.* Ames, Iowa: Civic Society.

Egan, Gerard. (1994). *Working the Shadow Side: A Guide to Positive Behind-the-Scenes Management.* San Francisco: Jossey-Bass.

Field, Jim. (1996). *Bully in Sight.* Oxford, U.K.: Success Unlimited. Available <http://www. successunlimited.co.uk>.

Fineman, Stephen. (1993). Organizations as Emotional Arenas. In *Emotion in Organizations*, edited by Stephen Fineman. Thousand Oaks, Calif.: Sage.

George, Jennifer M., and Arthur P. Brief. (1996). Motivational Agendas in the Workplace: The Effects of Feelings on Focus of Attention and Work Motivation. In *Research in Organizational Behavior* 18, 75–109, edited by Barry M. Staw and L. L. Cummings.

Giacalone, Robert A., and Jerald Greenberg. (1997). *Anti-Social Behavior in Organizations*. Thousand Oaks, Calif.: Sage.

Hatfield, Elaine, John T. Cacioppo, and Richard Rapson. (1994). *Emotional Contagion*. New York: Cambridge University Press.

Jaworski, Joseph. (1996). *Synchronicity: The Inner Path of Leadership*. San Francisco: Berrett-Koehler.

Lee, Blaine. (1997). *The Power Principle: Influence with Honor*. New York: Simon & Schuster.

LePine, Jeffrey, and Linn Van Dyne. (1998). Predicting Voice Behavior in Work Groups. *Journal of Applied Psychology* 83 (6): 1–16.

Lipman-Blumen, Jean. (1996). *The Connective Edge*. San Francisco: Jossey-Bass.

Lynn, Adele. (1998). *In Search of Humor: Lessons from Workers on How to Build Trust*. Belle Vernon, Pa.: Bajon House.

Mayer, Roger C., James H. Davis, and F. David Schoorman. (1995). An Integrative Model of Organizational Trust. *Academy of Management Review* 20 (3): 709–734.

Morin, William J. (1995). *Silent Sabotage: Rescuing Our Careers and What to Do About It*. Rev. ed. New York: AMACOM.

Namie, Gary, and Ruth Namie. (1999). *BullyProof Yourself at Work: Personal Strategies to Stop the Hurt from Harassment*. Benicia, Calif.: DoubleDoc Press.

Oshry, Barry. (1977). Power and Position. Position paper written for Power & Systems Training, Inc., Boston, Mass.

Pearson, Christine M., Lynne M. Andersson, and Christine Porath. (1999). Workplace Incivility: The Target's Eye View. Manuscript under consideration.

Peck, M. Scott. (1993). *A World Waiting to Be Born*. New York: Bantam Books.

Rachels, James. (1995). What Would a Satisfactory Moral Theory Be Like? In *Moral Issues in Business*. 6th ed., edited by William H. Shaw and Vincent Barry. Belmont, Calif.: Wadsworth.

Ryan, Kathleen D., and Daniel K. Oestreich. (1991). *Driving Fear Out of the Workplace: How to Overcome the Invisible Barriers to Quality, Productivity, and Innovation*. San Francisco: Jossey-Bass.

Van Dyne, Linn, Jill W. Graham, and Richard M. Dienesch. (1994). Organizational Citizenship Behavior: Construct Redefinition, Measurement, and Validation. *Academy of Management Journal* 37 (4): 765–802.

Whiteside, Linda. (1994). On Becoming a Butterfly. *ODPractitioner, the Journal of the National Organization Development Network* 26 (2): 27–32.

Yandrick, Rudy M. (1999). Lurking in the Shadows. *HR Magazine* 44 (10): 61–68.

CONVERSATIONS AND INTERVIEWS

Tim Field, Success Unlimited.
Kathryn Hall, publicist.

PART II

THE SIX ADVOCACY ISSUES IN THE WORKPLACE

ORGANIZATIONAL ADVOCACY®

Spontaneous value-added activities of workplace members that are significant to expanded achievement. These actions are meant to further the well being of themselves, their co-members, and the collective workplace community.

Advocacy participation influences the performance and achievement of the organization and the accomplishments of the contributing individual and his or her group. Being willingly responsible and accountable for his or her own workplace performance is significant to performing as an organizational advocate. Organizational advocacy includes the following issues:

Self Advocacy Actions of workplace members who appropriately promote themselves and their comembers as capable, productive members of the group and organization.

Leader Advocacy Member actions and activities that promote organizational leaders as competent, desirable leaders whose actions are beneficial to organizational achievement. Leader advocates also encourage and support the learning of those leaders who have much to learn about leading.

Member Advocacy Leader actions that promote individual and group members to others as beneficial performers, leading to expanded opportunities to contribute to organizational achievement.

Customer Advocacy Member actions of positively representing the company to the customer and the customer to the company. These actions are linked to performance with both internal and external customers.

Community Advocacy Includes member actions that promote the existence of an inclusive, integrative, and flexible internal workplace community while encouraging the organization to respond to the needs of the outside community.

Inclusion Advocacy The responsibility and accountability of the individual, whatever his or her role, and the organization in the quest to include and respect the worldview of all members in the expansion of individual and organizational potential.[1]

5

Self Advocacy

In present times, *ambition* may suggest equally a praiseworthy or a base desire; the concept is morally neutral. It is what we seek, not the basic drive itself, that involves moral issues.

Gilbert Brim (1992)

One has to be willing to say what our interests and capabilities are, because if we don't tell them ourselves, who will know?

Sheila McNamee, Department of Communication,
University of New Hamphshire

The United States has been chastised for having an achievement-oriented society that places a high value on success. One of the reasons given is that there is an entrepreneurial spirit in the United States that stimulates individual accomplishment and the desire for prosperity. This spirit attracts people with dreams from all over the world to come, work hard, and *become*.

Although these images of human nature may or may not be accurate as an individual or collective identity, it does appear that the desire to be very well-off financially is increasing in the United States. In 1985 it was a goal of 75 percent of American college freshman; in 1945, just 45 percent had the same goal (Brim 1992, 17, 21). Assuming that the trend continues, these changes justify concern as to how individuals choose to become very well-off financially. Will they do it at the expense of others or will they use their ambitious nature to also enhance the well-being of others?

Self advocacy is an important subset of organizational advocacy, and one of the most difficult to present as beneficial. It is not only difficult because it is often overlooked, but because of implications that self-promotion seeks possibly undeserved favor. To promote self was to be seen as self-serving, indicating actions of promoting self selfishly, possibly to the detriment of others.

Self advocacy is, by definition, a necessary ingredient to performing at our best for ourselves and others. Actions of self advocacy (questioning, supporting, promoting, responsibility, appreciating, acknowledging, performing, etc.) are significant to the achievement of feelings of success for ourselves and influencing the perceptions of others. Individuals who deny their self-advocacy urges sometimes decrease their value to their organization.

As a segment of organizational advocacy, self advocacy is defined as a members who are promoting themselves and their comembers as capable, productive members of the group and organization. Actively promoting the achievement and welfare of others helps create common understandings and positive partnering relationships. This removes barriers instead of putting them up or maintaining them.

Actions of appropriate self advocacy are important to achieving success for ourselves and others. The successful organization has many self advocates who have integrated the organization's best interests as part of their own success, while supporting the efforts of others.

The old understanding was that self-promotion was only done by the extremely narcissistic personality who was a highly self-interested employee. Seeking opportunities to be seen as an effective, capable, and contributing member was judged as brownnosing and posturing for the next opportunity or promotion. Of course, this was "bad." Nothing good could come of this selfishness.

As noted earlier, from a Western perspective these activities are known as "instrumental strategies" or actions: using the self and others as instruments for accomplishing personal goals. These activities smack of everything from egomania, nepotism, and social climbing to manipulation, corruption, and dependency. These views are not uniformly shared by other cultures. In some cultures, instrumental styles appear far less egotistical and narrow. The more indirect styles focus on the group, as opposed to the individual, widely distributing leadership and responsibility across the groups worked in. Relationships are important to exercising strong control within the group. These relationships ease the way, open doors, and offer otherwise unavailable opportunities. From this perspective, independent gestures are seen as egotistical and insensitive. Interdependence and emphasis on the group, brings respect.

While we as Americans remain quite proud of our independence, directness, and openness, leaders in Western society are now seeing the benefits of connectedness, influence, and interdependence. Lipman-Blumen (1996) says, "In a general sense, this new [connective] leadership model focuses less on the individual personality of the leader and more on the group, in all its diversity and interdependence. . . . Their most distinguishing characteristic is their willingness to call upon ethical instrumental action" (p. 229). The use of appropriate instrumental styles open up the path to community and supply a foundation of trust that supports partnering relationships (pp. 223–225).

Those practicing excessive ambition, narcissism, and self-interest, wherever located in an organization, have no qualms about undermining the organization for their own advancement or subverting it for their own needs. They feel no obligation or loyalty. They are essentially predators (Peck 1993, 52). These strong words are appropriate for members who seek accomplishment without consideration for the welfare of their comembers, their organizations, or the customers they take advantage of to achieve. In the new workplace new interpretations of ambition, narcissism, and self-interest support competence, worthwhileness tolerance, and achievement.

Ambition

Ambition is a workplace necessity, both for the person and the organization. A person's amount and focus of personal ambition is based on his or her motivation, self-interest, and personality. What one person is ambitious to achieve and is motivated by may be of little interest to someone else. As noted by Brim (1992), individuals can use ambition as a positive force for achievement for themselves and others, or it can be used to destroy the people in their path. Enlightened ambition, according to Menken (1988), "realizes there is greater power and benefit in cooperation, . . . Those who feel ambition and properly direct it become treasures of society, benefactors of progress, facilitators of common prosperity" (pp. 142–143). Destructive ambition drives highly competitive, ambitious people to take advantage, even to victimize others who get in the way of achieving their goals.

In order for an individual to act on ambition, he or she must (1) feel some hope for accomplishment, (2) have the time available to make it possible, (3) sense there are resources to support it, (4) feel it is worthwhile, (5) be willing to make the changes and sacrifices necessary to accomplish his or her goal, (6) understand that accomplishment is based on his or her own issues of competence, and (7) know that nothing worthwhile is accomplished completely on one's own. Ambition is redefined as including working together: cooperation, coconstruction, coproduction, and cocreation. The myth of the self-made man must be replaced with the "coconstructed person."

On the job, the workplace community either adds or detracts from one's belief in the accomplishment of personal ambitions through verification of an "abundance mind-set," the sense that there are sufficient resources and gains available for every member to benefit. The abundance mind-set sees actions of advocacy as beneficial to shared accomplishment. The "scarcity mind-set" (there is not enough opportunities to go around) detracts from the sense of availability and contributes to competition (Covey 1989, 219).

In actuality, healthy self-interest is a normal phenomenon and a healthy attribute of one's personality. Healthy self-interest allows us to dream about what is possible but still stay connected to reality. Some degree of self-interest is necessary in order to be willing to put energy into and take the risks necessary to achieve. It allows us to have a healthy concern for ourselves and contributes to self-esteem regulation.

Taken to the extreme, the highly narcissistic, self-indulgent personality is dependent upon others for good self-feelings. This personality is deeply in need of preserving self-esteem while appearing self-confident, invulnerable, and self-absorbed (Brown 1997, 645–648). In addition, the extremely narcissistic personality may interfere with normal, meaningful relationships with others or interfere with a person's ability to function adequately. Narcissism, as with other aspects of behavior, ranges along a continuum. At the extreme, a narcissistic personality is

- highly defensive and unwilling to accept responsibility for misdeeds.
- threatened by uncertainty.
- unable to judge his or her own limitations, taking risks that exceed his or her authority and capability.
- unwilling to acknowledge the contributions of others.
- connected only to the few who feed his or her paranoia.

James Fisher, Jr. (1999), consultant and author, emphasizes that in order to feel the freedom "to do our own thing," which is a privilege rather than a right, "workers are selfish in the sense that they clearly have a high need to please themselves. Yet they are much less self-centered than those of the please-other mentality. Self-interest creates enthusiasm, which is catching and directed toward the service of others. In this sense they display the antithesis of narcissism" (p. 11). Charles Handy (1989, 64) suggests that a "proper selfishness" is responsible selfishness. The properly selfish person is interested in a future that includes growth and improvement for himself or herself and others and is willing to make sacrifices that make it possible while benefitting others at the same time.

As with ambition, self-interest can equally be a praiseworthy or a base desire, or it can be morally neutral. It is in what we do and how we serve that moves it from fulfilling base desires that are highly self-centered to self advocacy, a praiseworthy, contributive focus concerned with the welfare of oneself and others.

Competence

Individual competence is a building block toward accomplishment of personal and organizational goals. Of course, a person can be competent in things that are completely irrelevant to what needs to be accomplished organizationally. Competence and employability must be actively sought in things that matter to our areas of accountability in the work being done. Since we individually decide what matters, competence is a personal issue. No one can force us to learn the right way to do the right things. Because each person decides on his or her own, an increase in competency is a purposeful act. Even when new skills are learned in informal ways, the member makes a choice to respond and repeat what has been learned or not respond and ignore what was observed or offered.

There are five competency characteristics. They include *motives* (what drives, directs, and selects what we must do to get where we want to go), *traits* (physical characteristics and consistent responses to situations and information), *self-concept* (a person's attitudes, values, or self-image), *knowledge* (what one knows about a certain thing that is relevant to accomplishment), and *skill* (the ability to do a certain task) (Spencer and Spencer 1993, 9–11). These member characteristics impact the ability and opportunity to achieve ambitions and contribute to organizational excellence.

These characteristics are also basic to being a successful self advocate. Questions abound around these same characteristics: What drives this person to promote his or her comembers and organization? Can this person be relied on to be a consistent advocate in the right way? Does this person see himself or herself as a victim or as a contributing partner in the group? Is this person capable of communicating effectively about his or her own needs and the needs of the group and organization? It is within these characteristics that it is realized that one cannot succeed alone: that the contributions of others are essential to personal accomplishment, that no one person can do everything well, and that each person has strengths as well as weaknesses. Organizational accomplishment is the unfolding of the efforts of many.

Worthwhileness

An action is seen as worthwhile when it is measured as worthy by observers. The worthwhileness of a goal or ambition is judged based on what it is contributing to the overall goal of the group. Is it contributive to do what is being done? Questioning worthwhileness may bring the integrity of the goal into stronger focus for the group as a whole. Of course, an individual's or groups' collective motives are not always out in the open to see and discuss. Motives and traits may be evaluated through observation of actions as well as listening to statements. People usually act in ways, consciously or unconsciously, that contribute to something personally valued (seen as worthwhile): a goal, a relationship, a sense of security and safety, or the like.

Tolerance

Self-advocacy gestures of tolerance include openness and discovery. When we are closed minded, we see the people around us as guilty or innocent, often with few grey areas. This is a self-protecting device. Levels of tolerance range on a continuum from intolerance to tolerance. Intolerance is, for some, guided by a search for self-designed concepts of "perfect." For the perfectionist, looking for perfect is a never-ending quest for someone or something that does not fail or betray. For others, the acceptance of what is seen as imperfect makes tolerance possible.

When our intolerance for a person we see as guilty is high, we react accordingly—and it is often visible. A negative reaction, if we look at a medical model, indicates problems. If we take medication and we break out in hives, we are having a bad reaction. If we take medication and our symptoms get steadily better, we are, as the doctors say, responding to the medication. We are tolerating the medication that is being used as an intervention to bring improvement. This would suggest that intolerance can change to tolerance if we take steps to learn and change our intolerant reactions.

Self advocates practice being open to discovery, a learning activity. Discovery is to see (to listen, read, associate, merge different things together) the same world and to think differently. Discovery often happens as a result of being purposely or accidentally in the right place at the right time. Serendipitous discovery can be enlivening. Of course, being able to see the discovery and then to turn it into a source of competitive advantage is noteworthy. The discovering member has the experience necessary to make new sense through efforts to reframe, reenvision, reform, or reassemble into something new and contributive.

A STORY OF REGRET

Recently a talented leader told me a story of regret. This leader is a highly capable, highly trained, credible, relational leader who has had many successes in his career—a person to be admired. In fact, this story happened as an outcome of his earlier successes and an opportunity he had as a result of those successes. I will call him David.

David was a vice president of a large, national organization. He had started in the field working beside the workers, worked under the guidance and watchful eye of strong, successful leaders in the corporate office, and then was moved to run a division to hone his leadership skills. He had become very visible to the CEO and chairman of the board because of his ideas and abilities. His future was bright. Even in the far hinterlands he was innovative and productive. He designed and piloted a new service and proposed it back to the corporate office as a focus for the future. He returned to start the application in a new division. This was a risk, as this large company was, and remains, a status quo organization.

David and his hand-picked group of entrepreneurs flourished in the new division. It was exciting and challenging. Early on, it made money. The potential in the future was obvious. But something went wrong.

David and his group's energy and success did not go unnoticed by another leader. This leader, we shall call Robert, was bored with his position. He had been president of the largest division of the company for many years. The recent years had been difficult. Profits had dropped; his workforce was complacent, competitive, and difficult to work with. His own vice presidents were feuding. He was a charismatic leader and there were always ready excuses for the division's problems, but would they remain acceptable for long? He was tired and ready to move on.

Robert looked around and saw the new division. He also saw the leader as vulnerable: David's experience, although strong, was less than his own, and David was not taking advantage of opportunities to shine light on what was happening successfully. This left the door open for Robert to get the chairman's attention. He could leverage the weaknesses and vulnerability of the new division to get what he wanted. After all, he was the more experienced leader. Over the next months Robert routinely got the ear of the chairman, telling him what he could do with the now successful fledgling division. He magnified the normal challenges and campaigned within the leadership group about what could be done, if he was running the new division, to move it faster, increase productivity, and "get the job done."

It was easy to get the blessing of the chairman, who was impatient for expanded performance in the new division. Also, the chairman was looking for a place to move Robert without it appearing to be a step backward. This could be the move. After all, he thought, this would be an opportunity for David. He was young and bright—he could learn from Robert's experience. Soon Robert was moved in above David and things turned sour. Within six months David and his entrepreneurs were either moved out of their jobs, had someone put over them "with more experience," fired, or made the choice to leave. This was not the new workplace they had been hired into.

What Could David Have Done?

In looking back on what had happened, David realized there was much he could have done to protect himself and his people from Robert's piracy. His main regret was that he forgot to be a self advocate, to actively create strong positive images regarding the group to those who mattered. He could have been more aware of the political maneuvers around him and protected his group during the early, more vulnerable times.

David was an innovative, productive, relational, and capable leader. His people supported his strengths, challenged his weaknesses, and responded to his leadership by developing a new successful and futuristic division in a status quo organization. He led his people in new ways toward goals that were not fully understood by the top leadership of his company. Without gestures of advocacy it left him, his comembers, and his fledgling organization vulnerable to the envy and lust of a more seasoned political fighter, Robert.

David had not leveraged self-advocacy opportunities to lessen the vulnerability of himself and his group. Like it or not, a key role of leaders is to keep themselves and their groups seen as successful in the eyes of those who count, without ignoring discrepancies. People see what they are reminded to see. The following are some self-advocacy activities that are beneficial.

Blow the Horn

Very few people have accomplished much without the support and goodwill of others. Self advocacy promotes as appropriate your own activities and the activities of others. It is blowing the horn and letting people know what is coming from the group. It is to influence and promote the accomplishments of individuals and the collective accomplishments of the group as beneficial, productive, and advantageous to the performance of the organization.

Benchmark Beneficially

Tell top management what has been done elsewhere, how the group is meeting the challenge, and the benefits these activities provide to the workplace community as a whole. This reassures them that good decisions have been made on their part to put the advocate in the leadership position. Errors in judgment must not be withheld; providing explanations clarifies what has occurred and what is being done to move forward. It also reinforces the assumptions that the advocate and the group members are making appropriate decisions to continue group achievement.

Develop Relationships That Count

Both inside the workgroup and within the higher leadership group it is important for the leader to seek out and work with others to create internal and external partnerships and alliances. It is within these relationships that top-performance opportunities occur. It is also within these partnerships and alliances that gaps in performance can be addressed. When alliances external to the group work well, information is provided, suggestions are made, and concerns are voiced when there is a sense that something may be amiss. Successful relationships provide opportunities to work in partnership in addressing these concerns, strengthening relationships and connections between individuals and groups and encouraging buy-in by observing others into the success of the group.

Remind Others Why You Are All There

Don't let those external to the group forget that you and the people you are working with are the best ones for the job, and why. Speak up about what is working, why it is working, and who is doing it. Strengthen the belief that this can only be done if you and your people are the ones doing it. Remind them through reinforcement of the message, recognition of who has done what, and inviting them to celebrate accomplishments.

Actively Develop

Actively promote your people as the best in the business, and make sure they are. Take the time and money to invest in them. Keep their skills and enthusiasm growing through challenges, empowerment, recognition of what each has done, and expansion of capabilities. If the money is not readily available, encourage self-investment. It is through these people that the organization learns lessons, remains in a mode of growth, and remains creative. Doing so yourself and honoring those who also do so demonstrates the value of being responsible for your own employability.

Be Authentically Enthusiastic

Let others know that there are synergistic characteristics in the group that cannot easily be replaced, while being open about how the group can improve. The enthusiasm displayed for the team and how it works energetically together expands credibility. By creating a sense that the group cannot succeed without each member already in place (and those to be added, if needed) the leader reinforces the importance and urgency of maintaining the group. This lessens opportunities for others to undermine the group. Consistency and authenticity around what is said regarding the group establishes a foundation for what observers believe about the group's accomplishments.

The following is an outline of the differences between high self-interest and self advocacy:

High Self-Interest	Self Advocacy
Forgets others are essential	Actively promotes the talents of self and others
Focuses on "me"	Says "we"
Holds information to themselves	Invites others to understand/add to information
Says, "I am the reason for this success"	Promotes why *we* are succeeding
Puts up barriers to involvement	Invites contributions of members and observers
Uses others as stepping stones	Pushes members to the forefront

LESSONS LEARNED

There are always things to be learned during disappointing times. David learned lessons he was to consider later in his work. Perhaps he was not in tune with the highly narcissistic activities of the other leader seeking redemption from past insufficiencies. Or perhaps it was not something that could have been avoided, because of the connection the "shark" had established over his years with the chairman.

The first lesson learned is that the assumption that others see and understand the goals, successes, and endeavors of the group one represents can be fatal. For a leader, the conscious and subtle promotion of himself or herself and the group as capable, essential, and productive is a priority and responsibility. Otherwise, others will fill in the blanks, often using less than correct information. The group (and the leader) is left vulnerable to the destructive self-interests of others.

The second lesson learned is that the success of an individual or group does not occur in isolation. To be integrated into the overall workplace community as successful (or striving for success), the group (1) must be seen as a high-performing group that is putting energy into a productive effort; (2) is innovative in achieving goals; (3) steps forward both individually and as a group when necessary; (4) is flexible, adaptive, and cooperative; (5) has resilience when change is required; (6) is individually and collectively enrolled in achieving group goals and the goals of the company as a whole; (7) is willing to seek input and support from other groups and individuals across the workplace community; and (8) has a formal leader (and group members) who knows and understands the importance of advocating the self and the group as successfully demonstrating these characteristics.

The third lesson learned is that there are always political realities to deal with. Political behavior was used by Robert to gain personal advantage to the detriment of the group. Few people can succeed when a high level of negative political activity is happening and they are the target. Robert was willing to take advantage for his own gain. His political activity filled in the blanks as he moved to fill the information void in his own way. It was too late when awareness came of the unscrupulous and irresponsible rival. Eventually the group floundered and the division failed.

HOW TO BE A SUCCESSFUL SELF ADVOCATE

The successful workplace community automatically performs activities that promote trust, inclusiveness, flexibility, resilience, and connection. In these organizations it is understood that (1) all members contribute to the welfare of the organization, (2) members participate in the construction and sustainability of the holding community and culture, (3) accountability is an exchange, and (4) members at all levels make positive personal choices about advocacy participation. The following describe the actions of the self advocate.

Other-Awareness Perspective

Self advocates have an other-awareness orientation that encourages them to seek and appreciate the contributions of others while being constantly aware of the impact of their own work on others (a systems approach). Other-awareness efforts bring balance to personal viewpoints through ongoing and purposeful consultancy with others and the development of contributive partnerships. Being aware of how to learn from and serve others makes it possible for all participants to perform at a higher level. Our ability to be aware of these opportunities often depends on our relationships and whether the organization makes it possible for people to take action. It may also depend on our behavior with others. Am I seen as responsible and trustworthy, and am I working well with others?

Messages of Belief

To attempt to influence others without a personal belief in what is being promoted is detrimental to connection. What we think, say, and do matters to successful organizational advocacy, stretching or following procedures and rules, and developing pleasant and beneficial relationships. The secret to this statement, often made throughout this book, is that we must believe in and appreciate what we are advocating.

We influence through choices we make, all the time, every day. We impact our own opportunities to become willing contributive partners. These daily activities create a "trail" for others to see, helping them to decide whether to be responsive to offers of partnership. The desire to be a willing partner is based on our willingness to influence with honor. For others, both inside and outside of the group, to believe what is said, there are certain actions and issues of self advocacy that must occur for messages of belief to be heard:

- The advocate is seen as sincere and authentic.
- What or who is being advocated is seen as credible.
- The message includes the willingness to take pressure on behalf of the group.
- Reciprocal relationships exist with those receiving the message.
- The message conveys hope, worthiness, and capability of the advocate and the group being represented.
- The advocate acknowledges setbacks without minimizing and without blaming others.
- The advocate asks questions and seeks the input of others.
- The advocate regularly evaluates the responses of others and feeds reliable information back to the group about how improvements can be made.

Advocacy messages require positive relationships. For this reason, the self advocate has strong interdependencies with members within and outside the group. Each person is a self advocate, performing actions of advocacy participation that stimulate top performance by all members of the group.

Challenge the Status Quo

An element of advocacy participation is challenging the status quo. Advocacy participation insinuates there may be several ways to "get it done" (if done is ever achievable). There is an openness to listening, risking, flexibility, experimenting, seeking different viewpoints, and acknowledging that approval and disapproval are all appropriate ways to provide information. A caveat here is that "appropriate" means just that—attacking is not appropriate. Exchanging information constructively requires respectful, honest, and open conversations connected to the situation, while deemphasizing personal agendas. (A measure of personal agenda must exist or disinterest becomes the natural response.)

Demonstrate Positive Intent

Demonstrating positive intent is a foundation point for self advocacy. Working well with others requires a shared sense of safety and that one does not threaten the welfare of another. Through working well together, more is accomplished than working against each other. Most demonstrations of positive intent start with an individual who is willing to promote mutual self advocacy in order to gain an understanding of a need. Mutual self advocacy provides openings for both parties to win, answering the question, "What's in this for us?"

Being a willing partner suggests a mutual consent to work on a shared interest, something the participants agree requires the skills, expertise, and investment of the partnering members. Putting caring energy into relationships makes it possible for each person to demonstrate his or her intent to be a willing, contributive partner. A successful partnership requires each participant to demonstrate a positive intent to

- put energy into the work to be accomplished.
- seek opportunities to exchange ideas or information while encouraging open collaboration.
- understand the benefits of individual uniquenesses.
- know that resources from outside the group can enhance accomplishment.
- be committed to shared and understood goals connected to the organization's overarching design.
- purposely build the partnering relationships.

In today's workplace people are looking for ways to work more effectively together, perhaps even new ways to organize and perform work. To do so is to assume individual responsibility and accountability and to actively demonstrate the willingness to personally and intentionally explore what can be done in a coconstructed workplace environment. To attempt to do so alone is futile. To attempt to do so without actions of self advocacy regarding your own performance and that of those in partnership with you is misguided and possibly futile.

Constructive Conflict

People are different in so many ways. Inclusion of all members and the conflict that results makes conflict a normal occurrence of organizational life. Successful partnerships build on differences and the constructive conflict that

comes out of those differences. Conflict can be seen as positive and beneficial or threatening and negative according to the mind-set of the group or the
individuals within that group. As noted earlier, groups made up of self advocates with an abundance mentality® know that there will be enough of the pie
to go around for everyone—that working well together expands the reward
opportunities for everyone. Constructive conflict often leads to increased alternatives, greater understanding, and higher group efficacy once members
realize it is okay to agree to disagree constructively. Innovation and creativity
happens through difference and the active contribution of new viewpoints,
ideas, and understandings from those who see things differently.

Meeting Expectations

Each of us offers rewards or punishments to others for how they work with
us on the job. Social contracts are established between members as to how
they will work together. Are they going to be competitive or cooperative?
Will they deal directly with each other or avoid doing so by finding other
ways to get information or perform their work? Once the contracts are established they are difficult to change without new, open, workable agreements.

We are human and our organizations are extensions of our humanness. It is
difficult if not impossible to have others, whether comembers, family, or
friends, consistently meet our expectations over time. What we expect of them
constantly slides on a spectrum from unrealistic to realistic. Our expectations
change, and we forget to let people know they have changed. Sometimes those
expectations are significantly met, more than could be expected, and sometimes there is dismal failure in doing so. Disappointment is the outcome.

Where a person is at a given moment and how he or she has in the past
handled disillusionment and disappointment designs a person's healthy or
unhealthy response to a situation. Mary Parker Follett called this the "law of
the situation" (Nohria 1995). Nohria, an associate professor at the Harvard
Business School, says, "Follett believed that in any situation reasonable people
could come to an agreement of who needed to do what to achieve the best
possible results" (p. 158). Expectations are then clearer and more realistic.

CONVERSATIONS

Conversations are not just talk. It is within this setting that people promote
their case, decide, listen, learn, disagree, challenge, question, describe, inform, learn, and so on. Understandings are reached or confused. Relationships are deepened, neutralized, or adversely affected. Somehow, in some
small or large way, each conversation impacts something or someone—somehow. For this reason we must pay attention to our thoughts, what we say, what
we do, and how we connect in our conversations.

Connective conversations are essential to advocacy participation. It is ongoing conversations that facilitate questioning, thinking, and action. Infor-

mal conversation reinforces connections and the accomplishment of work. Conversations lead to appreciation—or lack of appreciation. Conversations make it possible to identify

- the work and what is to be accomplished.
- what has been done in the past and what worked well (or didn't work well) and why.
- the people and interdependencies involved with accomplishment (and that solidify partnering relationships).
- the skills required to do the work.
- how the work will flow to accomplishment.
- the need for revitalization when energy has been lost.
- the messages of advocacy offered by others.

Advocacy participation, including self advocacy, requires us to pay attention to what is said in conversations. Conversations facilitate day-to-day activities that maintain our organizations. Learning and serving is benefitted by open conversations. What we do is most often "designed" by our conversations with others and the relationships developed and sustained through conversation. These conversations must be experienced as connected, authentic, and valued by those involved. Kofman and Senge (1993), in discussing connection, invention, and coordination in a learning organization, say, "When people talk and listen to each other . . . they create a field of alignment that produces tremendous power to invent new realities in conversation, and to bring about these new realities in action" (p. 18).

Constructive conversation brings agreements and disagreements into the open, making it possible to find the best way to approach issues and concerns. Can people genuinely disagree about who should do what and how and continue to communicate successfully? Absolutely. There will be cases where each clearly understands the interpretation of the others but they still disagree. It is through conversation that members (and customers) feel genuinely heard and valued. Effective conversations move learning, serving, and accomplishment forward.

CONNECTION TO THE WORLD I WANT TO WORK IN

Self advocacy is significant to connecting with others. People seek to know those who are around them, what they stand for, whether they can be trusted, if there is a likelihood they will be there if needed, and what their individual capabilities and uniquenesses are. Exchanges of information through the conversations of working together provide opportunities to become part of the world we work in—to become "legitimate" members of our workgroup and world.

Having connected conversations is difficult when working in an organization where one is uncomfortable. The member becomes disillusioned and demoralized. Something has to change. The choices are to (1) actively work to neutralize or change one's own responses, (2) become involved in intentionally influencing or changing what is unacceptable, or (3) leave. To remain without making one of these choices can initiate self-protective and disconnected activities. Constructive participation in our working world involves connection not only with our comembers but also to the organization each member represents every day, both on and off the job. Connection cannot occur when an individual is self-destructive. Before the member can be meaningfully involved in transforming their workplace, one must first transform himself or herself.

Peggy Holman (1999), a writer and consultant active in whole systems change, believes that what facilitates transformation are the beliefs from which we act (p. 10). Holman uses a "picture" (Figure 5.1) in her work in large-scale change in organizations to affirm the importance of establishing understandings of the benefits of personal and organizational change. The importance of the model is in connecting the individual to the workplace community; connection and transformation makes it possible to be part of the move toward "The World I Want To Work In."[2]

One-on-one connection (see Figure 5.1) across the organization is vital to individual and organizational growth. One strong, positive relationship can make a difference. Companies and countries have flourished or failed based on a connection between two individuals. The friendship of Bill Gates and Steve Ballmer of Microsoft designed a company with worldwide implications. The friendship of Roosevelt and Churchill was significant to changing the outcome of World War II. In the fast-paced world of work, partnerships facilitate the advocacy of ideas and opportunities that may not otherwise be seriously considered. The design and construction of what is to be done in partnership in order to anticipate, design, implement, and sustain beneficial change depends on connected relationships and effective partnering. Ultimately, the efforts and energies of each person in partnership with others matters.

I, the Individual

Change starts with changing the worldview and understandings of individuals. Each person makes choices deciding whether he or she will examine his or her own worldview and explore the possibility of change. In this evaluation, the individual looks at himself or herself and his or her workplace as ways of being (his or her confidence as a person whose work and involvement as a responsible person on the job matters) and ways of doing (contribution as an accountable individual who is capable and willing to do his or her best).

Individual change is initiated by awareness of a need. To achieve change and sustain it over time requires an environment that nurtures change through encouragement (because there will be moments of despair), the tools to apply those changes (providing an opportunity to succeed), and connections across the community that acknowledge the change as beneficial and contributive

Figure 5.1
The World I Want to Work In

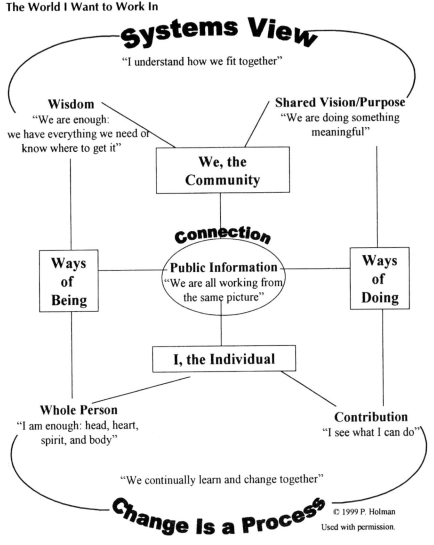

Source: Peggy Holman, Unlocking the Mysteries of Effective Large-Scale Change, in *At Work* (San Francisco: Berrett-Koehler Communications, 1999). Used by permission.

(to support and celebrate current and future progress). Without the support of the community and the rewards of accomplishment to support the new ways of doing things, the likelihood is that eventually the member will revert back to the old ways of being in the past. Connections across the workplace community are significant to establishing strong collegial relationships. Supportive relationships make it possible to overcome the discomfort of personal change. Self-advocacy gestures of support and encouragement help members to connect and value the being and doing of others during difficult times.

When organizational advocacy being and doing happens, individuals and groups get serious about making it possible for everyone to contribute. In this inclusive environment it becomes important that members be attentive to being interactive, to belong in meaningful ways, and to be open to uniqueness. Each person, whatever the reality is in their organization, is personally responsible for his or her daily contributions to the formation of the evolving community. Geoffrey Bellman (1992), organizational consultant and author, suggests that real contribution requires "adultness." He says, "As the individual who is in the middle of it, you can be an adult whether the climate is there or not; you cannot wait for the company to say that it is all right. It is up to you to lead your life, and your work is part of that life" (p. 268).

People who work together are looking for predictability and adultness. Each wants to know what to expect. Each person personally designs who he or she is seen to be through a pattern of what was done in many yesterdays and what is done today, resulting in an impression (reputation) that has to be lived with tomorrow and in the future. Self advocates design an image that predicts being cooperative, supportive, respectful, willing, and contributive. Building connecting relationships through positive ways of being and ways of doing helps others accept the contributions of the whole person—the total person— as being enough. Enoughness says, "As I am and as I will become, I am significant. What I think, say, and do matters to me, my colleagues, and the success of this organization."

We, the Community

Although change can start and even be sustained and made to work through the efforts and energies of one person, ultimately change requires the cooperation of many others: Connection is the basis for cooperation. The organizations we work in are what they are because well-meaning people have worked hard to get them where they are today. Connections and interpersonal relationships are built and sustained over time. These connections become the glue that holds organizations together in times of difficulty. Organizations have histories of things that have worked and not worked and ways of working together that don't always make sense. These ways of doing things have been established over time by past and current members, reflecting the culture and values of those members.

It is important that we are all working from the same overarching design. This makes sharing of information and connection essential to achievement. Reaching an understanding based on this design encourages actions that are ultimately sensible to participants understanding how we fit together. Wisdom (the ability to make decent sense of what we know and don't know) tells us that the picture is always changing and that the knowledge and understanding to make changes are ever present within organizations. Wisdom also tells us that when change is happening the overarching design (mission, vision, values, and purpose) must be kept in mind.

Because communities are always a changing design coconstructed by many and change in one area ripples into others (systems view), members at all levels must work together to constantly construct the design while on the run. It takes uncommon wisdom to know which pieces are to be kept and which ones are to be discarded. These decisions require the participation and sensemaking processes of a competent, involved, diverse membership.

It cannot be emphasized enough that formal and informal leaders must be involved. This includes labor union leaders, if they exist in the organization. Connection across levels and groups makes it possible for each person to make sense of what is happening—and to be involved. Achieving clarity when a whole system is involved requires tapping the wisdom and achieving the participation of members at every level. After all, we construct the organization. We *are* the workplace community.

Connecting Too Tightly

Of course, we can connect too tightly to anything. Doing so at work, a place where pressure to conform begins even in the hiring interview ("Does she fit?"), is more likely if one's group sees responsibility as represented by long hours of work and involvement to the extreme. Americans have a heritage that values hard work, affectionately called the "work ethic." The theory suggests that if you work hard, you will succeed. We are no longer always talking about the physical hard labor of decades ago. Much of the time we are talking about equally fatiguing mental work. Not only are we working longer hours on the job, in meetings, and doing our work, we are continuing to extend our workdays, adding working at home and in our cars. A recent study of 800 executives by Exec-U-Net verified the increase, at least at the executive level. The study indicated that average hours on the job per week increased for all executives from 55.6 to 56.4.

Women appear to be more sensitive to workaholism than men. In the same Exec-U-Net survey, women executives defined themselves as workaholics at 56.9 hours per week; male executives did so at 59.9 hours. According to Dave Opton, executive director of Exec-U-Net, it could be because women are more concerned about family, work, and personal interests, "some because they want to; others because they have to."

Workaholism (compulsive overwork) has for some become an addiction. People become so obsessed with their work that they cannot disconnect to take time to spend in leisure or even for a decent vacation. Even without the need, workaholics stretch their time on the job (hard workers put in the time when necessary but disappear when there is not a need to stay around). Workaholics are preoccupied with work. They work late and on weekends, whether it is a busy time or not. Eventually, workaholics become less productive than the person who leaves at quitting time.

There are multiple reasons why people become workaholics, including having supervisors and being in whole organizations that see overtime as an indication that an individual is committed. And, for some workaholism provides an escape for problems at home. For too many of us, work is no longer just about the money, it is about who we are and/or who our organizations expect us to be. Whatever causes it, the workplace will never successfully fill the painful gap in the workaholics life. Somehow, for the workaholic, there is a stronger need to be appreciated, taken seriously, and valued at work than at home. Workaholism is a dependent behavior; the individual loses themselves in work and eventually only depends on his or her organization to provide self-worth. He or she becomes connected too tightly to the organization to the exclusion of outside life. Family, friends, and other affiliations are subordinate to work.

There can be a seduction by the demands of the workplace resulting in a giving of more than is safe to give. Until recent decades we worked hard, but work remained secondary to other segments of our life. For too many, for better and for worse, work and life outside work have blurred into each other. Is this part of advocacy participation? Must one lose oneself in work in order to be seen as a committed, enrolled member? Of course, the answer to the question is complex.

Because work is personal, we all respond accordingly—personally. This suggests members must be open to a lot of different emotions about our work, without guilt. To be successful self advocates, it is important that we be both attracted and repelled by our work and our organization. It must become habit to see, evaluate, and respond as learning and serving participants. Members must care about the welfare of themselves, their comembers, and the organization while "having a life" (meaningful relationships and activities) outside of work.

PARTING THOUGHTS

The final message of this chapter is offered to you from the writings of James R. Fisher, Jr. (1999), on the culture of contribution. It is within the reality of this culture that organizational advocacy happens:

Workers need to think like victors, not victims; to be purposeful, not personalities; to take risks, not be obsessed with security; to cooperate, not simply comply; to be creative, not mirror expected behavior; to be proactive, not reactive; to focus on what is right, not what is wrong. They need to act like adults. And, yes, they need to be selfish, not selfless. (p. 10)

The proactive, ethical, and slightly selfish adult puts energy into his or her workplace and the outside-the-workplace world. Both worlds are taken seriously and attempts are made toward balance. He or she knows the limits and boundaries that are needed to keep both worlds healthy, rewarding—and separate. Self advocacy is not selfishness. Self advocacy includes contributing because it is meaningful to the member, a selfish act, while remaining aware at all times of the need to do so in ways that are beneficial to oneself, others, and the organization being represented both on and off the job every day. It supports the need to have a place for advocacy participation in both places, at home and at work.

NOTES

1. © 1999 Jane Galloway Seiling.
2. The model used, "The World I Want to Work In," is changed from Peggy Holman's "The World I Want to Live In." Her willingness to allow this alteration is appreciated as well as her generosity in allowing me to use it.

BIBLIOGRAPHY

Bellman, Geoffrey. (1992). *Getting Things Done When You Are Not in Charge.* San Francisco: Berrett-Koehler.

Brim, Gilbert. (1992). *Ambition: How We Manage Success and Failure Throughout Our Lives.* New York: Basic Books.

Brown, Andrew D. (1997). Narcissism, Identity, and Legitimacy. *Academy of Management Review* 22 (3): 643–686.

Covey, Stephen R. (1989). *The 7 Habits of Highly Effective People: Powerful Lessons in Personal Change.* New York: Simon & Schuster.

Fisher, James R., Jr. (1999). How the Culture of Contribution Gives Your Company a Grow-Up Call. *Journal for Quality & Participation* 22 (4): 6–13.

Handy, Charles. (1989). *The Age of Unreason.* Boston: Harvard Business School Press.

Holman, Peggy. (1999). Unlocking the Mystery of Effective Large-Scale Change. In *At Work*, edited by Alise Valencia. San Francisco: Berrett-Koehler Communications.

Kofman, Fred, and Peter Senge. (1993). The Communities of Commitment: The Heart of Learning Organizations. *Organizational Dynamics* 22 (2): 5–23 (Special Issue on The Learning Organization.

Lipman-Blumen, Jean. (1996). *The Connective Edge.* San Francisco: Jossey-Bass.

Menken, Daniel Lee. (1988). *Faith, Hope and the Corporation: Sharpening Your Business Philosophy and Business Ethics.* St. Paul, Minn.: Phronthisterion.

Nohria, Nitin. (1995). Mary Parker Follett's View on Power, the Giving of Orders, and Authority: An Alternative to Hierarchy or a Utopian Ideology? In *Mary Parker Follett: Prophet of Management. A Celebration of Writings from the 1920s*, edited by Pauline Graham. Cambridge: Harvard University Press.

Peck, M. Scott. (1993). *A World Waiting to Be Born.* New York: Bantam Books.

Spencer, Lyle M., Jr., and Signe M. Spencer. (1993). *Competence at Work: Models for Superior Performance.* New York: John Wiley & Sons.

Tyler, Kathryn. (1999). Spinning Wheels. *HR Magazine* 44 (9): 34–40.

Weick, Karl. (1995). *Sensemaking in Organizations.* Thousand Oaks, Calif.: Sage.

CONVERSATIONS AND INTERVIEWS

Peggy Holman, The Open Circle Company.
Sheila McNamee, University of New Hampshire.

6

Leader Advocacy

Don't get in the habit of broadcasting your boss's sins. Don't let yourself become a victim of your boss's weaknesses. And stop looking for evidence (in clandestine water cooler sessions with your colleagues) to justify your feelings about your terrible boss. . . . If you fall into these habits, you'll become afflicted with the "metastasizing cancers" of the workplace: complaining, criticizing, comparing, and competing.

Stephen R. Covey (1999)

Actions of co-members in supporting and promoting their leader as competent, desirable, and beneficial to the organizational group are important to the leader's ability to perform. Members who advocate initiate a flow of understanding directed toward their leader.

Jane Galloway Seiling (1997)

As group members we influence leader opportunities to succeed through our own influencing activities. Our verbal appreciation or denigration of those in a formal leadership role influences their acceptance and their opportunities to lead effectively. As positive or negative advocates of our leaders what we think, say, and do and the symbolism of our appreciation of them influences those around us. Leader advocacy is defined as member actions and activities that promote organizational leaders as competent, desirable leaders whose actions are beneficial to organizational achievement. Leader advocates also encourage and support the learning of those leaders who have much to learn about leading. When members promote the success and achievement of their leaders, somehow it always supports their own opportunities to reach maximum achievement.

For formally assigned leaders, leading is tough if it happens at all when support is lacking from those in a "reporting to" role. Daniels and Spiker (1994) say, "Although subordinates generally are in a less powerful position in the superior–subordinate relationship, they certainly are not powerless. They can and do attempt to influence their superiors and may well use some unsavory tactics such as threat and aversive stimulation in the process" (p. 214).

Unsavory influencing tactics by those being led are negative behaviors that include (1) giving suggestions in ways that signal "you are doing it wrong—again," (2) dominating strategies (withholding information, blocking partnerships with others, etc.), (3) efforts to control (the desire for freedom to act on our own may activate attempts to control those we sense are controlling us), and (4) being judgmental (activities of open cynicism, lack of cooperation, and being disrespectful). Perhaps each of us should be reminded that our work lives (as well as our personal lives) are shaped and directed by the accumulation of many common events and our responses to those events occurring over many days, weeks, months, and years of working together. Negative influencing tactics are problem generators, not problem solvers.

Whether they acknowledge it or not, leaders are most successful when those who work for them are willing to work with them. Members exert higher levels of effort, responsibility, accountability, and appreciation when there is shared respect and positive regard for the achievement of each other, our leaders, and comembers. Wilfred Drath (1996), a research scientist at the Center for Creative Leadership in Greensboro, North Carolina, says, "The effectiveness of leadership is determined by the extent to which people take responsibility for participating in leadership—not because some leader has figured out how to 'share' leadership but because leadership is a property of the relationships people form when they are doing something together" (p. 2).

Americans don't like to be told what to do. When listening in on conversations, it is common to hear complaints and admonishments about those in charge, or those who think they are in charge, and to hear comments on how things should be done. Few of us work where these comments are welcomed by the leaders we are talking about. There is a sense that there would be repercussions—or that no one really listens anyway. So we talk to each other and nothing is changed.

It is not commonly felt that leaders need and desire support and acknowledgment from those in subordinate positions. When comments are made in praise to a leader, they are often received as suspect. If constructive feedback is given (often even when requested), the member feels vulnerable. Once in a superior position, it is assumed that learning only comes from above.

More and more in today's workplace the intent and motives of those in leadership roles are automatically suspect. We don't always offer others the benefit of the doubt, especially those in management. Even with explanations we ask ourselves and others, "Why are they doing/saying/wanting/providing that?" We don't always trust what we hear or what we see.

Katz and Kahn (1978) define leadership in behavioral terms as "*any act of influence on a matter of organizational relevance*" (p. 574; italics orig.). To suggest that the role of influencing is limited to formal leadership is contradictory to how work is being done in today's workplace. Activities previously performed by formal leaders are now being done by those doing the work, those who know the job the most. The broad sharing of leadership functions contributes to organizational effectiveness under almost all circumstances. Formal leaders, informal leaders, and leaders of the moment are vital to organizational achievement. At any given moment the leadership abilities of organizational advocates are called for—even insisted upon—no matter what their assigned role.

Responsible members take ownership of their actions (or inaction) in all their relationships in the workplace, including with the management group. The concepts of membership emphasize personal responsibility and constructive accountability and that leaders are also members. Membership suggests involvement and heightened personal responsibility for what one does and says. Leader advocates intentionally support their leader, reinforcing the actions of integrity made by the leader. They know that the constructive exchange of ideas and information requires respectful, honest, and open conversations that deemphasize personal agendas.

Leader advocacy suggests successfully partnering with those in charge. Comfortable relationships require effort by all participants to maintain ongoing, productive partnerships. Partnering suggests people are willingly working together on something they are interested in—something the participants agree requires the skills, expertise, and investment of energy by the participants. Putting energy into constructing good relationships with our leaders over time demonstrates the willingness to work with them in partnership.

Yet to attempt leader advocacy without a belief in the person being advocated is pretty near impossible. Somehow the message comes across with a lack of truthfulness. We tell our truth through gestures, choices, and even body language. Somehow the signal will be that there are some things to be concerned about here.

Constructive Conflict

Differences and disagreements between members of different levels and different groups create conflict, a normal occurrence of organizational life. Leader advocacy is often difficult when people are different in many ways. Conflict can be seen as positive and beneficial or threatening and negative according to the mind-set of participants within the group. As noted earlier, groups made up of advocates with an abundance mentality® know that there will be enough of the pie to go around for each person—that working well together (especially with those we work with every day) actually expands the reward opportunities for everyone. Constructive conflict, where each can openly contribute their own view for consideration, often leads to greater understanding and group learning. Innovation and creativity happens through partnerships that encourage new viewpoints, ideas, and understandings from those who see things differently.

Contributions of Energy and Value

Instead of small things being done through compulsion, larger things happen with new excitement when organizational advocacy is a reality. Heightened connection stimulates greater involvement; energy increases levels of personal responsibility and a sense of significance. Feelings of being valued and that "what I do matters" increases beneficial accountability. When members know they can influence how and why things get done, things change.

"The only way we really know that the organization has changed is when people's behaviors change," says Edward Marshall (1995), author of *Transforming the Way We Work*. He adds, "Leaders usually do not implement change. The workforce does" (p. 134). They can talk all they want, but a change management process does not work unless the members decide it needs to be done and that it is workable and beneficial. In the end, the culture of the organization and the people who construct it decide whether change has occurred. Do the members demonstrate the values, principles, commitment, beliefs, pride, energy, language, habits, customs, integrity, and loyalty that is called for to demonstrate change has happened—and that it is for the long term?

THE ENLIGHTENED MEMBER

In 1991 Ed Oakley and Doug Krug wrote *Enlightened Leadership: Getting to the Heart of Change*. Oakley and Krug describe enlightened leadership as performed by "leaders who not only have the vision but who have the ability to get the members of the organization to accept ownership for that vision on their own, thus developing the commitment to carry it through to completion" (p. 19). These leaders function as organizational advocates. They believe in their vision and the people who make it possible. Oakley and Krug add, "Enlightened Leaders create an environment or culture that unlocks the creativity and energy of the people, an environment that supports their natural desire to make a contribution and that has them *want* to make a contribution" (p. 230). One would assume, when change is real, that the members are also enlightened. A description of enlightened members also reflects the beliefs and activities of organizational advocates. Enlightened members

- see their future connected to the growth and welfare of their organization.
- know and identify with the overarching design of their organization.
- regularly evaluate their own contributions and value the contributions of others.
- are open to innovation and experimentation.
- understand that learning and serving attitudes are vital to personal and organizational growth.
- positively impact the climate of their workplace community and what is happening.

These characteristics are reflected by the willingness to constructively support and challenge the ideas and activities of others, whatever their place or role in the organization. Primary in the membership concern is the effectiveness of the leadership. They want to work with enlightened leaders.

It is common thinking that 20 percent of the members of organizations usually look for the benefits of change and move to embrace it early on (these are the enlightened members). Sixty percent are hesitant (want some proof), reluctant (need even more proof), or resistent (tough but changeable). The remaining 20 percent are those who will never be convinced. Unfortunately, without a lot of support and encouragement, the 60 percent can be influenced by the disconnected 20 percent, potentially defeating change efforts.

Showing the members what it looks like to adopt the change and reinforcing the expected changes regularly makes it possible for change to take hold. New attitudes become possible when members recognize what the new attitudes make possible and what the benefits will be—and are willing to let go of less productive processes and behaviors. The top 20 percent will showcase what has to happen—if they know how the change supports or changes the overarching design and how they can reflect it in their work. Enlightened members are capable of letting go while honoring the past and engaging in coconstruction of a new organizational future.

Letting Go

Before people let go, they have to know what to let go of, what the benefits to do so are, and what to move toward, both personally and professionally. Of course, different people have different things to let go of, so it makes sense that there is no hard rule or list. Self-examination—and the caring suggestions of others—of what is putting up barriers to top performance provides a more suitable list. The following are offered as some suggestions.

Letting Go of Perfection

The movement to advocacy participation requires us to let go of expecting perfection of those around us. "Perfection is in the eye of the beholder—it's the way I would do it, what I perceive as 100-percent right" holds true here.

Seeking perfection makes people continuously dissatisfied with the efforts and capabilities of those we work with. Expecting my version of perfection in others will eventually lead to resistance, resentment, and unpleasantness. The perfectionist's "one right way of doing things" is not perfect. Other options may be more beneficial. The expectation of perfection might hide or disguise new ways of doing things as undesirable. Eventually the perfectionist faces the disappointment that perfection is not attainable by those around them.

Letting Go of the Past

This is a hard one. Present attitudes reframe the past to become useful to shape what is needed for today. We see the past through colored glasses. A supervisor, when in orientation for a new job, spent three days out in the field. During that time she repeatedly heard about the strike that happened thirteen years previously. Two different stories were told about one incident. One described it as a funny story, and the other repeated it in bitterness, like it was yesterday. Yet both were on the same side of the strike. Forgiveness, requiring adultness, is part of letting go, even if one cannot forget.

Letting Go of Limiting Others

The workplace is designed by the "best guesses" of members in how to do their work. Dictating and demanding others do their work in certain ways, at certain times, and with certain resources limits the results (and may create detrimental consequences). Creativity and innovation is stifled by restrictive rules and regulations (an exception would be in areas of safety, where rules and limitations must be enforced).

Letting Go of Inflexibility

Workplaces and the people in them continually change and evolve. New ideas, new customers, new processes, new viewpoints, and even new members require us to be open to adjustments, new directions, and new spheres of influence. Inflexibility in an individual or an organization limits performance in the increasingly complex environment of today—and will do so even more in the future.

Letting Go of Conformity

Conformity suggests too much obedience. Letting go of conforming behaviors awakens, even requires, deepened participation in doing things differently. The assumption that someone else knows all or knows best is a dangerous assumption. Ongoing opportunities to learn and opportunities to serve others in rewarding ways are lost when unquestioning conformity (which suggests dependence) is the normal way to work.

Letting Go of Lack of Acceptance

Our actions demonstrate acceptance or rejection. Rejection is often based on a personal agenda of anger, resentment, or guilt. Lack of appreciation signals lack of acceptance. As humans we have ways to protect ourselves from the known and unknown. Letting go of self-protecting devices opens us to looking at and accepting new ideas, new opportunities, even people who were previously ignored.

Letting go is not easy. It involves reflection and new understandings and possibly "ah-ha" moments that define a different future. It also requires support. Without the support and energy of others, resilience will wane, questions will not be asked or answered, and barriers will become insurmountable. Letting go makes possible new enthusiasms, new experiences, and new partnerships that have not been possible in the past.

RESPONSIBILITY-ORIENTED ORGANIZATIONS

The nature of membership in organizations is changing. Because the broad sharing of leadership functions contributes to organizational effectiveness under almost all circumstances, it is now accepted that leaders exist everywhere in the workplace. The existence of effective formal, informal, and occasional leadership is significant to organizational achievement. At any given moment the leadership abilities of individuals across the organization are called for—even insisted upon—no matter where their assigned role.

The U.S. Environmental Protection Agency (EPA)—Region 10, in Seattle, Washington, emphasizes within its Leadership Philosophy the following statement: "All employees are leaders." Julie Bowen, an organizational effectiveness consultant in the Office of Innovation, says

This is an important perspective that is emphasized through our Leadership Philosophy [see Appendix A]. Our Leadership Philosophy and the Supervisor of the Future have been touchstones in our culture change journey over the past five years. Both have served as guides in our recruiting, selecting, and evaluation of both employees and supervisors. As we continue to develop our personal and organizational ability to be adaptable and strategic in this ever more complex work of environmental protection, our Leadership Philosophy identifies our expectations that all Region 10 employees be leaders as part of their work performance. Without this focus on everyone being leaders, I'm sure that the progress we have made would have been more difficult. The environmental problems are big, complex, and many. It takes courage to choose to say, "We are going to focus our efforts here and not here." (personal correspondence)

There are two things that EPA—Region 10 has done that has helped make extreme progress toward their goal of being adaptable and relevant as an environmental agency among a host of other players focusing on protecting the environment. As noted by Julie Bowen, the first is the "Assignments Not Positions" philosophy. This philosophy states that no one owns their position. They are expected to rotate every four to six years or so. 1999 brought a major rotation project. The executive level had several major shifts, with some people moving into the executive level and some moving out to nonsupervisory assignments. First-level supervisors also completed their rotation, again with some major shifts. At the staff level, a total of forty-seven staff, or 8 percent of the workforce, rotated to new assignments. This round of rotations was punctuated with both a sense of excitement at the possibility of moving to another assignment and a sense of fear and trepidation. In the words of Chuck Clarke, Region 10's Regional Administrator, "It is up to each of you to take charge of your own career to make it an exciting and challenging one. The region will continue to be open to rotation opportunities or ideas at anytime."

The second initiative, according to Bowen, is "Supervisory Feedback." "EPA—Region 10 is in the third year of supervisory feedback. This process evolved from being very 'one size fits all' the first year to one of clear responsibility and expectations with very broad guidelines. Supervisors and executives are expected to work with a staff design team and a facilitator to design and implement a feedback meeting to develop reciprocal agreements between them and their staff. Professional coaches are provided for supervisors if they want the support to make real shifts and changes in the actions and outcomes they are getting." (From my perspective, it is constructive accountability in action.)

Many organizations are actively seeking to provide an internal environment that stimulates performance generated by higher levels of individual and group responsibility, encouraging people to be leaders of the moment. To do so makes it possible for workplace participants to light an internal spark that brings new ideas, expands energy, and nurtures positive attitudes that encourage advocacy participation. This spark propels them and their organizations to excellence brought about by increased personal motivation to perform.

The role of the individual in participating in the orchestration of a better place to work cannot be emphasized enough. We have habits of passing the buck, blaming others for our own discomfort, poor performance, and lack of confidence, diminishing our willingness to accept responsibility for our own performance or lack of performance. According to William J. Morin (1995), chairman and CEO of Drake Beam Morin, "Neither our government nor our other institutions themselves are causing a crisis of confidence in society today. You and I are!" He calls it a values crisis. "We are becoming a people without rudders, real values, and vision. The values we do cling to often have very little value at all. This, in turn, has given birth to a new phenomenon, a rarely examined social disease I call, 'Silent Sabotage' that is tearing each of us and the very fabric of our society apart from within." He continues, "Silent sabotage is so deep and so pervasive that I'm not sure anyone fully understands its scope or where to look for a solution" (p. 4). Silent sabotage is a demonstration of irresponsibility.

Perhaps a step in the right direction for organizations is for each person, wherever he or she works in the organization, to step back and examine what he or she has purposely done in the last three months to contribute to the growth and welfare of their organization. Was there something that was significant enough to be memorable? If not, why not?

Leaders are now carrying the message that addressing the crises in our organizations starts with placing the responsibility for change on each individual at every level. Success depends on the willingness of each person to examine what is happening within their own accountabilities. Am I striving to contribute something of value each day to move the organization to a higher level of performance? To continue to blame and shame others for what is happening won't initiate a positive shift—nor will it encourage other members to "hang in there" during times of instability. According to Charles Handy (1989, 64), there are those who every day, without crises, are demonstrating a "proper selfishness." They

- take responsibility for themselves and for their future.
- have a clear view of what they want that future to be.
- want to make sure they get it.
- believe that they can.

Highly responsible people strive to be resilient. They know it is no longer enough to adapt, cope, or adjust to whatever is happening. Nor is it appropriate to point fingers at those above, beside, or reporting to them. Responsibility starts in the shoes of each person doing what they can to contribute to achievement. Because of the need to work at top performance in more complex, unpredictable, and global environments, it is suggested that those who learn and serve best are those who are most comfortable with change—those who are most resilient in times of uncertainty.

Personal and organizational success requires personal responsibility and accountability that is spread across the organization to every person and position. Personal responsibility provides the impetus for each person's willing, proactive involvement in future achievement not previously possible. It is no longer appropriate to be merely cooperative. Effective contribution requires each person to work consultatively and collaboratively with others, no matter their status, title, or work assignment. Organizational advocacy becomes part of the way work is accomplished.

Responsibility starts with the purposeful contributions of each member. Cross-organizational partnerships and member involvement are invited and accepted. New freedoms come with responsible performance which include new risks and vulnerabilities. Willing participants in the new freedoms of value-added participation become leaders of the moment. These new freedoms, including empowerment, decision making, involvement, and so forth, ensure that members support the move from a competitive, rigid, or even abusive workplace to a cooperative, interactive, and strengthened member-oriented community.

Exchanges of respect typically grow with demonstrations of personal responsibility. The amount of energetic responsibility we decide to put into a task is often adjusted by the amount of respect held for the person, organization, or process. The amount of urgency felt in doing a task is also adjusted by the amount of respect we have for whoever or whatever makes the task necessary. Respect is spirit lifting. Respect contributes to civility. Respect encourages letting go. Respect supports the willingness to be involved in exchanges of learning through accountability. Respect is designed into the leader advocacy stories we tell that impact the reputation and significance of our leaders and organizations. Respect for our leaders makes it more likely we will take things seriously enough to take action. The willingness to be an in the moment leader is stimulated by respect.

To expect members to be positive advocates and to claim a leader as beneficial when respect is nonexistent is to increase disconnection. When a leader is not respected, they are tolerated, and the amount of productive work by those tolerating the leader is lowered. In healthy comember relationships with leaders, respect always exists.

Trust

Trust has long been known to be the basis for cooperative relationships, yet it has not as yet been openly discussed in this book. As an issue inside organizations, the trust factor has called for full books and will continue to do so. Of course, organizational advocacy calls for a reemphasis on trust in organizations where advocacy participation is possible: Trust is crucial to the activation and maintenance of advocacy participation.

According to some, trust in U.S. organizations at this time is very low, and the probability is that it will fall even further. Whitener, Brodt, Korsgaard, and Werner (1998) state, "Interpersonal trust has a significant relationship with many organizational variables, including the quality of communications, performance, citizenship behavior, problem solving, . . . and cooperation" (p. 513). Their definition of trust reflects three facets: "First, trust in another party reflects an expectation or belief that the other party will act benevolently. Second, one cannot control or force the other party to fulfill this expectation—that is, trust involves a willingness to be vulnerable and risk that the other party may not fulfill that expectation. Third, trust involves some level of dependency on the other party so that the outcomes of one individual are influenced by the actions of another" (p. 513).

Benevolence, defined as a desire to do good to others, consists of three factors that may lead others to perceive trustworthiness: (1) showing consideration and sensitivity for the needs and interests of others, (2) protecting the interests of others, and (3) not exploiting the vulnerability of others for the benefit of one's own interests (Whitener et al. 1998, 517). It makes sense that we cannot force benevolent behaviors on others, but if one treats another benevolently, there is a possibility it will be returned. Reciprocity has long been acknowledged as a factor in how people treat each other: When one offers trust, it often is reciprocated. What one gives out, often comes back.

In a leader and subordinate relationship, the leader is assumed to be the initiator of benevolent activities. In some cases the group waits for signals of trust and respect before responding. The leader advocate, the promoting member, instead assumes trustworthiness and benevolence even if it has not been previously offered by the leader. Effective group dynamics includes the routinization of benevolent relationships.

Jones and George (1998, 536–537) suggest there are three distinct states or forms of the trust experience: (1) distrust, (2) conditional trust (both parties are willing to work together as long as there is appropriate behavior), and (3) unconditional trust (each person's trustworthiness has been tested and is now assured). Members, because of the need to cooperate with comembers, often become vulnerable to the actions of another. Being vulnerable is taking a risk. When a new member is hired into the group, conditional trust is activated by comembers until the new member proves he or she is worthy of unconditional trust. If the member proves to be untrustworthy and does not meet the expectations of the group, a distrusting relationship may be the outcome. Trust is a changing or evolving experience. People can trust someone in one situation and question their trust of the same person in another.

Once trust has been earned and becomes unconditional, participants become confident in the performance of the trusted person. Unconditional trust suggests that a "lapse" in behavior is more likely to be overlooked or forgiven. Past trusting behavior helps the offended person to ignore what is happening. In some cases, there is a choice made to not notice the lapse. The situation may also signal the wronged member that something needs to be done, bringing attention to what is happening: A test of the trusting relationship has occurred. The offended person may, based on the desire to ignore behavior that is counter to what is desired, choose to tell himself or herself what has been seen is inaccurate. He or she wants to explain away the situation, making it unnecessary to deal with it. But if either person responds with an offensive emotional outburst, trust that was previously unconditional may switch to conditional, or the relationship may become distrustful (McKnight, Cummings, and Chervany 1998, 484). The outburst has signaled strongly the need for a change in behavior to maintain or reclaim unconditional trust. The relationship is renegotiated. Forgiveness, if requested and agreed to, may restore the relationship.

A leader's investment in time, benevolence, and support is a long-term endeavor requiring considerable effort and organizational resources. If experienced as believable by members, these investments may lead to an exchange of trusting relationships and gestures of leader advocacy. The three levels of trust (distrust, conditional trust, and unconditional trust) also "decide" the level of a member's investment in advocacy participation and the activation of leader advocacy gestures.

Organizations are constructed through the energies applied toward the establishment of relationships by the people, consciously and unconsciously, incident by incident, person by person, group by group. The actions of the collective group honor or dishonor those investments. Each individual member controls their investment of effort; each "spends" or invests energy as he or she chooses. Each person, through what is thought, said, and done, the elements of invested energy, impacts what his or her group will become. Leader advocacy is especially vulnerable to the interactions of the group through shared suspicions or understandings of leader competence.

Commitment

Organizational leaders implore us to be committed. Consultants talk endlessly about the dire outcomes if everyone is not committed. Confrontations happen when people are not seen as committed. But we are human. For both the individual and the group, commitment, like respect and change, is an emotional activity that takes time. It is a process—and for some, it can be a struggle.

Kofman and Senge (1993) tell us, "Building learning organizations . . . requires basic shifts in how we think and interact" (p. 7). This is a challenge for the Western world, because of the tendency to be competitive and to use competition as our way of improvement and the desire to look good (p. 11). Making changes requires members to use their psychological and social sides while focusing on relationships, respect, and motivation. The goal in organizations is to design communities that are diverse and committed. Where in the past leaders told their people to be committed with limited success, inclusive, enlightened leaders now know they must earn it. It requires them to honor and value their members, build an environment where trust is possible, and make long-term commitments to the welfare of the people and their organization through actions of integrity. This is a long-term journey. Commitment to an inclusive organization is the basis for sustaining that journey.

Commitment proceeds in stages (Schenkel 1984, 105). Moving toward commitment is what is to be expected. Commitment is an outcome constructed over time, requiring the following:

- Leaders who provide information and reinforce that information over time.
- Trust, responsibility, and enrollment.
- A reasonable expectation of success.
- Availability of learning, both formal and informal.
- Recognizing and working with leaders and change agents at all levels.

- Recognition that commitment is demonstrated differently by individuals.
- A sense that those leading the process are evaluating (and listening to our evaluations) on a regular basis.

Gaining the involvement of the critical mass of members (whatever that number may be) does not mean commitment is automatic. Oakley and Krug (1991) suggest, "Enlightened Leaders know that the hearts and minds of their people can be won when they are working toward a purpose they find worthwhile, are involved in the planning and decision-making, and feel appreciated by leadership" (p. 247). People try things out and watch for the consequences. They check to see if they have "full," trustworthy information. To withhold negative information to gain participation and commitment is to betray the efforts of those who accepted the challenge, are participating as change agents, and are actively advocating for the change.

SIGNALS OF DISRESPECT

Abusive behavior can be translated as signals of disrespect. These signals thrive on fear and environments that nurture feelings of insecurity. In many organizations, exchanges of negative influencing tactics create norms of borderline (or actual) uncivil behavior. Incivility in these organizations goes unacknowledged and unchallenged. It isn't seen to be a threat to individual or organizational performance. It becomes acceptable behavior. Management members subtly abuse and lean on those who work for them. Those being leaned on often grouse and complain, even mimic the abusive behavior, while lowering their willingness to contribute their best. Disrespect and uncivil behavior become the normal way to work together. If people tread on my toes, I can "let 'em have it," either to their face or behind their back. Management members in noninclusive organizations claim the right to be disrespectful and occasionally downright nasty to those in less-than positions. In response, leaders are not respected by those not being respected. The cycle of disrespect is constantly being activated by one group or the other.

As noted earlier, Namie and Namie (1999) call it "bullying" (the term chosen to use in this text). Davenport, Schwartz and Elliott (1999, 20) note it as "mobbing" when comembers, superiors, and subordinates repeatedly attack a person's dignity, integrity, and competence for weeks, months, or years. (In the 1980s the term "mobbing" was used by Dr. Heinz Leymann in Sweden and Germany in discussing how people identified and treated those who were "difficult people" (Davenport, Schwartz, and Elliott 1999, 21). Carter (1989) labels nasty people who pick on others in insidious ways as "invalidators." There are many names for the behaviors used to control in a devaluing workplace. According to Wright and Smye (1996, 5), behaviors they diagnose as "corporate abuse" include discrimination, overwork, harassment, systematic humiliation, arbitrary dismissal, demotion without cause, withholding of resources, and financial manipulation. Wright and Smye add, "People who are intensely ambitious often enjoy the feeling of power and control that they get from treating others badly. Dishing out abuse becomes addictive, a drug for the ego" (p.60). Its more subtle manifestations include lack of support, penny-pinching, micromanagement, constant miscommunication, hidden agendas, surveillance, inverted priorities, and smothering corporate cultures. Unfortunately, these activities sound all too familiar to all too many people.

Being civil creates far more opportunities for connection than actions of incivility. It makes sense that being pleasant and less threatening to others lessens stress and lowers anxiety for those on the receiving end as well as those handing it out. Giving up efforts to control others can bring more rewards than continued efforts to control and the maintenance of fear tactics.

Leader actions and attitudes limit or invigorate member participation and put up or take down barriers to member performance of leader advocacy. Positive or negative assumptions about individual members are played out in what leaders say and do, teaching future leaders these same abusive leadership tactics. The willingness to cooperate or not cooperate can be decided by member observations of how a leader behaves with someone else.

Moral duty suggests there are rules to follow. And having rules suggests there are sacrifices to make because written or unwritten rules have to be followed. But what if a leader sets up an objectionable unspoken rule, such as, I can be abusive to you but you must be kind and thoughtful to me—all the time. Or, I can shout and call you names, but you cannot do it back; you must stand there and take my bullying. Or, I say what you do and you do what I say without back talk or questions. The uncivil leader is offering you an opportunity to be civil according to his or her rules. In this leader's definition, being civil means doing as he or she says.

When the abusive leader is unwilling to sacrifice his or her own impulses to control, punish, and seek certainty, it may be risky to suggest change is needed. If you tell this leader that he or she is uncivil, he or she may claim innocence: I'm just doing what it takes to get the job done. That's just me. Or, tell someone who cares. And the person who protests to HR or management regarding the abusive and bullying behavior will eventually pay for his or her insubordinance. The outcome is that people are quiet and the abusive behavior continues—potentially worsening.

In most organizations, those in charge don't want to hear about or deal with disrespectful behaviors. It upsets them. They want to ignore disruptions. They want to think that if they ignore it, it will go away. They don't want to get involved. If you complain, you may be told to deal with it yourself like a big person. And then the problem (and possibly you) will be ignored, or you may be labeled and treated as a problem person, someone who complains about "little things." The choice is to either tell him or her in a civil way that the behavior is uncomfortable and difficult to handle, or to cope with it and get on with your work. Or leave. In many cases, if you could go away, you would.

In the case of peer bullying, like it or not, leaders are accountable for the behavior of individuals in their group. What the leader does or does not do and what is said or not said about abusive, bullying behavior in the group models what is acceptable. Leader messages of what is appropriate behavior become clear over time. When a coworker's behavior is borderline civil (today it could be abusive and tomorrow everything is pleasant), letting it go by makes it more likely to happen again and again. It becomes normal behavior. Over time, everyone participates in the construction of shifts in the culture of their organizations. Leaders partner with their comembers in setting the tone of the environment.

Working in a Punishing Environment

But what if we are working in a dismal environment of repression, punishment, and bullying, an organization where dignity and respect is withheld? Is it possible to take ownership in this environment? What if we choose to be in this degrading environment?

The environment we work in may be limiting as to what can be accomplished, but our actions and attitudes need not reflect the limiting atmosphere. Mihaly Csikszentmihalyi (1990) tells us we can learn to provide rewards to ourselves. As humans, we have the ability to find enjoyment and purpose, regardless of external circumstances. He says, "This challenge [to reward ourselves] is both easier and more difficult than it sounds: easier because the ability to do so is entirely in each person's hands; difficult because it requires discipline and perseverance that are relatively rare in any era, and perhaps especially in the present" (p. 16). Tough it may be, but it can be done.

Members are personally responsible for their own responses to what is going on around them. "The devil made me do it" or "You made me do it" don't work anymore. It means looking for opportunities to learn from others and to serve in ways that make a difference, even in the worst of circumstances. There will be hurtful failures in doing so. Environments of distrust cause struggle and disconnection. People may choose not to "let go" and forgive themselves and others about things going badly long ago. To not let go is to sink constantly deeper into a resolve of victimhood. Victimhood eliminates opportunities to appreciate even the smallest things that could make it possible to claim ownership of what is personally contributed every day.

In a culture of blame and shame someone else is always at fault. Instead of collectively working on solutions, a constant flow of intimidation around "who did it" and how to punish him or her is the primary effort. People at every level are constantly trying to avoid being the one who made the mistake. In order to make sure one is not the Scapegoat of the Day, blaming and shaming of others is an active sport. Innovative ideas and enthusiasms are covered up. Eventually, silence, sadness, saving face, and anger become the way to survive. There is no longer a possibility of asking the right questions and finding the most effective answers that stimulate ideas and innovations. No one is daring enough to speak up anymore. If the company starts spouting the usual slogan of "our people are our most important asset," the workers snicker and share stories about why it isn't true. In a culture of shame and blame, leader advocacy gestures are limited to promotion of the few extraordinary leaders. Fortunately, they do exist.

Members, it is assumed, are very aware of working in a punishing environment, yet they are unaware of how it is affecting their work. Responses to shame and blame lowers performance without the slightest thought of increased involvement and energy. This environment is stressful, even for leaders. Stress, something to be survived, is aggressively present in the devaluing, inflexible workplace. A stressful workplace can destroy one person and still be tolerable to others. It is the response of people to circumstances and the stressful events they experience that decides if they are coping or defensive.

Volumes are written about handling stressful workplaces and life situations. The central message is that something has to be done to gain some control over what is happening. The goal is to at least neutralize personal responses instead of becoming helpless and hopeless (defensive). Many people do not attempt to change a stressful, hopeless situation into a bearable situation— they slowly descend into victimhood. Others refuse to give in to despair and know that in order to do well in the best or most deplorable situations, one

1. trusts one's own ability to cope and contribute successfully.
2. is flexible, focuses on the needs of others, and adapts and contributes even in the worst of situations.
3. gets involved in identifying new solutions and opportunities, learning new skills, and committing to constructing something he or she can be proud of.
4. is available when talents, skills, and experience are needed.
5. lets others know he or she believes that change is possible.

Inaction or standing on the sidelines questions and/or destroys the sense that a meaningful contribution can be made. Feelings that energy and value have been wasted lessens trust in our own ability. Being inactive makes it possible for others to undervalue contributions, even to withhold opportunities for growth and learning in the future. One must do something, get into the center of things and get involved.

Creating Partnerships with Leaders

Leader advocacy cannot happen when disconnection occurs. Unless something or someone seeks to make changes, to blur the lines between levels, nothing changes. The customs, culture, and dominant personalities of a group will keep things going in the currently preferred direction unless someone does something. Although it is the role of the formal leader to encourage members to create and nurture new kinds of partnerships, the member may need to signal openness to creating a new way of working together. A member can seek opportunities for involvement by seeking more open connections with their leaders. Informal activities of exchange can start the process. Offering support when support is needed establishes opportunities to work together. Inviting others into opportunities for new relationships helps them to understand it is beneficial even though it is uncomfortable. If it doesn't work at first, it is essential to keep trying. There are rewards for softening the atmosphere, if only for the individual who is attempting to do so. You can say, I tried and I'm willing. It can make new partnerships possible, potentially blurring the lines in place in the past.

PARTING THOUGHTS

We see what we expect to see; and then we justify what we've seen. Each person constantly sets baseline levels of what he or she expects from others. One watches for confirmation of already-in-place assumptions. Thus, the willingness to say and do what confirms our leader as a competent, beneficial leader (leader advocacy activities) is limited by not letting go of negative experiences with leaders in the past. Unfortunately, expectations are often set against the low performance of previous superiors. People don't always take time to reevaluate and support leaders who are attempting change. The assumption is, another supervisor, same behaviors, same abilities, same impatience, same leadership style. Been there, done that. Same thing again.

But, the nature of leading in organizations is changing. Because the distribution of leadership functions contributes to organizational effectiveness under almost all circumstances, it is now often accepted that leaders exist everywhere in the workplace. Comember recognition and acknowledgment of the best performances of leaders, whoever they are, contributes to the leader's feelings of accomplishment. Someone noticed. Someone knows they had to sacrifice to make changes and to get the work done. Someone understands that leaders need support and acknowledgment too.

BIBLIOGRAPHY

Bardwick, Judith M. (1991). *Danger in the Comfort Zone*. New York: AMACOM.

Bowen, Julie. (1999). Personal correspondence.

Carter, Jay. (1989). *Nasty People: How to Stop Being Hurt by Them* Without *Becoming One of Them*. Chicago: Contemporary Books.

Covey, Steven R. (1999). Don't Let Yourself Become a Victim of Your Boss's Weaknesses. *Fast Company* 23: 96.

Csikszentmihalyi, Mihaly. (1990). *Flow: The Psychology of Optimal Experience*. New York: Harper & Row.

Daniels, Tom D., and Barry K. Spiker. (1994). *Perspectives on Organizational Communication*. 3d ed. Dubuque: Brown & Benchmark.

Davenport, Noa, Ruth Distler Schwartz, and Gail Pursell Elliott. (1999). *Mobbing: Emotional Abuse in the American Workplace*. Ames, Iowa: Civic Society Publishing.

Drath, Wilfred H. (1996). Changing Our Minds about Leadership. *Issues & Observations* 16 (1): 1–4.

Handy, Charles. (1989). *The Age of Unreason*. Boston: Harvard Business School Press.

Jones, Gareth R., and Jennifer M. George. (1998). The Experience and Evolution of Trust: Implications for Cooperation and Teamwork. *Academy of Management Review* 23: 531–546.

Katz, Daniel, and Robert L. Kahn. (1978). *The Social Psychology of Organizations*. 2d ed. New York: John Wiley & Sons.

Kofman, Fred, and Peter Senge. (1993). The Communities of Commitment: The Heart of Learning Organizations. *Organizational Dynamics* 22 (2): 5–23 (Special Issue on The Learning Organization).

Leonard, Bill. (2000). Employee Loyalty Continues to Wane. *HR Magazine* 45 (1): 21–22.

Marshall, Edward M. (1995). *Transforming the Way We Work: The Power of the Collaborative Workplace*. New York: AMACOM.

McKnight, D. Harrison, Larry L. Cummings, and Norman L. Chervany. (1998). Initial Trust Formation in New Organizational Relationships. *Academy of Management Review* 23: 473–490.

Morin, William J. (1995). *Silent Sabotage: Rescuing Our Careers, Our Companies, and Our Lives from the Creeping Paralysis of Anger and Bitterness*. New York: AMACOM.

Namie, Gary, and Ruth Namie. (1999). *BullyProof Yourself at Work!: Personal Strategies to Stop the Hurt from Harassment*. Benecia, Calif.: DoubleDoc Press.

Oakley, Ed, and Doug Krug. (1991). *Enlightened Leadership: Getting to the Heart of Change*. New York: Fireside–Simon and Schuster.

Schenkel, Susan. (1984). *Giving Away Success: Why Women "Get Stuck" and What to Do About It*. New York: McGraw-Hill.

Seiling, Jane Galloway. (1997). *The Membership Organization: Achieving Top Performance Through the New Workplace Community*. Palo Alto, Calif.: Davies-Black.

Whitener, Ellen M., Susan E. Brodt, M. Audrey Korsgaard, and Jon M. Werner. (1998). Manager as Initiators of Trust: An Exchange Relationship Framework for Understanding Managerial Trustworthy Behavior. *Academy of Management Review* 23: 513–530.

Wright, Lesley, and Marti Smye. (1996). *Corporate Abuse: How "Lean and Mean" Robs People and Profits*. New York: Macmillan.

CONVERSATIONS AND INTERVIEWS

Julie Bowen, Office of Innovation, EPA—Region 10.
Chuck Clark, Regional Administrator, EPA—Region 10.

7

Member Advocacy

Leadership is a function of every level and what needs to be understood—and practiced—is that leadership is a function not only of action, but of character.

Stephen R. Covey (1989)

When a manager has a low opinion of a staff member, the employee usually lives up to that expectation by making mistakes or otherwise performing poorly. Then, the poor performance reinforces the manager's beliefs about the employee, and a vicious cycle has begun.

Rebecca B. Mann (1993)

In a recent issue of *Fast Company* the results of an informal poll on their Web site were noted. The question was, Is your workplace toxic, or are people truly valued? The results were as follows:

My workplace is toxic   48 percent
My workplace values people   52 percent

In other words, if you drive down the road, whether in an industrial park or retail center, it appears that almost half of those companies you drive by have the possibility of being a toxic organization. This less-than-perfect sampling by *Fast Company* suggests that the actions of advocacy—questioning, informing, promoting, decisioning, learning and serving and performing—are less than rampant in our organizations. There is a probability that deconstructive "negative advocacy"—shaming, blaming, withholding, mediocre performance, disconnection—is normal and not noticed as out of place or inappropriate in these organizations.

Destroyers of Motivation

In our organizations there are people at every level who are destroyers of motivation. Leaders complain about and degrade their subordinates (the people "working for" them) as incapable of top performance. They do not advocate their group to other leaders as capable performers. The strengths of the less-than member go unnoted and his or her weaknesses are highlighted mightily. Only the favored few are held up as top performers. Later the leaders are surprised when other leaders are reluctant to accept the work of their disrespected subordinates.

Repeated denigration by a leader of his or her subordinates influences what others think and assume. Leaders who complain about their people are negative member advocates and possibly bullies, setting themselves and the people they are degrading up as low performers. Promoting comembers as nonproductive warns others of the leader's inability to lead, train, coach, or support improvement. While pointing out inferiority, the leader is heightening awareness of his or her own leadership inabilities. This leader is not an advocate for the members he or she is managing.

Member advocacy is defined as leader actions that promote individual and group members to others as beneficial performers, leading to expanded opportunities to contribute to organizational achievement. Member advocacy promotes and supports the existence of ability, potential, and significance of the leader's reporting group. We make assumptions about the actions of others through perceptions established in the past—and verified by others. Member advocacy, as performed by leaders, supports their role of influencing the perceptions of observers and, ultimately, the teams in which they participate. Member-focused advocacy participation also includes actions of sponsoring and supporting members as capable, learning, and serving members.

THE RESPECTFUL LEADER

Leaders in a respectful organization regularly examine their own roles in designing how the workplace is experienced by others. Examination includes looking around to check the amount of energy people are routinely putting into their work. If there is a lack of energy and initiative, they should ask themselves the following questions:

- What are the signals and messages I am giving to those around me about how work gets done here?
- Do I actively support and contribute to the performance and efficiency of those around me?
- Am I willing to hold others constructively accountable for their performance?
- Am I willing to be accountable for my own actions and activities?

As noted previously, there is a place of flow between anxiety and boredom where energy and ownership occurs (Csikszentmihalyi 1990). To contribute to the accomplishment of flow by others and to support them in achieving a sense of respect, dignity, appreciation, and efficiency, leaders

- are visionary and/or enhance the vision of others.
- know that leadership occurs at all levels of the organization.
- are knowledgeable, supportive, appreciative, and accountable.
- plan with those who do the work and acknowledge the results.
- align everything that is done with the overarching design of the organization.
- know that leadership and membership are based on relationships.

To suggest that these activities are located only with formal leaders limits the coconstruction of partnering relationships by the collective membership. Successful, beneficial partnerships are based on these activities being performed well by all members, wherever and whatever their work involves. The understanding that these activities are key to high performance for themselves and the organization as a whole is significant to what all members (including leaders) think, say, and do—and what they appreciate about each other and their organizations.

Leader Naysayers

Those sitting on the top of a hierarchical pyramid occasionally become naysayers and justifiers of problems. The leader-naysayer laments, "No one wants to work anymore. They just don't listen. Why do they insist on questioning everything?" Ideally, the naysayer attitude will pass without notice. The leader who values everyone, believes in them, and knows that the involvement of people's minds and hearts in their work is important will rarely be a negative advocate. This leader-member invites everyone to be part of the achievement and maintenance of success and vitality of their workplace, making pride, responsibility, productivity, and advocacy possible while enhancing profitability. This leader, in partnership with others all across the organization, actively works with the membership to stimulate the belief that "this organization is a good place to work and what it does matters."

Leadership happens when members are willing to partner with the leader in accomplishment (leaders have to work with someone or they are not leaders). Leadership includes valuing the contributions and concerns of those being led and seeing them as coconstructionists. Contributing comembers willingly participate in these relationships developed across the organization, ignoring status, title, or position and supporting accomplishment built on positive, productive partnerships (all organizational participants are members, including the CEO, receptionists, supervisors, marketing representatives, and so on).

Leaders, through member advocacy, draw attention to seen and unseen contributive behavior. Others then "test" the represented picture. If experienced as true, discrepancies between past assumptions and repeated positive performance calls for new understandings regarding the performance of the advocated member and brings new possibilities of partnership.

THE MEMBER ADVOCACY ROLE

The advocacy role of performing as a beneficial representative of others is not new in the workplace. The HR professional has performed (or was assumed to perform) as an employee advocate, routinely dealing with employee-related issues and concerns. HR departments not taking on this role have been seen as paper pushers, compliance or policing persons, and expediters of processes for entrance to and exit from organizations. A new realization is that HR is a contributing business partner as well as a strong advocate of the members. Human resource professionals, as well as organization development professionals, are being integrated more closely into a business performance focus and are expected to yield a measurable impact on the human and financial bottom lines. HR is becoming a more complex activity.

As a member advocate the HR person is the representative of the member to the company and the representative of the company to the member, often in the same conversation or meeting. Unfortunately, balance is often difficult or even impossible or not called for. The activity of highlighting the importance of advocacy participation is in the role of managers, supervisors, and HR persons—as well as the members themselves. Organizational advocacy is a business-partner role and a personal responsibility, whether performed in a union or nonunion organization.

Power With

Mary Parker Follett, a social worker who became interested in employment and workplace issues, wrote and consulted with many large corporations. Although she died in 1933, her writings were well before her time. She lived during the classical management era but her thinking was more in line with the behavioral and systems management outlook. Follett's emphasis on the functioning of groups in organizations, though written in the 1920s, is being looked at and read widely as contributive to best practices in leading today's organizations.

Follett's ideas around power and authority were based on the principles of "power with" rather than "power over." Power with is the ability to influence and bring about change through power that is jointly developed, a cooperative effort of working together. Follett noted, "No one has a greater asset for his business than a man's pride in his work. If a worker is asked to do something in a way which he thinks is not the best way, he will often lose all interest in the result, he will be sure beforehand that his work is going to turn out badly" (Graham 1995, 126).

Power with is without limits in its ability to energize and focus people. It is not necessary for members to go for permission for things they know are right and appropriate for successful performance in their work. In organizing, working with suggests that members are capable, contributing, empowered members, and, as such, should be actively working in partnerships and networks with others. Members contribute to organizational decisions, make decisions in their own areas of expertise and within their own accountabilities (their assigned work), and carry out their own decisions and the decisions of others that affect them. Their energy is higher when they have helped decide.

Enhancing Member Credibility

A leader's behavior enhances or diminishes the credibility of contributive members, both inside and outside of the group. Besides being capable, trustworthy, and responsive, a member advocate uses "sponsorship tactics," including listening, supporting, promoting as capable, developing, truly empowering, challenging, and coaching his or her comembers. Positive impressions and images that are generated regarding individual and group activities are relevant to performance, nurturing member feelings of goodwill and pride in group membership. These impressions and images also impact leader credibility. Member advocacy is demonstrated through effective sponsorship. The following are things to know about sponsorship:

- Sponsorship is a leadership function. Leaders sponsor each member to the group and then sponsor the group as a whole to other organizational groups as a capable, likeable, appropriate, and contributing person or group others are justified in supporting.

- Sponsorship, by necessity, is an exchange. As an exchange, a leader's member advocacy activities, when seen as authentic, stimulate leader advocacy activities and advocacy participation on the part of group members. Actions of group members of supporting their supervisors and managers are also significant to the leader's willingness to be an active sponsor.

- Sponsorship is a long-term approach. Just doing it once doesn't cut it. Sponsorship by the leader over time makes it possible for the group to be seen as productive and credible, reinforcing the effectiveness of the group and its participants.

- Sponsorship assumes that what each person thinks, says, and does matters. Each individual in the group can have an effect on the success of the group and, ultimately, the organization. For this reason, each new group participant is chosen wisely in partnership with the group.

- Sponsorship includes providing and seeking development opportunities for group members. Being constantly alert to the learning needs of members enhances confidence and their interest in the work being performed now and in the future.

- A leader can also negatively sponsor. A skeptical comment shared with someone else, a thoughtless response to a group member that is heard or observed by others, an inappropriate explosion in front of others, a cynical response when a department person is trying to make a point, or sharing with others "concerns" about this person that may or may not be valid, are all devaluing tactics that happen almost unconsciously. The effective sponsor has to be alert to what he or she says and does.

What is said by a manager or supervisor in meetings and in discussions with others regarding group members is reflected inside the group. Negative member advocacy is disempowering. Disempowering talk eventually comes back in the work being done and how members sponsor their leader to others. Activities of credible, positive sponsorship increase the likelihood of success for the manager or supervisor, each participant in the group, and the group as a whole. Leaders must regularly remember they are comembers with others performing at all levels.

The following is a comparison of sponsoring and mentoring (Seiling 1997):

Sponsorship	*Mentorship*
Automatic responsibility	Voluntary responsibility
Professional relationship	May be a personal relationship
Highly visible	Not always visible
Directly impacts group acceptance	Indirectly impacts group acceptance
Internal to the organization	May be external to the organization
Advocacy/coaching role	Counseling/guiding role
Long-term relationship	Short-term relationship
Acceptance and development issue	Growth issue

Between Work and a Hard Place

In some cases much of how people work together in today's workplace is represented by our recent political arena: laying blame on others, pointing fingers, and "suggesting" or verifying inadequacies and activities that are unforgivable. Inevitably, this brings the possibility of top performance as individuals and groups to a crawl. Ineffective partnerships create few opportunities for participants to step beyond their job descriptions, work together to solve problems and issues of concern, and/or shed light on what each needs to do to collaborate effectively.

Problems that come up in this environment are commonly defined by people on one side of an issue pointing to others and saying, "it is their fault," causing people to take solid stances of separation. The outcome is competition, rivalry, and stalled opportunities for partnering and interdependence. When cooperation and collaboration is nonexistent around a problem, the problem grows, causes disconnection, and spawns other problems and conflicts. An exchange of actions of mistrust begins and continues.

Conversely, in an organizational advocacy environment, leader actions of member advocacy promote effective movement from seeing problem employees to seeing valued members wanting to contribute. The focus on cooperation with others, support and sponsorship, perceiving things differently, and being open to the power-with and working-with mentality that fosters constructive exchanges of accountability diminishes blaming activities. To do so strengthens the probability of collaborative partnerships across the group. Integrative power (empowering those who are most capable of making beneficial decisions) is heightened and the group becomes more aware of creating opportunities for all members to contribute at their best and in ways which are meaningful. The resulting increased energy strengthens commitment, expands informality, and more easily blurs lines across status and title.

In the past, members who pushed from the edges of the circle of inclusion were often seen as "mavericks." Mavericks made others at every level uncomfortable. They did what participative advocates now do: They asked questions that were uncomfortable, they insisted on discussing undiscussables, they looked in corners for hidden opportunities not previously or properly examined, and they often did so without authority. They were seen as out of line—as troublemakers–but if they did good work they were tolerated. These contributive mavericks, often reflected the following characteristics:

- bright, industrious, curious, and talented.
- compelled to perform as change agents.
- disliked bureaucracy.
- impatient with normal progress.
- took risks and overstepped boundaries.
- attempted to influence beyond their status and titles.
- not always predictable.
- struggled with the admonishment "do the right thing." (They asked, "What does that mean?")
- flourished when they didn't have clear marching orders.
- unknowingly practiced and believed in advocacy participation in the workplace.
- disliked and struggled against the control behaviors of their leaders.

The characteristics of the contributive maverick now are accepted as gestures of organizational advocacy—the appropriate behaviors of deeper participation in the workplace. As noted, working with these members, as a peer or leader, may be stressful or even difficult. They never slow down. They never stop asking questions. They challenge when challenge may not be seen as necessary. They always seem to be on the verge of being in trouble—working between a rock and a hard place. Seeing a maverick as beneficial and productive would be a stretch for many leaders and their peers. These are not dependent members. They lean toward "exclusive independence" (working on their own outside of relevant partnerships when they alone see the need). The goal is to encourage them to participate more fully in consultative ways of working, to be inclusively independent (able to work alone while willing to work well with team members and others, while keeping others informed and continuing the exchange of information) and being interdependent in order to effectively achieve common goals (Seiling 1997, 47). It is the role of the leader to actively promote these behaviors as the way to expand possibilities in the workplace.

It will take energy and determination on the part of the leader to work with both the organizational advocate and the advocate's comembers—as well as the other leaders the mavericks tend to frustrate—in making it possible for all to see the benefits of working in this way. To understand that the energies of advocacy participation will occasionally be out of line—and to see it as productive—will have a vital role in coconstructing a better future for the organization.

PERFORMING BADLY

Every day, members bring themselves to work. They do not leave the desire to be successful at home. Members also do not want to feel inadequate or guilty of not doing their jobs well. They are unhappy about poor and inadequate personal performance. Yet many do perform badly. Their contributions are sloppy and/or their attitudes are bad. Most of us don't want it to be this way.

If we don't want it to be this way, why does it happen? Why do people do sloppy work; why do they stay home when they should be at work; why do they not get along with those around them? It is normal for us to value our own contributions. When those contributions are not valued by those we value, it affects our judgment of our own value—our self-esteem. To increase our own self-esteem, we fight back; we protect ourselves, even at the risk of causing ourselves further harm. We do sloppy work, act as negative advocates, become cynical, and so on. We act against our own self-interest and our organization. We have an attitude.

Whatever our role in an organization, it is best we understand the four major feelings to be dealt with when sustaining relationships with those we work with. These feelings are human and are reflected in our behavior. When our own assessment of ourselves as being a valued member is low, and when others treat us as ineffective and undervalued, we feel it and respond. There are four major feelings.

Affection

Affection is a sign of appreciation and acceptance. People want to experience positive regard in their work. People want to be appreciated and valued in all their relationships. Since we are on the job more than any other affiliation, this is a primary place, along with our relationships at home, for establishing our self-worth. The level of appreciation and encouragement experienced from those worked with provides messages of affection or disaffection. When there is a loss or lack of opportunity to experience affection and appreciation, it is a blow that is not easily overcome.

Anger

Anger is a natural human response that is controllable through responsible choice. Our actions when angry, whether constructive or destructive, impact relationships and, when inappropriate, have consequences for the future. Unfairness, criticism, or constantly being forced by supervisors, comembers, and/or customers to do work seen as meaningless or unnecessary initiates feelings of anger and/or denigration. Those in leadership roles should be alert for demonstrations of impatience and anger and work with the member to constructively deal with those feelings.

Dependency

Those who prefer to control want dependent, work-for subordinates instead of work-with comembers. The realization that one has little or no control over what is happening brings a sense of being helpless. Members want to be interdependent. They want to be part of the decisioning process in the performance of their own work and in the work done with partners. Supervisors who prefer dependent members will struggle with advocacy participation. Advocates are not dependent: They ask questions, want to have reasons, seek to have the tools to perform well, and tell those who should provide resources what their needs are. They bother those in charge and are leader advocates seeking to contribute to the welfare of their leaders and the organization.

Self-Esteem

Member advocacy activities by a leader, such as encouragement, coaching, and representing them as capable, contributing members, encourages feelings of increased self-esteem. Valid ongoing acknowledgment and appreciation expressed by comembers also contributes to one's self-esteem. People constantly evaluate their own performance and competence through the eyes of others. When treated as doing work that is contributive to the achievement of their group, they value their work as important. Bullying and denigration by leaders and/or comembers eats away at the self-esteem of individuals—and the group.

Effective leaders regularly step back and evaluate the relationships within the group. Does the group regularly tear down the efforts of comembers or a specific member? Does anger and frustration boil to the top on a regular basis? Is dependency the accepted behavior within the group? Do the members regularly support the efforts of others in the group, without being asked? Do you hear appreciation or denigration? Is there laughter and playfulness? The work tone of the group signals the potential for accomplishment. Like it or not, what they appear to think, say, do, and appreciate also signals their willingness to contribute, both individually and as a group. The wake-up call is that leadership activities are often reflected in the level of participation performed by group members. Effectively addressing any identified issues is an act of member advocacy.

ADVOCACY IS ABOUT LEADERSHIP

Leaders exist across blurred lines of status and title. Advocacy participation includes acts of random leadership, whether by a formal or informal leader or someone "on the line." Leader actions of member advocacy are about direct and indirect influence and leadership. The willingness to support and encourage others to top performance is based on the premise that all members influence the thoughts and viewpoints of others.

The U.S. Environmental Protection Agency—Region 10 (see also Chapter 6) recognizes that all members, when called on, can be leaders and many, without realizing it, are leaders every day. Bowen, in discussing the change process started in 1994, states, "The Environmental Protection Agency—Region 10's Leadership Philosophy underlines their belief in the leadership role of all members. What has happened so far has proven to be beneficial to what we are charged to do. We know this is an ongoing process. We continue to initiate the changes that go with our Leadership Philosophy. We are quite proud of what we have accomplished so far." The following is the introduction in their Leadership Philosophy (see Appendix A for the full document):

We expect all Region 10 employees to be leaders as a vital part of their work performance. Leadership is not a position that someone occupies; it is how we all strive to behave. Leadership is the art of inspiring and motivating ourselves and others to realize our personal and collective best.

All Employees are Leaders

A leader inspires, prepares, and mobilizes self and others to accomplish organizational goals consistent with Region 10's Vision and Mission. A leader embodies and displays tolerance and respect. A leader values diversity, allows and encourages others to lead, perseveres in the face of adversity and stress, and remains accessible and approachable. A leader has compassion and empathy for others. A leader is dedicated to making personal accountability a reality. A leader is able to appropriately acknowledge and share in the learning from accomplishments and mistakes. A leader is committed to personal and professional growth for both self and others. A leader is self-confident, but appropriately humble.

As noted in the EPA—Region 10's Leadership Philosophy, the leader behaviors that are required to influence the commitment of members are wide ranging. If members observe these behaviors and see that they are offered consistently and reliably, they are more likely to see that management is serious about leadership. When change efforts are happening, as they are now in EPA—Region 10, leadership includes the following:

• Framing and clarifying the changes to be made.
• Coconstruction of the climate for the change with the members.
• Establishing and demonstrating the practices that facilitate the change.
• Expecting the desired behavior and rewarding that behavior.
• Supporting the individuals who are willing to give early input.
• Providing training essential to the change being made.
• Monitoring, rewarding, and renewing the process over time.

Research has shown that commitment to a new strategy increases when incorporated into the work performance of the members. "Acting as if" appears, for many people, to be a prerequisite to understanding the benefit of the new strategy and buying into it.

Everyone Is a Member Advocate

To insinuate that only those in leader roles are credible advocates of members is to limit the effectiveness of organizational advocacy. Member advocacy is a role every member performs, making it possible to contribute to the success of comembers at all status levels in the organization. Member advocacy

• increases possibilities and perceptions of support from respected others.
• stimulates the achievement of legitimacy (acceptance) by members.
• encourages members to see a larger possibility of success beyond what has been previously achievable.
• lessens the impact, proliferation, and acceptance of cynical and detrimental attitudes.
• increases expectations of others.
• is contagious.
• increases feelings of significance on the part of those advocating and those being advocated.

People are unlikely to try new behaviors unless they are aware of the benefits. Each person sees the new holding environment happening and hears why to do it and how to do it. Giving vague admonitions for new behaviors once (a normal process in today's workplace) and then expecting perfection is ludicrous. Ongoing education on what is to change, with regular messages modeled by those respected in the organization, regularly emphasizes the new way to work together.

New understandings of the environment where advocacy participation can flourish are learned through testing the authenticity of what has been represented. A supervisor becomes aware of his or her own tendency to criticize instead of encourage, and experiences a different response when he or she encourages instead of criticizes. A member who has previously kept suggestions to himself or herself makes a suggestion that is acknowledged, implemented, and rewarded. New messages of competence and significance are given and heard. The change will be gradual. With intentional nurturing by those who believe in it and do it and attention paid to those who are blocking it, advocacy participation can become the way work is accomplished in the organization.

Consultancy

The opportunity to influence others and be influenced by others becomes part of performing as internal consultants. Members strive to become successful as internal consultants regarding their own work with others. The organization with individuals performing as willing internal consultants will be innovative, productive, and more connected to the overarching design of the organization. As members become confident in their ability to influence and contribute, they will become more involved and more interested in their daily work. Each person will share information more openly and seek out information as needed.

Becoming a consultative advocate does not come without active, willing, and energetic learning, nor does it include blind trust. Being inquisitive and searching for information and knowledge requires effort and curiosity. The member who obeys too fully does not question—nor does he or she step outside of the limitations of lines drawn in the past. Not giving input when decisions are made in your own work is assuming decision makers know everything. This assumption is dangerous. Even the assumption that you personally know is dangerous. Being an advocate invites everyone to be alert to looking for the unknown while working together.

The willingness to appropriately challenge, seek, and share information in partnership with others is an extension of awareness, relationships, motivation, action, pride, and conscious effort. It is physical, intellectual, and emotional work. These are all important attributes of the consultative advocate. Members willing to accept a stake in what is going on and who know that what they do is important will practice how to be consultative members. It helps them to lay claim to the purpose and vision of the organization as worthwhile. They have a reason to be consultative.

Awareness is the foundation of knowledge and reasoning. Knowledge and reasoning gives us the "why" of consultancy. *Relationships* create the opportunity for connections across the circle, providing support and initiating partnerships that expand the "who" of consultancy. *Motivation* expands the desire for one's work to be significant to personal and organizational accomplishment, another "why" of consultancy, increasing the willingness to do our work well. It also increases the desire to learn from and serve others and to be a consultative organizational advocate. *Action*, the "what" of consultative participation, requires member enrollment and is a catalyst for pride and/or the outcome of advocacy participation. Pride is related to happiness. Pride in what we do is an outcome of our purposeful contributions to the achievements valued by ourselves and those around us.

There is a gap between just doing work routinely and pushing to accomplish what one can be proud of doing. We want to stand back and say to ourselves, "Well done." We want to know that we did it well because we are competent, empowered, and feeling challenged. We want to know that what was accomplished is significant to the organization we work for every day. Accomplishment expands personal pride and energy while contributing to the welfare of comembers and the organization.

CHAOtic RESPONSES

Organizations, whether local or global, are never static. For most people, the workplace is a turbulent, chaotic, fast-paced, ever-stressful, and demanding environment. As such, organizations are potential seedbeds for hostility and cynicism or enthusiasm and ownership. The leader who is a member advocate recognizes signs of cynicism, the lack of consultancy activities, and decreased contribution or cooperation—signals that members are rejecting ownership.

The CHAOtic Responses Model of Performance (Figure 7.1) is individual performance focused and situation based. Each of us is somewhere on the productivity spectrum and, as a productive, mediocre, or nonproductive member, we are the company. Every day we represent the company by how we work and how we respond to situations. The actions and responses of others are also related to how we respond during incidents and situations. A downward spiral is described as related to member responses to incidents of negative chaos.

The CHAOtic Responses Model has three segments: good chaos, incident, and bad chaos. Understanding these phases encourages us to be alert to our own responses during difficult situations and to know when to seek the support and encouragement of a trusted and respected comember.

Figure 7.1
CHAOtic Responses Model

Good Chaos				Bad Chaos	
Phase I: Entry	**Phase II:** Learning	**Phase III:** Earning	**Phase IV:** Incident(s)	**Phase V:** Burnout	**Phase VI:** Entitlement

C autious	**C** ooperative, curious	**C** oncientious	**C** ompromising	**C** autious	**C** ompetitive
H esitant	**H** umble, honest	**H** onoring	**H** orrifying	**H** esitant	**H** ostile
A wkward	**A** cquiring	**A** ction-oriented	**A** ssumption of guilt	**A** voiding	**A** ssuming
O pportunity-focused	**O** pen-minded	**O** wnership	**O** verwhelming	**O** n-coming train	**O** pposing
S eparate	**S** earching	**S** elective	**S** uspended effort	**S** ad, separate	**S** arcastic
				in- **E** ffective	**E** mbattled
				D epressed	**D** ependent

The Phases of CHAOtic Responses

The first segment of the model is good chaos. This first phase involves the member's entrance and eventual achievement of productivity in a new position and/or group. This time is stressful, but it is also exciting.

Phase I: Entry

Entry includes the hiring process or promotion and the initial stages of performance. The new person is uncertain and faced with issues of acceptance. He or she may feel awkward because of "not knowing the ropes," and be anxious to learn what good performance means in this new accountability. As the newcomer, he or she doesn't want to appear "pushy," so may be guarded and hesitant even when having the knowledge to perform the work. Feelings of being a little separate from the group are common at this time, yet the new member will be alert to opportunities that will support getting comfortable and productive in the new job and new group. The need is to "figure out how things work around here." The job and its possibilities are taken seriously.

Phase II: Learning

This is the phase where the new member puts his or her head down, learns the new job, and starts performing. Curiosity and openness to listening to others support the learning process. Getting valid information, having learning opportunities, and focused training are important in this phase. Being open and honest about what is needed to learn and actively search for answers to questions is also important. This time is critical to long-term abilities and contributions on the job. Although not as yet highly productive, he or she feels challenged and anxious to learn. (It is important for members to understand that learning is an open-ended phase for as long as they are on the job.) The new member's ability to contribute in the future is grounded in this phase, even if moved to other jobs in the company. Attitudes regarding future feelings of significance are initiated at this phase. Uncertainty begins to subside.

Phase III: Earning

Earning is a time of contribution, conscientiousness, commitment, and productivity. What needs to be done on the job is now clearer. The new member takes it seriously and has initiated a level of responsibility that makes it possible for him or her to claim ownership of what he or she is doing. He or she is selective about how and what is done, and strives to do the work well. Time is used efficiently and effectively, and contributions are seen as productive for his or her amount of experience on the job. The new member has become part of the group—has achieved "legitimacy" and acceptance. Constructive exchanges of accountability occur between the member and his or her mentors and sponsors, contributing to further knowledge and growth. He or she is enthusiastic and involved and appreciates the opportunity to work in a company he or she sees as a good place to work and expresses this to others both inside and outside of the organization. He or she is potentially an organizational advocate.

Phase IV: Incident

Eventually even the best member is faced with an incident or situation on the job that causes frustration, anger, fear, and even feelings of betrayal. When incidents happen, and they always do, resilience may be tested to the limit. The member's personal responses and those of the people he or she is working with are significant to the member's ability to remain an earning member. It may not be one specific incident. It may be a series of happenings that lead to a sense of defeat that temporarily or permanently changes how the member does his or her work (Figure 7.2).

After an incident in the member-oriented organization, the member is (1) encouraged to make recovery efforts and (2) be coached as to how to make a better judgment call if the situation is repeated. Although repercussions of the action may continue, the member is not labelled as a problem. Being perfect is not in his or her job description, and forgiveness is readily given. The member does not continue into entitlement. In this organization, the member returns to the learning segment of the model and then again into the earning phase of performance.

Figure 7.2
The Downward Spiral

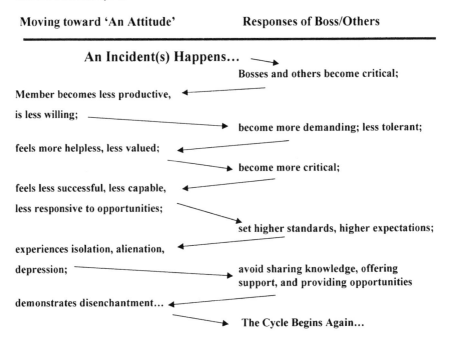

In these member-oriented organizations, most people stay positive and productive most of the time. "Stuff" happens, but they do not become permanently frustrated, unforgiving, and/or negative. People can make mistakes and take risks and even fail. Incidents do not sear to the bone for long. In competitive and punishing organizations, the feelings of being burned are often triggered by overload, feelings of unfairness, abusive/bullying treatment, and/or a costly, unforgiven mistake. In these organizations, people do not admit mistakes. Competition and punishment result in unresolved feelings of hopelessness, powerlessness, and insignificance. A lot of energy is wasted on conflict.

In the competition-based organization you don't make mistakes. As an "employee" organization, lack of forgiveness is evident. You pay, and you may continue to pay forever. The incident may or may not be of much significance, but it triggers distrust from the people around you. The member steps back; he or she is hesitant to move ahead, cannot move ahead, or is blocked from the opportunity to attempt to do so.

Issues of punitive accountability flash into the mind of the member and concerns regarding the incident affect performance, self-image, and personal pride. The possibility of loss of desirable material resources (e.g., the support of others, promotions, prized assignments, budget allocations, authority, equipment) are significant to the member's response. The member becomes less productive and disenchanted by what is happening.

The member appears to be incompetent in the eyes of others. Comembers and the leader become more demanding and less tolerant of his or her work. His or her response is to feel more helpless and pressured to do something, anything, to deal with what has occurred. He or she thinks through what can be done to rescue the situation, or considers looking for someone who can offer assistance. He or she feels sad and separate. The spiral continues downward when the leader becomes even more critical. Now it feels even more devastating. Desperation causes mistakes, miscalls, and miscalculations. The member feels less successful, less capable, and less responsive to the needs of others and to his or her work. It is difficult to maintain (or regain) productivity. The leader puts on more pressure, intensifying the feelings of failure. And the spiral continues downward (see Figure 7.2).

Unfortunately, the cycle is self-perpetuating. Another incident will happen and the cycle will start again with even more intense responses on the part of everyone involved. Eventually, any previous potential for growth and valued participation becomes more and more improbable.

The Choice to STOP

Some look for alternatives. This member hasn't hit the wall yet. Due to his or her own resilience and backed by the support of others, he or she chooses to STOP what is happening. The choice to return to the learning and earning stages can be made. The efforts involved with stopping include suspend judgment, take time, organize, and perform. Ideally, these efforts are performed with the coaching and sponsorship activities performed by the leader.

STOPping

When an incident happens we have two choices, suspend judgment or use defensive reasoning. Defensive reasoning supports the choice of justification. The defensive member looks around to identify reasons (excuses) for why the incident occurred; the goal is to avoid personal responsibility. Justifying breeds disenchantment and disappointment. Performance is lowered. When the choice is to *suspend judgment*, be personally responsible, and seek opportunities to learn through exchanges of learning and accountability, it is possible to remain connected to the situation and recover. Performance is maintained and the member *takes time* to do a "personal reality check" by asking questions:

- What is happening here?
- What is my role in this?

- What are the options available?
- What are the consequences of those options?

Judgments by comembers and the leader may be made at this point based on the member's response. It is beneficial for the member to commit to action and gain involvement of those in the group that can support the process. With the support of others he or she can now move to *organize*. This step may be the most difficult because he or she is still feeling burned. But to not organize and move on can be disastrous.

Improved *performance* is now possible. Taking action makes it possible for the member to reenroll in the group, moving back into Phase II, learning, and eventually reentering earning. The learning stage provides opportunities to learn from the incident.

The opportunity to STOP is not available in a punishment-oriented organization. Previous competence will suddenly come in question. The downward cycle of exchanged negative responses by the member, his or her supervisor, and peers is reactivated by the inevitable, watched-for next mistake, suggesting one must now be perfect. The target of the cycle, unless he or she has superhuman resilience, is feeling depressed, incompetent, negative, and insignificant. Burnout is inevitable.

Phase V: Burnout

In the America @ Work study conducted by Aon Consulting of Chicago in 1998, the percentage of employees reporting job-related burnout increased from 39 percent in 1993 to 53 percent in 1998. These numbers speak of people working longer hours with lowered productivity and feeling overworked and overburdened. Also notable was that of seventeen factors that indicate workforce commitment, salary did not make the top ten. The top five were (1) an employer's recognition of the importance of personal and family time, (2) the organization's overall direction, (3) opportunities for personal growth, (4) an employee's ability to challenge the way things are done, and (5) everyday work satisfaction. These top-five factors are notably significant to top performance. Is anyone hearing what they are saying?

The burned-out employee displays many of the same behaviors he or she demonstrated when in the entry stage, with the added ingredient of an "attitude." Caution and even secretiveness about work is now part of the way to work. A lack of self-confidence causes hesitant, guarded exchanges with co-workers. The employee avoids doing anything that puts him or her in jeopardy of another incident; the level of responsiveness and responsibility is lowered. A sense of separation and alienation from the group starts to surface. The previously challenged, productive employee is now less involved. Eventually, something happens again and the downward spiral is reactivated.

This employee no longer feels competent or significant in his or her organization and the likelihood that he or she will choose to become empowered is limited. They panic and turn to coping techniques of "good" behavior, self-protection, seeking safety and solace in rules, and leader protection (Bardwick 1991, 37–40). The employee knows that another downward cycle will start with another "mistake" or failure. Eventually, if he or she stays, this previously productive member becomes a captive employee. He or she no longer wants to be challenged—there is too much risk and potential for more humiliation. This member is "just there." The best day of the week lasts a few minutes when the paycheck is distributed.

Phase VI: Entitlement

Research tells us that previously positive and productive members can swing radically to being less productive, even resentful, behavior when there is a perception of unfair treatment. The member becomes frustrated and angry. He or she may say, "After all I've done for this company," and/or "I don't deserve this treatment." As noted by Judith Bardwick (1991) in *Danger in the Comfort Zone*, "You can't have a team psychology when people are preoccupied with protecting themselves" (p. 54). The previously high-performing member may fast become an entitled employee. This person often has a feeling of security and of being in no danger of being fired or demoted. He or she assumes that past performance, the ability to appear to work (mediocrity), and perceptions of friendships with those who matter will shield them from danger. In one situation, a manager had been head of a division that had lost dramatic amounts of money because of poor management for several years. When moved from the position, he was resentful, actively spreading rumors and excuses. He became a negative advocate, denouncing the company with mythical and exaggerated stories. As in most cases of entitlement, he became dependent and resentful instead of grateful for what the company continued to provide: a job where it was possible to move back to learning and earning, a new opportunity. He felt he had earned the right to certain things that the organization "must provide" because he "deserves it." Forgotten were the huge losses because of lack of performance. "Entitlement creates people who keep asking what else is going to be done for them. And what is done is never enough," notes Bardwick (1991, 26). Entitled employees become demanding, angry, and even abusive when they are denied something seen as earned in the past. They become greedy.

The quality movement and cutbacks have brought headlights to the performance of employees—especially those practicing entitlement. Organizations are forced to address issues of entitlement. The entitled employees are being replaced with high-energy, performance-oriented members, or their positions are being eliminated completely. In some organizations where unions in the past were barriers to addressing issues of entitlement, the union leaders are becoming partners in doing so. Global competition and survival is dictating the need for high involvement of all members. It is no longer possible to protect those who are potentially threatening the jobs of others.

Entitled members demonstrate the phase they are in by their behaviors. In entitlement, loyalty is not apparent and higher levels of cooperation, for the most part, are a thing of the past. The employee doesn't have a good thing to say about the company on or off the job. Perhaps an incident that happened years ago, still remembered or long forgotten, was the impetus for his or her negative, entitled stance.

In hostile, competitive organizations there are many obvious and even more not so obvious incidents. Things get nasty and the person experiencing an incident feels shut out, shut down, and shut off. Often supervisors with abusive management styles instigate the need for self-protection, or the nonsponsoring, unresponsive supervisor sits by while the downward spiral occurs and people "fight it out." High stress lowers the performance of those directly and indirectly involved. Feelings of uncertainly and disconnection prevail in their work. It is no fun to experience the incident part of the model in this organization.

After an incident the member who does not STOP feels drained, tired, and victimized. If sponsorship and support is withdrawn, he or she withdraws to regroup and heal wounds. He or she pulls inside himself or herself and hopes the incident will go away or be forgotten. Every workday feels like an eternity. Frustration and fear have brought a sense of being out of control. A choice to withdraw further or to become bitter and more angry, openly or silently blaming others for what has occurred, is not uncommon. Performance diminishes; commitment disintegrates; relationships deteriorate. Bad chaos occurs. The member may psychologically walk away. For some with the alternatives to do so, the choice to leave the organization will be made. When working in an unforgiving or punishing organization, opportunities to relearn and to earn will be withheld. Dismissal may occur. The goal for the member is for the nightmare to be over.

Stopping the Downward Spiral

Leaders in all likelihood make assumptions about the commitment of members through observation of job performance and behavior, often without wondering if there is a reason why the members are acting that way. Members are "categorized" (lazy, a good citizen, committed) (Shore, Barksdale, and Shore 1995, 1594), and this categorization influences the information the leader (whatever his or her level, CEO or first-line supervisor) attends to, remembers, or recalls. These assumptions affect distribution of recognition and rewards, influence the leader's routine exchanges with the member, and change what is expected. The leader's decision to offer support and constructive feedback versus leaving a member to flounder influences the downward spiraling exchange.

With support, encouragement, and sponsorship provided by the member's leader and comembers, the nastiness and defeat of an incident can be avoided. With positive intervention and empathy, responses can be "redesigned." With new commitment by the member, entry, learning, and earning phases are revisited, making restoration of the member's previously high levels of responsibility and productivity possible. By purposely working together to deal with situations, the progression to entitlement can be avoided.

Protect the Voices

People who want to contribute, experiment, question, and learn ultimately "get out of line"—they don't keep concerns to themselves. These productive, committed members are often organizational advocates who give voice to their beliefs, make suggestions, and ask why. Heifetz and Laurie (1997) say, "Giving a voice to all people is the foundation of an organization that is willing to experiment and learn. . . . Such original voices routinely get smashed and silenced in organizational life. They generate disequilibrium, and the easiest way for an organization to restore equilibrium is to neutralize those voices, sometimes in the name of teamwork and 'alignment'" (p. 129).

Withholding the opportunity to feel safe in stretching boundaries maintains feelings of insecurity, separation, and alienation. When people feel powerless, meaningless, isolated, and estranged, they seek ways to find a voice. In some cases, "People feel less alienated (powerless) when they are members of organizations that have some potential for influence in matters of importance—labor unions, professional societies, political organizations, and other voluntary associations," state Katz and Kahn (1978, 383).

Alienation has increased in recent years in some areas of American society and the workplace. It is natural that for some a stronger attachment to their union would be the outcome. Through the union, face-to-face confrontation can be avoided—and their concerns are still being addressed. Nancy Mills, director of the AFL–CIO's Center for Workplace Democracy, emphasizes the point that statistics indicate that once unionized, the union members rarely choose to give up that additional and more powerful voice at work. She says, "Workers want to have their collective voices heard around issues that have historically been management issues–issues that in the past have not been seen as appropriate for union involvement. They see a need for and have an attachment to the traditional union functions: bargaining over wages and benefits. They also want to give a voice to their desires and have meaningful, contributive work in providing quality goods and services they can be proud of. The key is that they want their own needs met as well as the company's. When the union, it is assumed, is seen as successful in providing this voice, these members will be even stronger advocates for their labor union, as well as even stronger advocates for workers making proactive and positive contributions to the success of their employer."

There are strong memories of when giving unwanted suggestions brought the reward of a pink slip. Security became even more of a concern with downsizing and rightsizing. New technology is making long-term members obsolete, and technology also means the need for fewer members. To expect them not to be concerned is reaching too far. The question that stands out is this: How is it possible for members to be organizational advocates in a union environment?

THE NEED FOR NEW PARTNERSHIPS

In the past, relationships between union and management were a struggle; that was "the way it worked." To work in obvious cooperation somehow implied there was no need for a union, automatically bringing up thoughts on the part of both the organization and union leadership groups of a vote "to get the union gone." It was beneficial for the union to keep messages of the struggle alive and ongoing.

Because of fear and distrust of management, unions proliferated, but in recent years it has been different. From 1983 to 1998 there was a steady decline in union membership; 1999 brought a slight increase (Leonard 1999, 64); 2000 again saw a decline. Expansion of unions based on fear is no longer as successful as it was in earlier decades of unionization. With or without a union, organizational members are now seeking new ways of moving toward individual or collective cooperation, or at least there is conversation about cooperation.

Even the staunchest adversaries can learn to focus on the same goals and work together in accomplishing a beneficial future. The success of the American workforce, and the country, depends on management and labor becoming successful partners. The Eighth National Labor–Management Conference Summary, 1996 brochure states, "The American workforce is the basic foundation of the U.S. economy, and the ability of American business to compete worldwide relates directly to workplace performance. The workplace labor–management relationship, therefore, has major economic implications, because it affects the product quality, productivity, and profits of firms, and the jobs and employment security of workers" (p. 1).

Whole organizations have passed from the scene because one or both parties were not willing to go through the discomfort of finding and believing in new ways of organizing. In these organizations, one or both of the leadership groups (union or management) stood their ground to keep things as they were, often to the detriment of the workforce. Both pretended the only way to survive was through forcing compliance by the other group.

Management and union leadership alike are facing the need to bite the bullet and experience a new form of discomfort: working together. Somehow both leadership groups are justifying partnering in a way that builds the capability to move forward. If they do not, they are realizing there is a possibility of facing extinction. It takes cooperation at all levels for organizations to stay alive and well.

In many organizations both leadership groups have decided it is best to find new ways of surviving; they know their future is depending on it. Previously frozen attitudes of separation and competition are no longer seen as beneficial or productive. Through these changes, the two leadership groups are seeking ways to act together as rational and relationalchange agents, calming their people and encouraging them to accept the changes as opportunities to become new, stronger people and workplaces where all can benefit together. The assumptions of the past, hopefully, will be replaced by new workplace realities without destroying the basic principles that nurtured the two internal organizations in the past.

There is also a need to have new, more inclusive values that assume all members, management and union, contribute to and make possible organizational existence over the long term. Old, counterproductive efforts to keep the groups separated and alienated, creating the them versus us mentality of the past, is now seen as counterproductive. They are being replaced with productive efforts toward coconstructing an environment where both groups are engaged in designing a new future together. Quoting a Department of Labor study, Nancy Mills says, "The least productive workplace is the traditionally unionized manufacturing facility and the next productive is the non-union 'high-performance workplace.' However, the most productive workplace by double is the unionized high-performance workplace" (Leonard 1999, 64). Mills adds, "There are four reasons why manufacturing organizations with unions outperform non-union facilities; (1) employee security (the job may change within the organization but their employment is as secure as possible in these days of increasing insecurity), (2) employees get their share of rewards in an ordered way (the union–management bargaining process insures that information about corporate performance is considered and there is a structured way to advocate for their share of the gains achieved through an employee involvement process), (3) increased investment in these organizations on education and training (ways to increase competence), and (4) in a unionized environment, the combination of the first three reasons allow for a truly 'collective yes' when workers say they are ready and willing to participate in workplace decision-making" (interview, 2000).

In recent years Wall Street has honored those organizations that have actively downsized, rightsized, and stripped themselves of knowledge and energy through making financially focused, short-term decisions to invite and escort people at all levels to the door. Some, through poor or misguided management, had gotten "fat"; some did not see it necessary to look at the long-term social and human bottom lines of the organization along with the financial ramifications. It is slow coming, but these same organizations are seeing the futility of "cutting costs" through cutting the brain muscle and the memory from their ranks. (It can be dangerous to move decisioning to those who do not have the information or training to do so.) There have been less than adequate rewards for these actions. Many are paying out more than was saved in replacing previously available talent and knowledge. Restoration of the organization's knowledge bank can be painful. Perhaps as an outcome of watching communities and people struggle because of these cuts, a Labor Research Association poll of 952 people in August 1999 reported that 51.4 percent of likely voters think labor unions have a positive effect on the United States (down from 56.1% in January of the same year). This number, according to Greg Tarpinian, director of the prolabor group, rose from 49 percent in 1995. (Those voters who think unions have a negative effect was reported at 37.2%, increasing from 28.5% in January 1999.)

Recently, a union member shared a story. He had watched experience and knowledge "pushed out the door" and was being offered few alternatives but to perform work he felt unqualified to perform. Slowly he learned the new skills—with little support from top management. His supervisor stood by him giving him encouragement and training that could be obtained with the few dollars available for education. He regained his confidence in his work and became closer to his supervisor in the process. He said, "Recently one of the guys who cut us to the bone came in yelling that things weren't getting done, that he needed something done *now* and proceeded to tell me what had to be done to do the job. I told him that, number one, he brought one vial of fluid to be tested and if he wanted all that work done he needed to bring gallons. And, number two, all those tests weren't needed to get the information he wanted. He called me a name and headed for the door while yelling and insulting my intelligence. My boss walked right with him telling him in no uncertain terms that I *do* know what I am doing and if he wanted the work done he'd better pay more attention to how he treated the people doing it. And let me tell you, he paid a price for telling him that." This supervisor was performing as a member advocate. Disconnections are the norm as a result of downsizing, but occasionally connections are made also.

Two-Leader Groups

Many companies are working to create positive partnerships that work well across the boundaries of status and position, and across the boundaries held so tightly between management and unions. Members at all levels want to regard others as cosponsors of the welfare of their organization. To do so, it is important that both groups see the benefit of recognizing the importance of working together to coconstruct a strong, growing workplace community.

Organizations with active unions have two management teams (or more) that separately or together must seek the welfare of the organization and the people they are leading. To attempt to lead an organization while leading in opposite directions is both ludicrous and outrageous. Decades of doing so has created an oppositional mentality at all levels and it leads to the disintegration of high-potential projects, even whole organizations. While leaders in the management ranks feel content that they are in control, the union managers know that nothing can be accomplished without their input and cooperation. And yet neither group, in many cases, is willing to set aside the desire to win separately instead of surviving and growing together.

The younger, more educated union member is demanding a more cooperative working environment. In some cases, their union leaders are not listening. A union member in a West coast utility says, "I can go somewhere else and make even better money but the time I have here holds me captive. I'm not able to be rewarded differently even though I really do a good job. The company says, 'Go talk to your union.' The union says, 'We all get the same compensation, that's all there is to it.' Why should I care how hard I work?" He added, "The good ole boys are retiring and the younger people, unfortunately, aren't interested in being union leaders. Somehow they [the union leaders] have to listen to the people's needs or the union is going to disappear. We are no longer working in Ralph Cramden's organization of the 60s when the reward for putting a suggestion in the box was a pink slip. Our unions have negotiated the security of workers to get us past that . . . but there is more that we need and it includes flexibility by our own union leadership."

Union leaders are beginning to listen. Margaret Blackshire was elected as the first woman to lead the Illinois AFL-CIO with 60 percent of the votes after a hard-fought election. She is expected to be an aggressive, inclusive leader. Blackshire has vowed to shape an agenda that "includes a focus on family-friendly legislation and transforming the federation from a top-down organization to one that's more inclusive and supportive of individual union efforts." Almost as if she was responding to the west coast union member, she also said, "People will see that we will listen" (*Chicago Tribune*, Internet). As an information point, Mills notes, "Blackshire's opportunity to locally impact in this may be limited as employer relations has traditionally been the purview of national unions. As an example, the current national AFL-CIO has created a national Corporate Affairs Department with a Center for Collective Bargaining to coordinate and support these local initiatives. For this reason, the whole question of how unions deal with partnerships or employee involvement, etc., is not really her purview. State Federations are expected to 'listen' on these matters. National unions will or should" (interview, 2000).

We hope that the next decade will see the expansion of union–management partnerships in companies with the two leadership groups. One way or the other, younger organizational members or those insisting on being heard and individually recognized are being rewarded for each person's contributions.

Evaluating Labor–Management Partnership Status

There are already many organizations on this journey. For some, trusting partnerships—and organizational advocacy—are a long and arduous journey.

Only the determination of change agents in both groups will sustain the journey. There will be those who struggle with participation because of past relational history. The following, the Labor–Management Partnership Status, suggests the journey is a progression:

5. An ongoing, successful business partnership exists contributing to a thriving union and organization.
4. Active participation is occurring in the coconstruction of a partnership.
3. Individuals across the organization are discussing the possibility of partnership.
2. People are silently thinking that there must be a better way to work together.
1. There is active posturing and verbalization of the stance of "them" and "us."
0. The company and jobs no longer exist.

5. An ongoing, successful business partnership exists contributing to a thriving union and organization.

Successful partnering relationships exist all through the organization, making it possible for information, ideas, activities, and relationships to thrive across blurred lines of status and title. Working with is now the language of participation, replacing working for. It is realized that (1) because the people are human, partnership is an ongoing quest, and (2) internal and external environments are factors in the success of the collective organization. The question is, How can these realizations strengthen ongoing efforts to coconstruct an organization that can thrive around these factors?

4. Active participation is occurring in the coconstruction of a partnership.

Leaders in both the union and organization have been convinced that a partnership is appropriate and possible. Formal and informal leaders are actively working together to design new ways of working together. Education, training, and activation of new expectations are based on coconstruction of new principles of how to work successfully to the benefit of all members, not just a selective group of members. The question is, How can we together construct an organization to be proud of?

3. Individuals across the organization are discussing the possibility of partnership.

There are now change agents who believe that partnership is possible. These change agents are in discussions based on these beliefs and seeking opportunities to introduce the concepts of partnership to formal and informal leaders across the organization. These change agents are being scoffed at, even warned to not take this further by their peers and, if located in vulnerable positions, their leaders are also doing so. The question is, Why not? or, Is there an alternative?

2. People are silently thinking that there must be a better way to work together.

Individuals exist who believe there are reasons to find more successful ways to work together that do not threaten the growth or existence of the organization and the collective bargaining unit(s) as working and managing entities in the organization. These members realize the old way of working is no longer effective. These may be the very members previously active in posturing and verbalizing the power of threat and coercion. The question is, How can we bring this out in the open for discussion?

1. There is active posturing and verbalization of the stance of "them" and "us."

Members at all levels are cynical and secretive. Blaming and shaming activities cause people to destructively challenge without constructively questioning, oppose without examination of reasons, and assume the worst without seeking possibilities. Trust is not offered or sought as a basis for working together as cocontributors to an organization all believed in enough to hire into and stay. The company is struggling. There are ominous signs, but no one is trying to bring down the barriers to working together or to deal with them. The question is, How do we make them do it our way?

0. The company and jobs no longer exist.

The dysfunctional organization has died an agonizing death, or moved to start again elsewhere, possibly repeating previous mistakes. The activities of individual members at all levels and the membership as a whole have led to the destruction of a once thriving organization. All members have mutually shared in the destruction through noncollaboration, withholding personal responsibility, and individually and collectively refusing to share accountability for the achievement or nonachievement of the organization. The members refused to work together to design an organization that could survive well over time. The question each is asking is, What do I do now?

Many unions are seeing the light on education and participation. At the same time, they are increasing funding for organizing. They are shifting their focus from manufacturing to service and, with the new service economy, seeing new opportunities that have been ignored in the past. "Unions," says Nancy Mills, "are a way—and as far as we can tell, the best way—to provide an avenue for workers to claim their share, and therefore, free them up to make their maximum contribution to the success of the employer" (Leonard 1999,

64). Two questions might be, Will the Generation Xers see the benefit of being in a union for the long term? How will "Generation I" (identified by Bill Gates as the generation born after the Internet) respond to unionization efforts? The unions are betting a lot of money on their response.

The issue is not whether there should or should not be a union. For management, if or when a company has a union, the company management group must work well with the union and the union management group. For the union, to seek to work well with the company management may make a better future. The leaders from both groups signal how people should work together. Learning and serving well together is vital to the success of both groups and the organization they all represent on and off the job every day. Only if both groups succeed—and are strengthened—can the organization thrive. A successful labor–management partnership, whether a formal or informal relationship, can contribute to future growth, even survival, for both leader organizations.

Labor Advocacy

Effective union–management partnerships will require both leadership groups to (1) see the benefits of working together; (2) convince their comembers that it is the right way to go; (3) be committed to shared benefits and the preservation of long-term profitability of the company; (4) educate, reinforce, and expect contributive participation; and (5) provide the tools to do so. In doing so, a definition of an additional advocacy issue, "labor advocacy," could be coconstruction of a culture of trust, openness, fairness, and support for all, making it possible for union and management groups to work together for the success of the organization as well as the union. Those firms that do so will have the advantage over those whose labor relations are stuck back in the oppositional mode.

PARTING THOUGHTS

Organizations are seeing the benefits of getting serious about the role of leaders in the responses of workplace members. Leaders have to stop insisting on and waiting for members to change their behaviors without making sacrifices themselves. Some leaders do things differently. They know that it is important to begin with acceptance of others. Commitment is an emotional experience; how can members be expected to commit to leaders and organizations who are obviously questioning the worthiness of the contributions they make every day? Exchanges of respectful gestures are important to the occurrence of productivity and civility. Members are no longer willing to tolerate the abuse coming from those who have a grandiose sense of their own self-importance. As noted by Manfred F. R. Kets de Vries (1994), "In their interpersonal relationships, leaders . . . should bear in mind what I term the three Hs of leadership: humility, humanity, and a good sense of humor" (p. 88). The same holds true for all organizational members.

BIBLIOGRAPHY

Aon Consulting. (1998). Study: America @ Work. Chicago, Illinois.

Avery, Christopher M. (1999). All Power to You: Collaborative Leadership Works. *Journal for Quality and Participation* 22 (2): 36–40.

Bardwick, Judith M. (1991). *Danger in the Comfort Zone: From Boardroom to Mailroom—How to Break the Entitlement Habit That's Killing American Business*. New York: AMACOM.

Boulding, Kenneth E. (1989). *The Three Faces of Power*. Newbury Park, Calif.: Sage.

Covey, Stephen R. (1989). *The 7 Habits of Highly Successful People: Powerful Lessons in Personal Change*. New York: Simon & Schuster.

Csikszentmihalyi, Mihaly. (1990). *Flow: The Psychology of Optimal Experience*. New York: HarperCollins.

Eighth National Labor–Management Summary. (1996). Brochure for the 1996 Biennial Labor–Management Conference, Chicago, Illinois. Sponsored by the U.S. Department of Labor, Federal Mediation and Conciliation Service, State and Local Government Labor–Management Committee, and the National Labor–Management Committee.

Glasser, William. (1984). *Control Theory: A New Explanation of How We Control Our Lives*. New York: Harper & Row.

Graham, Pauline, ed. (1995). The Giving of Orders. In *Mary Parker Follett Prophet of Management: A Celebration of Writings from the 1920s*. Boston: Harvard Business School Press. Reprinted from L. Urwick, ed., *Freedom and Coordination: Lectures in Business Organization by Mary Parker Follett*. London: Management Publications, 1949.

Heifetz, Ronald A., and Donald L. Laurie. (1997). The Work of Leadership. *Harvard Business Review* 75 (1): 124–134.

Katz, Daniel, and Robert L. Kahn. (1978). *The Social Psychology of Organizations*. 2d ed. New York: John Wiley & Sons.

Kets de Vries, Manfred F. R. (1994). The Leadership Mystique. *Academy of Management Executive* 8 (3): 73–88.

Laabs, Jennifer. (1998). Why HR Can't Win Today. *Workforce*, May, 63–74.

Labor Research Association. (1999). Labor Union Report. Submitted by Zogby International. (Press Release: Majority Thinks Unions Have Positive Effect on America.)

Langer, Ellen J. (1983). *The Psychology of Control*. Beverly Hills, Calif.: Sage.

Leonard, Bill. (1999). The New Face of Organized Labor. *HR Magazine*, 56–65.

Mann, Rebecca B. (1993). *Behavior Mismatch: How to Manage "Problem" Employees Whose Actions Don't Match Your Expectations*. New York: AMACOM.

McCall, John J. (1995). Participation in Employment. In *Moral Issues in Business*, edited by William H. Shaw and Vincent Barry. 6th ed. Belmont, Calif.: Wadsworth.

Seiling, Jane Galloway. (1997). *The Membership Organization: Achieving Top Performance Through the New Workplace Community*. Palo Alto, Calif.: Davies-Black.

Shore, Lynn McFarlane, Kevin Barksdale, and Ted H. Shore. (1995). Managerial Perceptions of Employee Commitment to the Organization. *Academy of Management Journal* 38: 1593–1615.

Tetlock, Philip E. (1990). Accountability: The Neglected Social Context of Judgment and Choice. In *Information and Cognition in Organizations*, edited by L. L. Cummings and Barry M. Staw. Greenwich, Conn.: JAI Press.

Tough Talk, Fast Action, On the Web. (1999). *Fast Company*, April, 38. Available <http://www.fastcompany.com>.

Tsui, Anne S., Susan J. Ashford, Lynda St. Clair, and Katherine R. Xin. (1995). Dealing with Discrepant Expectations: Response Strategies and Managerial Effectiveness. *Academy of Management Journal* 38: 1515–1543.

Webber, Allen M. (1998). Danger: Toxic Company. *Fast Company*, November, 182–183.

CONVERSATIONS AND INTERVIEWS

Ron Bigler, LRA Consulting.
Julie Bowen, Office of Innovation, EPA—Region 10.
Nancy Mills, AFL-CIO Center for Workplace Democracy.
Dave Opton, Executive Director, Exec-U-Net.

8

Customer Advocacy

No matter how great an organization's potential, no matter how good its product or service, it is the influencing abilities of members at all levels that determine its success.

Jane Galloway Seiling (1997b)

Perhaps the most important single accomplishment of modern consumerism is the recognition that consumers have certain rights. In 1962, President John F. Kennedy in a *Special Message on Protecting the Consumer's Interest* outlined consumer rights as: (1) the right to safety, (2) the right to be informed, (3) the right to choose, and (4) the right to be heard.

C. Glenn Walters (1974)

This chapter is the outcome of the author's internal work as a customer advocate in a company where the service provided was its main differentiator from other companies of its kind. The company is in a previously highly regulated industry that has been deregulated. The role of the customer advocate was seen as an attempt to smooth over some of the edges of the arrogance that had developed over the years as an outcome of knowing the customers were captives. It was, until deregulation, a monopoly. Things were going to change drastically when customers found they had a choice. Eventually, customers could get the service they needed without dealing with a company that they might perceive as not treating them well in the past. They would—horrors—have other choices.

ON BEING "THE COMPANY"

This chapter is also about the person who is in the place of contact with customers. The person who is the company to the external customer. Hopefully, he or she is also a customer advocate. Customer advocacy is defined as member actions of positively representing the company to the customer and the customer to the company. These actions are linked to performance with both internal and external customers. This definition places the advocate squarely in the center of the activities between the company and the customer (see Figure 8.1).

This positioning of the advocate places him or her in a place of vulnerability. When working in a "toxic" company this is a place of stress, tension, anxiety, anger, and low morale. In an organization that values and takes care of its internal members, customers become connected to the company by the services or products being provided through actions of the advocate. The company becomes tightly focused on the customer's needs also through the actions of the advocate. The member performs as a representative of the organization with every service activity. In the best of the customer service world, the member identifies with the customer, positively connects with the customer, and is committed to serving the customer—while also performing in the best interests of the company. The advocate becomes a liaison. This customer service person is a vital contact point for the company.

Figure 8.1
The Customer Advocacy Role

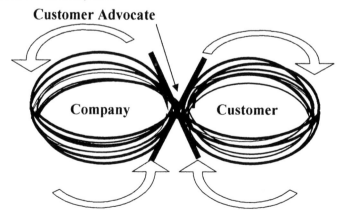

Customer advocacy is essential to individual and organizational achievement. Members make choices about how well they will serve the customers they come in contact with each day. The responsible customer contact person contributes to the growth and success of their organization. Through highly responsible service they connect to the customer; the customer potentially becomes loyal to the product or service being provided, and the customer can then become an advocate of the product or service to others (see Figure 8.2). Offering only "adequate" service potentially limits future opportunities to serve the customer.

The Meaning of Customer Service

To expand the meaning of service to the customer, the organization (1) commits to serving its own people, (2) hires advocacy-oriented people—those who want to learn and serve, (3) clearly defines what a successful customer advocacy role is, (4) emphasizes the message of advocacy through education and accountability while tying it to the company's overarching design, and (5) clearly knows that the place where marketing for the organization really happens is at the place of customer contact, with both internal and external customers. Members are always marketers, whether on or off the job. It is the organizational leader's role to constantly advocate for customers by reminding the members what advocacy participation means in customer service. Leaders do this by doing the following:

- Creating an awareness on the part of all members that customer advocacy is a marketing activity. Marketing occurs with all customers through demonstrating good work and appreciation.

Figure 8.2
Customers as Advocates

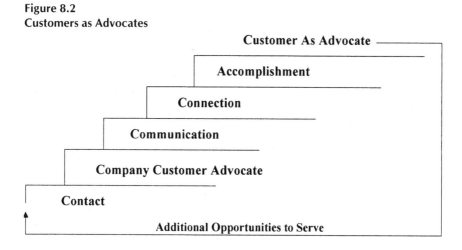

- Checking for ideas about organizing people, capital, technology, and services in ways that are value-added for members, customers, or clients.
- Establishing and rewarding organizational values that hold to ways of serving related to integrity, dignity, and trust.
- Demonstrating and expecting a level of energy on the job. To do so creates and sustains partnerships with internal and external customers.
- Knowing that edge comes from the willingness to make decisions; openness to new approaches; and the ability to reliably and consistently combine skills, information, and process with caring service.
- Carrying the message that advocacy of comembers, the product or service, and the company as beneficial, reliable, and believable is a role of each and every member of the organization.
- Being there when things are tough and when things are good with support, empathy, and appreciation. A little understanding goes a long way.

When promoting the company as good and the product or service as excellent, external customers also serve as advocates. Over the long haul, loyal customers are the ones who determine the success and longevity of the company and the members of the organization.

Customers as Advocates

The goal is to have many customers who act as marketers and advocates for the organization. As a customer advocate, the author saw it as a process (Figure 8.2):

1. Contact is made with the customer.
2. Communication is established between the advocate and the customer.
3. Connection is made (both participants decide they can work together).
4. Accomplishment of the service.
5. The customer as advocate promotes the product/service/serving actions of the organization to others.
6. Other opportunities to serve will occur.

The process does not always go smoothly, even when all participants are seeking to have a good exchange. At the communication level, there are efforts to establish what is needed and appropriate. Ideally, the exchange goes well. At times it is more difficult. Not misunderstanding the customer's needs calls for additional information, possibly causing frustration by the customer. When a clear understanding is reached, the participants establish a connection. Both participants become involved in doing what needs to be done to get to accomplishment. Accomplishment can also be difficult. If the customer's needs cannot be met, or if the advocate can only partially accomplish what the customer needs, there will be disappointment. Yet the customer still may become a customer acting as an advocate. It is in the successful interaction between the company representative and the customer that determines if it will occur. Even with disappointment, if the customer feels he or she has been treated well, when a need arises again that the company can provide there will be additional opportunities to serve.

The successful customer advocate is a partner in the moment with everyone he or she has the opportunity to work with, whether an external or internal customer. There are times it is tough because there are tough customers to partner with: Some are hard to get to accomplishment. Customers who reach accomplishment also may not, even with excellent service, become advocates. Although customers are always unpredictable, it is predictable that organizational members will occasionally run into customers such as the following:

Inconsiderate Customers. This person treats providers as "less thans." Demanding more and grunting when being encouraged to look at the advantages of the product are typical. One could say they have no manners.

Crisis Customers. Waiting until the last minute is their game. Everything is urgent and life threatening. They like working under crisis conditions ("This is how I work my best") and assume others do too. They keep you on your toes.

Nitpicker Customers. Nothing is ever right. In the end they will always be looking for a better product and a more perfect service provider. These customers are rarely satisfied—and they are always looking for the next provider to meet their standards.

Entitled Customers. These are the people who believe that as customers they are always right. And they will settle for no less than what they demand. They can be (very) difficult and they are rarely going to be in the role of customer as advocate. (Seiling 1997, 326, adapted)

A difficult customer can become a loyal customer when he or she experiences a positive connection with the company's representative. A pleasant exchange can make a difference in whether the customer enjoys the experience or not.

Getting Connected

In recent years we have all heard the dire words that service is declining. At the same time, the demands of customers have increased, leaving companies facing a double bind: The customer is expecting bad service while wanting (demanding) more service. A positive connection has to be made in order to find out what the customer's needs are and/or provide the service. And it can be a challenge.

In the case of a customer who is being delivered a package or the exchange is minimal, communication can be limited to addressing them respectfully and asking them *the* question: Is there anything else I can do for you? For the customer service person who is fielding a call or talking directly to a customer, communication can be pleasant, less than pleasant, or horrible. The key is to establish a connection.

As noted, working well with a customer requires us to know what they need. This requires both participants (advocate and customer) to exchange information and dig for what can be done to meet the customer's needs. Having a positive connection with the customer is essential, whether working with the customer directly or not. Giving cues of acceptance and the desire to meet the customer's needs is meaningful. The rules of connection include the following:

- Always assuming the customer contact will be pleasant.
- Knowing that the best approach is to
  —Be pleasant while directly addressing the customer and the customer's needs;
  —Listen to and ask questions to clarify;
  —Be knowledgeable in your area;
  —Be empathetic;
  —Be openly customer oriented;
  —Always keep promises made by you and the company.
- If a customer is bringing a problem to be solved, meet the needs of the customer as best you can or take the concerns of the customer to those who should hear them.
- If the customer is passed off to someone else, follow up to check if the customer's needs have been met.

Full accomplishment, in many cases, is tough, even impossible. Partial accomplishment or "almost accomplished" may be all that is possible. For the customer, this may be satisfactory if the customer accepts the circumstances and that the serving member has done his or her best. A full explanation of what has occurred makes acceptance by the customer possible. This customer may still serve as an advocate for the organization.

Follow-up, when called for, may be the differentiating factor. Customers no longer expect follow through. They have been disappointed too many times. They feel discounted and underserved. When good service is given, they are pleasantly surprised. It is the role of the customer advocate to set a high standard of service and to meet or exceed that standard routinely. Customer advocacy is not to be accepted as an extra-role activity. This is an assigned accountability.

When dealing with customers, especially upset customers, sometimes you have to negotiate the opportunity to serve them. This occurs in the communication and connection stages of service. Unfortunately, many customers already expect the worst from service providers. Many have felt victimized by insolent, uncaring providers, just as providers have experienced insolent, abusive customers. Negative service providers and the responding customer create a cycle of difficult exchanges, sometimes for no reason. It is the negative interactions the customer remembers, eventually creating an expectation of bad service. They are on the defensive before they even lay eyes on the customer service provider.

HEWLETT-PACKARD AND CUSTOMER ADVOCACY

Manuel Diaz has a new title. It is, "Retired." But trying to get hold of him is still hard: He still has meetings to go to, an assistant, Johnny Ince, who tries to keep track of him, and a strong loyalty to his company, Hewlett-Packard (H-P). It was his title when he was on "active duty" that brought me to contact him, with Hewlett-Packard's assistance. His title was senior vice president for customer advocacy. One could say this title is rare. This was a conversation that had to happen.

Organizational history has always been that nothing works unless you make your customers happy. Hewlett-Packard from its beginning was focused on their customers. H-P did not make a product and then look around for customers. It made sense to reach out first to the customers to find out what they needed. Unfortunately, it got harder to do as the company got bigger and more sophisticated. Sometimes urgent things of the moment were pushing the contact with the customer to the side.

In 1997, it was decided to rethink how customer service was being done. In the early years of the company, H-P was a one-of-a-kind company. In recent years there have been other companies added to the industry who could offer the same products. The urgency of being there with the products the customer wants is basic to survival. In 1997, the question was asked, "What can Hewlett-Packard do to find out more clearly what the customer really wants?" The answer was customer advocacy. The new role then and now reports directly to the president, now Carly Fiorina. The role serves as a liaison between the company and the customer. Manuel Diaz, who previously had thousands of people reporting to him, was asked to make a dramatic change in his role with the company. His new title would be senior vice president for customer advocacy. As such, he would design and lead the new departments. Diaz says, "At the end of the day, companies have to go out and find out what the customer needs and bring that information back to the people who can make it happen—while at the same time carrying to the customer the messages of what the company can do for them." His new role became his passion. Diaz states, "It worked well and, for me, it was the most fascinating job I ever had. Representing the customer to the company and the company to the customer puts you in a place where innovation happens. That's important to the company." He adds, "I feel very good about what was accomplished. They have actually enhanced the position since I left. It is obvious that the need for the work of the group has been recognized and is valued."

Manuel Diaz's role with Hewlett-Packard in some ways combined the corporate advocacy role and organizational advocacy: It was an assigned role, but there was a level of spontaneity because it was also a role of connecting the customer to the company and the company to the customer. It was a two-way conversation. The customer advocacy activity at Hewlett-Packard is certainly a learning and serving activity.

As with Hewlett-Packard, the products or services of most organizations can eventually be duplicated elsewhere. It is the provision of superior, purposely offered customer-guided service and innovation that gets and keeps the loyalty of customers. It is important that customers experience a "customer orientation" and know that the company—as well as their service provider—are meeting their needs. The service-provider role of the customer advocate is to

- represent the company positively to both internal and external customers.
- represent the customer to the company.
- facilitate recovery of the concerned customer back to satisfied (or at minimum, neutral) in the event of a service problem.

Unfortunately, every day companies squander opportunities with their customers. Every day companies are more concerned about the paperwork people fill out to get things done than what the customers themselves want. Every day mediocre people give mediocre service to customers. They commit the seven sins of service: apathy, brush-off, coldness, condescension, robotism, rule book, and runaround (Albrecht 1988, 14). Unfortunately, only good service and providing the product and service the customer wants translates into profits. The result is that many organizations are struggling when they could be soaring.

A LEARNING AND SERVING MIND-SET

Customer advocacy requires a margin of an unselfish frame of mind—a mind-set of serving. Unselfish customer service includes a mind-set that "doing enough" is not enough for the customer. Especially in the service industry, going beyond doing enough gives a signal to customers that they are valued and their satisfaction is important to the individual (and the organization) serving them. Customers can then feel a personal connection to the company and the person they have enjoyed working with as the company's representative.

Service is part of the success equation for all companies, whether they deliver intangible (services) or tangible (products) goods. For tangibles the quality of the product matters. Intangibles include the relationships and experiences that come with what happens within the service received. The intangibility of experience is indicated by receiving the service (seeing a movie, buying popcorn at the movie, noting whether the theater is clean or not) and then walking away with the memories of the movie, the consumed popcorn, and that the theater was clean. Intangibles are provided, experienced, and consumed at the same time. It is the interaction of the delivery of service and the acceptance of that service that determines whether it was a good experience, acceptable, or not a good experience.

The end users of the product or service receive the benefits of members getting along well on the job. Good treatment usually indicates the member does not feel exploited, does not feel helpless, is getting the cooperation of comembers in dealing with problems, and is valued by the company. People tend to feel better about themselves and their jobs if they are treated well. Customers know (make assumptions) about whether they are valued through their own experiences of being treated well (or badly) by organizational representatives.

The members at the edge of the circle are the ones most likely to get information that may be vital to a company's future. It is there that the opportunity is available to listen to comments, identify opportunities, and collect innovative ideas from those who use the product or service regularly. Customers are learning resources that companies are beginning to utilize. Through gathering information and acting on it, it is more likely customers can become partners in innovation.

The top twenty categories of 8,000 responders on a corporate equity survey by *Fortune* and Yankelovich Partners indicates the following (Gronstedt 2000, 71):

- Customers consistently recommend their products.
- Employees recommend these companies to other prospective employees.
- Industry colleagues recommend them to joint venture partners.
- The public stands by the companies in times of controversy.
- Investors find their stocks attractive as investments.

These findings reinforce the value of organizational advocacy and having a competitive product or service as a premise for organizational success. It appears that members and customers recommend companies they value and that it starts a flow of connecting activities that significantly impact the financial bottom line of organizations. Companies like Saturn and Xerox are carrying the voice of their customers all through their organizations in order to connect their people to the need to have satisfied customers. At Xerox, says Gronstedt (2000), "Front-line workers are empowered to act as 'customer advocates,' doing what it takes to please the customer" (p. 30). He adds, "Xerox has taken the voice of the customer and used it to redefine itself" (p. 31).

These members are being responsible customer-influencing agents of their organization. Customers expect and receive courteous, respectful, and reliable service and the product or service that meets their needs from a company they value. The willingness of the member to promote the company as a customer advocate is an outcome of many factors. Successful customer advocates are members who

- enjoy the role of being in contact with customers and demonstrate those feelings of enjoyment to the customer.
- care about their organizations success.
- are proud of the organization they work for.
- are "energized" by the opportunity to serve organizational customers.
- know that satisfied customers mean job security for themselves.
- have a positive outlook.
- are willing and able to make appropriate decisions on the spot to meet the needs of the customer (Seiling 1997a, 324).

One by one, every day, customers decide the fate of organizations. Customer advocates influence the future by what they think, say, do, and appreciate about their customers and their organization.

Sliding into Defensiveness

Members cannot get past the seven sins of service unless they want to do so. Although it may not be a conscious decision, it is a choice made regarding the interest and energy (level of responsibility) to be put into serving a customer. Slipping into routinely doing these "sinful" activities doesn't usually happen quickly. There is a slide into being a negative advocate; a descent into demonstrating feelings of defensiveness, anger, and frustration—even to becoming a bully who cares little about whether he or she is driving customers away.

People often overestimate how well they are serving others. Assumptions around what is wanted or needed and if customer needs are being met also may be way off track. The organizational advocate checks to see if what has been done is significantly meeting the needs of the customer. When customers don't communicate that their needs have not been met, the member is not learning how to serve them.

Effective customer service is often limited by policies, systems, and procedures that interfere with member opportunities to serve. There is no more distracting and infuriating statement than, "Sorry, this is company policy." Although this is common as a statement to external customers, internal customers hear this same maddening excuse. A feeling of helplessness is the response of the internal customer. The external customer, also feeling helpless, will look for other resources for the desired product or service.

Training Customers to High Expectations

Service providers become mentally overwhelmed and exhausted when they are constantly being bombarded by internal and/or external customers who have been trained to have very high, even unachievable expectations. Customer entitlement, according to Peter Block (1999, 11), has resulted from the customer-delight obsession that has made customers unreasonably demanding. Customer entitlement starts with greediness, turns to crankiness, and ultimately becomes nastiness because of entitlement attitudes.

Internal customers can also become unreasonable and demanding—some for good reasons. People are working "lean and mean." They are overworked and under stress. Things are falling through cracks they didn't even know existed. No one appears to be listening to their cries for help, or when they do listen they do nothing about meeting their needs. It is in the assumption of management's lack of listening or caring about what they hear where high turnover and the descent into bad service begins. Blaming and shaming becomes a way of working while continuing to scramble to perform reasonable and unreasonable internal and external customer demands. Eventually, everyone is burned: the customer, suppliers, members, and the organization. Healthy partnerships become strained and disconnected. Addressing these issues is an accountability of management.

Everyone Serves Customers

Not everyone will like to hear that all members are serving customers. In the past decade we have been hearing the message about internal customers—that everyone around us is a customer at one time or another. And that we are also their customers. We have been admonished to "identify your customers" until we don't want to hear it anymore. The answer is to treat everyone as a customer. Find out what they need from you. Listen to what they say. Work as partners in getting things done. Work with them because you want to! And make sure they get that message. Make them feel appreciated. Again, we get back what we hand out.

Customer Pride and Advocacy

Customer pride that leads to customers as advocates is obvious in talking to customers of Harley-Davidson Motor Company. Pride and connection spreads to the dealers selling the product. Mike Forszt, a coowner of Harley-Davidson of Valpariso, Indiana, notes that the company sponsored the formation of a Dealer's Council to which he and his brother and partner, Mark Forszt, can go when there are problems or concerns. He added, "But I don't always use the Council. I can go directly to any of the vice presidents, and I do. They pick up the phone and talk to me about whatever I have on my mind each time I call." This dealer is feeling connected to the organization who provides his product. He is an enthusiastic representative and advocate of Harley-Davidson. In this scenario, a call to the vice president puts a leader into the role of being a service provider and customer advocate.

An organization's positive customer orientation is communicated to internal and external customers by members through the following.

Positive Attitudes

The behavior and demeanor of the service provider helps the customer make purchase decisions. At a minimum, customers expect members to be positive about their own organization, the product or service being provided, and the people they work with while delivering excellent service and exceptional products. Customers confirm to themselves that they are buying a good product or service from a good company by observing the actions and activities of the service providers.

Demonstrations of Credibility

Highly trained representatives answer questions in their areas of expertise and, when they do not know, find the answer for the customer or refer them to those who know the answer. And they do it cheerfully and on a timely basis. Company credibility is experienced and expanded or diminished through the effectiveness of company representatives.

Company participants willingly participate in effective partnerships. Whether short- or long-term activities, partnerhips create opportunities to gain extra knowledge to work for the welfare of those with needs—whether co-worker, external customer, or the company.

Vocal Support

What the member thinks, says, and does tells the customer what to think. The advocate is training the customer what to think about the company with every word he or she says and every action he or she takes. It has been said that when we think no one is looking, everyone is looking. What we say and how we say it matters. Being verbally responsible is significant to the personal success of the member and the success of the organization.

Having Realistic Expectations

Customer advocates do not expect perfection of themselves or the customers they deal with. Everyone is human. Specifically for management, care taken regarding the well-being of members who are in continual contact with people all day makes them more likely to do it well. Regular intervals to relax and gather their wits helps them continue good service. Taking the time and responsibility to regroup and revitalize when things are going badly helps them see things realistically.

In recent years there has been a realization of the stressfulness involved with customer service. It has been labeled "emotional labor." Emotional labor is any work in which a person's feelings are the tools for getting the work done. Customer service is definitely emotional labor. When they do their job, psychological, emotional, and even physical responses or reactions are involved with at least some aspects of how they accomplish their work. The number of people served and how upset or distressed the people are every day can impact their health and well-being. These jobs require being fully alert and being able to fully concentrate on the customer and issue being dealt with at the moment. At any given moment, it can be tough. Psychologists, according to Karl Albrecht (1988, 111–112), author of *At America's Service*, have identified regular one-to-one contact with many, many people as potentially involving "contact-overload syndrome." People vary in the amount of personal contact they can bear on a constant basis. For some people, this kind of job is even unhealthy.

In recent years emotion has taken on a new validity in the workplace. In the past, objectivity without "all that feeling stuff" was the way people were expected to work. Rationality and financial-bottom-line thinking was the superior mover in the workplace. To consider the human or social bottom lines in decisioning was seen as being less than effective. Now it has been realized that good judgment, making sense, and rational thought are vitally dependent on our emotional signaling. If we feel pain, remorse, guilt, fear, empathy, doubt, and pride we learn, change, and grow. Without emotional signals, we become rigid and uncaring.

Emotions such as appreciation are part of making good decisions. Some will not like to hear that decisioning is emotional and rational. Clearly, thinking is undeniably based on emotion.

Commitment to Our People Leads to Customer Advocacy

Some organizations claim to be customer oriented while those expected to provide the great customer service are treated badly. The reality is that in many instances what customers experience is significantly different from what is claimed, because the service providers are passing on how they are treated on the job by those in charge. The experience of the member inside their organization is the place where customer orientation is tested.

Advocacy participation includes positive exchanges. Positive reciprocity requires work environments that make it possible to perform as advocates. According to Mike Beyerlein, Director of the Center for the Study of Work Teams at the University of North Texas, "Significant components of performance are not up to the individual and, hence, not due to lack of physical, emotional, or intellectual ability. Our own studies suggest that 50–90 percent of the failures of teams are due to lack of alignment of support systems with team needs. This suggests that significant influences on performance by individuals comes from outside the individual." This is unquestionably true of those who want to serve their customers well but are not provided the necessary skills, tools, or information to do so.

Members who are working with customers want to believe that they are supported and valued and that they have the authority to do their own work. Being supported suggests working in a place where the following is true:

1. Serving members have the authority to act when action is called for.
2. They are provided the information to make good judgments and their leaders back up their decisions.
3. There is open acknowledgment when doing their work well.
4. Their role is valued by the company.
5. Management is there when they are needed (availability).
6. The members ask for help as well as give help.
7. Partnering works well across groups and levels.
8. It is an atmosphere where one can be relaxed and appropriately professional.

Southwest Airlines is an example of these practices. The operating strategy of Southwest is low fares, frequent flights, and fun! fun! fun! Customers every day, on every flight, experience this strategy, filling flights while feeling that "no frills" is fine—when the service that is provided includes pleasant contributions of fun! and surprises. Customers are rewarded with genuine smiles and appreciation from attendants who sing funny songs, chant, or say poems to get the customers to listen, really listen to the flight instructions at the beginning of their flights. Passengers laugh, applaud, and pay attention—even though it may be the tenth time they have heard it—because it is fun! Passengers who are grumpy and in the toleration mode on other airlines are moved to another mood: appreciation. "Hey, this is a fun place to be." Southwest Airlines is noticeably different. Even Southwest's telephone message while you wait to talk to an agent is funny.

The mission of Southwest Airlines says it all. And it is a meaningful message. Attached to the mission is a message of commitment to their employees—and an expectation of the member's gestures of concern, respect, and caring of the customer—which are all part of advocacy participation:

The mission of Southwest Airlines is dedication to the highest quality of Customer Service delivered with a sense of warmth, friendliness, individual price and Company Spirit.

To Our Employees

We are committed to provide our employees a stable work environment with equal opportunity for learning and personal growth. Creativity and innovation are encouraged for improving the effectiveness of Southwest Airlines. Above all, employees will be provided the same concern, respect, and caring attitude within the organization that they are expected to share externally with every Southwest Customer.

Southwest has never had a furlough of its members. Their commitment is to competitive pay, regular increases, great benefits, and the hiring of members who will demonstrate "positively outrageous service" (POS) to both internal and external customers. Their goal is long-term employment of people who make a difference, while serving loyal customers who are advocates for Southwest to other potential customers. Through these commitments to their members and their customers, according to Libby Sartain, vice president of people at Southwest Airlines, "We get growth and profits. The result is a sustainable company where it is fun to work."

The profitable organization that is growing depends on its people to make it happen. In order to do so, learning and development happens through hiring the right people, providing opportunities to learn and develop, and having a culture (holding environment) and work ethic that makes growth possible.

Southwest Airlines has a People Department that hires for attitude and trains for skills. "Attitude," according to Sartain, "is a knockout factor." Southwest does not keep people when they don't fit. They believe in "tough LUV." The misery of the one who does not fit is catching. One person can, through their attitude, change an organization—for the better or for the worst.

Southwest Airlines was number one on the Fortune 100 Best Companies to Work For list in 1998, number four on the list in 1999, and number two in 2000. "We do this through our people," says Sartain, "It is our people who make the difference for their internal and external customers." While other airlines are "training" their customers to be in nasty moods, Southwest is training them to have fun. At Southwest, awareness, ideas, values, energy, edge, and advocacy happen and their customers experience it. They happen because of their people profile.

Southwest wants people with initiative, who are team players, who are intentional learners, and who have common sense and sound judgment. They also want people who don't take themselves too seriously. They are looking for people who

- Are adaptable. Things aren't always going to go predictably or realistically. Being adaptable matters.
- Have a sense of humor and fun! They are able and willing to laugh at themselves and with customers—and create humor under the worst of circumstances (inside a flying tube).
- Challenge traditional thinking. Customers will understand this is a better place to be when their experience is not the usual—which means noticeably better.
- Wear their professionalism loosely. "Professionals" need not apply here. Professionals, by Southwest's standards, are seen as straightlaced, do-by-the-numbers people. Southwest wants people who can "color outside of the lines." They focus on performance and attitude, not credentials.
- Empower others. Empowerment is a choice each member makes through an environment and intentions that make it possible—a choice that makes POS possible.
- Practice POS. Positively outrageous service is only possible when people feel supported, valued, and safe. Customers experience the same support, valuing, and safety being offered to them. And they become loyal passengers.

Through willing partnering efforts, clients and customers can be energetic participants in maintaining an organization's competitive position in the marketplace. Information and feedback are sought from internal and external constituencies, and feedback is responded to in a timely, meaningful manner.

SOME CAN'T SERVE EXTERNAL CUSTOMERS WELL

As noted earlier, there are people who are not well-suited for the work of directly serving the external customer. It happens more than it is admitted: People get into the wrong jobs, so they don't do well. Many of these same people can work well in other jobs, if given the opportunity. People want to feel good about doing something they enjoy. This is called "psychological success." They want to experience involvement to limits they see as appropriate, have the opportunity to grow through being personally responsible for their own learning, know that they have a degree of control over what they do and how they do it, and feel that their work is significant to the success of those around them and their company. They also want to be committed to a job where they are able to utilize their unique abilities. And customer service of external customers may not be it. They just don't like doing it. Every day is a struggle.

There are two people who are accountable for the member's opportunities to succeed. The first person is the member. The second is the member's supervisor. Being open and honest with the supervisor about his or her sense of accomplishment and worth in the job provides an opportunity to examine options. Keeping the issues to himself or herself won't get changes made. The member feels hopefully that his or her supervisor is concerned and empathetic to his or her needs and is supporting, not ignoring them. In an organization that is less caring and supportive of its people, it is less likely that the person would see much hope in approaching his or her supervisor. (Of course, there are caring leaders in the worst of organizations.)

Things We Need to Accept about People

People are going to have bad days. Whether we are serving internal customers or external customers, we have to assume there will be problems. Personal relations at work are often complex. We work with people we like, people we tolerate, and people whose very presence we question. There are things we need to accept about others, especially if we are fully aware that those around us are our customers. Unfortunately, the list could be a lot longer:

- People have gifts to share; not everyone is interested in sharing their gifts.
- People ask dumb questions; people ask good questions.
- People "assume" because they do not know.
- Not all people want to be developed or highly involved.
- Not all people want to be leaders or be empowered.
- Not all people are "adults."
- There are evil people who like creating painful moments.

Some of the items on this list are easier to accept than others. It is often impossible to understand the behavior of others unless you take on or experience their perspective. Ask yourself, If I were him or her, what would I feel? What would I not understand? What would I need from the other person (you)? How would I protect myself? What would others see in the actions of the other person (you)? For some, it is difficult to ask these questions. We have to constantly remind ourselves that "we are here for the long haul" (which, in the new working world, may only be next month). Whether it is one month or many years, the thought of the long haul helps us see the reason to be empathetic and understanding—without joining others in their misery. An additional question is, Do I really want to even deal with this? The answer is, if I don't, who will? Serving and valuing internal or external customers may be difficult, but it can also be meaningful—for all involved. Acceptance is the foundation of serving. It means acceptance of our needs, feelings, and outlooks, and the willingness to accept the same in others.

Kennedy's Consumer Rights

In President Kennedy's consumer rights statement it states that consumers have (1) the right to safety, (2) the right to be informed, (3) the right to choose, and (4) the right to be heard. These rights don't sound all that tough or unreasonable. Unfortunately, our customers do not always feel safe, informed, heard, or able to make informed choices. In many cases it is not that the provider does not want to support the protection of these rights; often the customer service providers do not have adequate information to honor those rights. The problem goes back to the organization being represented: the lack of taking the time and paying the cost of informing and training the people who are in everyday contact with customers. It is difficult to "learn as you go" and be successful without the knowledge necessary to serve customers well.

Performing as a customer advocate and meeting the meaning of President Kennedy's statement means performing in ways that include routinely and authentically practicing the following serving behaviors. This is where the rubber meets the road:

Responsible Acceptance

The customer wants to experience the feeling of being a valued customer who is accepted as a participant in the process of accomplishment of his or her need (see Figure 8.2).

Responsible Influence

The influence of the service provider can be significant to whether the product or service is purchased. This suggests some customers are vulnerable to the "slick salesperson." Mature purchasers know what they want and will only buy what they want. It is irresponsible to take advantage of customers who can be swayed easily. Being warmly expressive and involved in helping the customer at that moment without taking advantage of vulnerability goes a long way toward having a customer as advocate for the company and its product, even if they don't purchase the product or service.

Trustworthiness

The service provider is the representative of the company to inside and outside customers. Trustworthy actions are a significant part of establishing connections with others.

Civility

A key part of civility is to be empathic and sensitive to the needs of the customer or client at all times. The desirable service provider is caring, expressive, warm, and candid. They know that having a receptive demeanor and listening to customer concerns makes it possible for the customer to feel special and unique. It's called having manners.

Energy

The energy and enthusiasm for serving are key to performing these behaviors. Hiring appropriately, training sufficiently, and supporting the provider in his or her work are key to maintaining energy when serving customers.

• • •

It is through these behaviors that members are successful service providers and customer advocates for their organizations. It is the role of all members, especially management, to be ever alert to the needs of the people in this role.

A Myth: The Customer Is Always Right

Very frankly, this statement makes my blood boil. Being a customer advocate does not mean always, without question, giving customers whatever they want—especially if it is outrageous. When the company believes this myth, it puts a heavy burden on the customer service providers. Some people are unreasonable. It does mean working with customers, helping them understand that the company wants to serve them in every reasonable way. The key words here are "in every reasonable way." There are limitations. Not having the product. Not being able to meet unreasonable deadlines. Adhering to regulations outside the provider's control. No, the customer is not always right. But working with customers as partners can establish an understanding of what can be done. Then customers can decide if the best solution is to take their needs elsewhere.

If the customer goes to management and they provide what the customer demands ("I went higher up and they did it") they are telling the customer that the provider is uncaring, uninformed, and unreliable, if not downright telling lies. If management does not inform the service provider where the boundaries are and what is meant by "flexibility," they are leaving themselves open for these occurrences. It is important that the service provider be given the support and back-up that is necessary when the inconsiderate, crisis, nitpicker, or entitled customers arrive. To not provide support and backup is a barrier to the customer service provider being willing to be a customer advocate.

The End of Competition

Competition forces companies to focus on customer and member satisfaction. Is this focus diminishing? Peter Block (2001) called attention to the increase in mergers and super stores and how it has impacted both customers and members of organizations. Mergers have had an impact on everything from the use of airlines to the purchase of prescriptions. "The survivors of the merge and purge decades of the '80s and '90s now find that they are no longer so worried about competition and therefore no longer so worried about customers" (p. 11). The results include these:

- Competition has been reduced.
- Prior obsession with customers has shifted to obsession with cost.
- Automation is expanding.
- Investment in employees is lower.

Block adds, "When businesses were worried about customers, it forced them to worry about competition, and therefore customers. It forced them to worry about employees. . . . When you dominate your industry or segment, you stop worrying about customers and employees" (p. 11).

As customers, we cannot be fooled for long about the service we are getting. As corporate members, we notice we are being treated as expenses instead of assets. We may even give excuses for the treatment handed out by previously caring organizations. It may take a while for us to notice that the focus is back on cost instead of the customers both inside and outside the company. Learning and serving will then diminish. Obsession with cost and industry domination in the private sector clouds the need for advocacy by those who revert to command and control. In these circumstances, the likelihood that member advocacy will happen is lowered.

Block sees this occurrence as cyclical, as most recessions are, especially the ones of the human spirit. Is the result that I have wasted my time and yours in focusing on the customer in this chapter? I think not. Customer advocacy is an important segment of organizational advocacy and will not be dismantled by mergers. Even the big companies that focus on cost will continue to teach their claim of customer service—even as it fades into the background. But those who work there and those who buy there will insist on it returning to the forefront, and eventually the cycle will come around to a reawakening to the need to return to a focus on competition. Global and local competition will not allow it to go away; it only fades a little, temporarily.

PARTING THOUGHTS

There is no doubt that power is flowing downstream, especially when we are talking about customers. Customers now have much more power than in the past. No longer do they wait to see what the next innovation will be and buy it because the company who produced it says "here, you want this." Now customers are in on the design and they are demanding products be available better and faster by people and companies they can like and respect. Customer service is now decidedly the differentiating factor in organizational survival and the role of customer advocate performed by the learing and serving provider is significant to organizational achievement.

BIBLIOGRAPHY

Albrecht, Karl. (1988). *At America's Service: How Corporations Can Revolutionize the Way They Treat Their Customers.* Homewood, Ill.: Dow Jones–Irwin.

Block, Peter. (1999). Enough Is Enough. In *News for a Change.* Cincinnati: Association for Quality and Participation, June.

Block, Peter. (2000). Back to the End of the Line. In *News for a Change.* Cincinnati: Association for Quality and Participation, February.

Gronstedt, Anders. (2000). *The Customer Century: Lessons from World-Class Companies in Integrated Marketing and Communications.* London: Routledge.

Heath, Douglas H. (1994). *Lives of Hope: Women's and Men's Paths to Success and Fulfillment.* Haverford, Pa.: Conrow.

Seiling, Jane Galloway. (1997a). How to Be a Customer Advocate. In *The 1997 McGraw-Hill Team & Organization Development Sourcebook*, edited by Mel Silberman. New York: McGraw-Hill.

Seiling, Jane Galloway. (1997b). *The Membership Organization: Achieving Top Performance Through the New Workplace Community.* Palo Alto, Calif.: Davies-Black.

Walters, C. Glenn. (1974). *Consumer Behavior: Theory and Practice.* Homewood, Ill.: Richard D. Irwin.

CONVERSATIONS AND INTERVIEWS

Mike Beyelein, Director, Center for the Study of Work Teams.

Manuel Diaz, Hewlett-Packard, retired.

Mike Forszt, Harley Davidson Dealer.

Libby Sartain, Southwest Airlines VP of People.

9

Community Advocacy

> There's some kind of crazy belief that if you discard the responsibility to your country, to your city, to your community, to your workers, and think only of the immediate profit, that somehow not only your company will prosper but the entire economy will prosper as a result and I think it's dead wrong.
>
> Aaron Feuerstein, President,
> Malden Mills, Lawrence, Mass.

Communities are collections of people who individually and together sustain a shared existence. Chester Bowling, Community Development Specialist with the Ohio State University Extension, states, "There are life-giving elements that make it possible for all communities to exist. Communities are not just wood, brick, and concrete buildings. Without life-sustaining activities, they would eventually no longer exist." Although Bowling was discussing home communities, this statement is also true about workplace communities. The people in them "decide" by their activities and involvements whether the organization will continue to exist in the long term.

The American Productivity & Quality Center's International Benchmarking Clearinghouse and The College Center for Corporate Community Relations, in their study *Community Relations: Unleashing the Power of Corporate Citizenship,* examined how organizations performed a situation analysis to identify

- the company's reputation
- community needs, attitudes awareness, expectations, and evaluation of community involvement
- key community stakeholder groups
- critical community issues that pose challenges or opportunities to the business.

The purpose of the study was "to document and assist community relations with the transformation to a more strategic role in the corporation." The study "provides strong evidence that companies are managing their community relations operations in ever-more sophisticated ways with the intent of adding value for both the business and communities." Although this will continue to be seen as an evolutionary process, it is obvious that members of organizations are influenced by how the external community "sees" their employer. They want to work for the employer of choice which chooses to also be, as noted by the study, "the neighbor of choice."

This chapter discusses the community inside the workplace, referred to as the *workplace community*, and its relationship to the community outside the workplace, referred to as the *home community*. A workplace community includes departments, teams, lunch groups, partnerships, alliances, and so on, and all the relationships inside, across, and including customers, vendors, and so forth. The home community includes neighborhoods, cities, associations, businesses, service and social organizations, schools, church congregations, youth programs, and more. People who work in organizations also belong to, volunteer in, and support their home communities.

Community advocacy of necessity includes both the workplace and the home community. Community advocacy includes member actions that promote the existence of an inclusive, integrative, and flexible internal workplace community while encouraging the organization to respond to the needs of the outside community. It is impossible to separate personal existence in one community from another. At the beginning and end of the day, we carry our existence from one into the other. The influence of one community suggests how a person should think about another; one community can influence the connections—or disconnections—in another.

People create and sustain the communities they most want to be part of. How the members view problems, how they resolve them, and who says and does what is part of the way a community functions. The amount of personal responsibility and the constructive accountability exercised by those around the member influences his or her decisions regarding what level of involvement might be beneficial (a factor of contagion and belonging). Or a member can be the influencer by making decisions and seeking opportunities to influence those close by as well as remote others.

ACTS OF APPRECIATION

Conversations within groups reflect what is appreciated by the communicators. Conversations are also reflections of the empathy, appreciations, influences, and assumptions of the individuals and groups making decisions. Vickers (1965), in *The Art of Judgment,* notes that acts of appreciation (a process of merging judgments of what is real with judgments of what is decided as valuable) have an impact on our decisions as well as our conversations and what is hoped to be accomplished. Recognition and naming of problems, new or old, involves reaching an appreciation of how something works and what is "wrong" (if something is wrong), as well as evaluating intended and unintended outcomes.

What we appreciate and the behaviors that may happen because of what we appreciate have strong moral implications. These implications require us, as individuals and as members of many different communities, to consider the potential consequences from the standpoint of how it will affect others. It involves thinking through questions, such as, "If this is not done, what will happen?" If the answer is "not much," then one can consider the ethics of not doing it. Another question may then occur: If one is being compensated to do it, and it is a moral, beneficial, and legal act, is it ethical *not* to do it?

Civility is connected to empathy and appreciation. People sense whether they are appreciated and respond accordingly. The response creates an exchange of more civil behaviors and activities as reciprocal events, creating additional learning and serving opportunities. Stephanie Hemingway, a consultant in Seattle, in discussing her volunteer work with women immigrants, says,

Civility is the act of attempting to be beneficially together, sharing and making meaning, as humans on this planet. This act includes advocating for rights, working toward mutual regard and standing up for ourselves if we are not treated as equals or worthy. Nice is one definition, but it could ultimately be a passive life stance. Civility includes being assertive when society as it is constructed is based on a false or outmoded premise. Civility, ultimately, is the act of being a contributive civilian.

If you think about it, advocacy participation is about being a contributive civilian, as noted by Hemingway, rather than a militant. Civilians in organizations and countries advocating involvement practice the free will to participate in and influence their communities. Militant controlling atmospheres are designed for the participants with rigid rules and rigid ideas. As an involved civilian (and workplace member), we are more likely to give ourselves permission to be open to new thinking while having a choice as to whether we can or cannot safely present those ideas and thoughts to others. One can stretch the rules or act differently in militant environments, but it may happen at a high cost or sacrifice. "Civil" atmospheres value ideas and contributions that may lead to reevaluation of rules, procedures, and processes—as well as relationships.

One Can Make a Difference

The difference one person can make has been documented time and again. One person can mobilize movements that change workplace organizations, home communities, whole nations, even the world, as exemplified by Winston Churchill, Jonas Salk, Mother Theresa, Martin Luther King, and other known and unknown people who had strong beliefs and, through determination, took community advocacy to a phenomenal level. The patience and skills of these and the not-so-well-known advocates for recruiting others into their work and getting them to enroll is exemplary.

Bliss Browne of Imagine Chicago is an example. She is turning her appreciation and belief in the potential of those not included into action. Browne graduated from Yale and Harvard Divinity School and became an Episcopal priest, one of the first women to do so. She was the first woman priest to preach at Westminster Abbey in 1979. In 1976 Browne became a banker as well as a busy wife and mother. In 1991 Browne was in a job she loved as a division chief for First Chicago, an enviable place to be, when she saw a "new possibility of a human community." It took her about three days to decide to look at these new possibilities. Since then she and her colleagues have had an impact on the children of Chicago and, through the Leadership Formation Program, have developed grassroots community leaders who have made a difference in many urban Chicago communities. Provocative and innovative community projects have been the outcome of her energy and belief. Also, the Urban Imagination Network of Imagine Chicago links urban Chicago public schools and museums to learn in innovative ways about science and social studies. For Browne, her work at Imagine Chicago is enlivening. It is the beginning of achieving her image of "a city economy in which nothing and no one is wasted, like in God's economy."

Leatra Harper started a retail business called the Nature Reserve, a health food and natural products store in Bowling Green, Ohio. As a result of her desire to "walk the talk" of social responsibility as a business owner, and with the hope of raising funds to aid local environmental causes, she began an Earth Day celebration in the college town of Bowling Green. Since its inception in 1994, on the last weekend of April each year the Walk for the World has attracted city, county, and state officials as well as many private citizens and organizations to its cause, and promoted awareness of the importance of Earth Day. According to Harper, "The event has become larger than anticipated. I am very happy to see it flourish through the shared vision of what people can do when they combine their resources with their love and appreciation for the Earth." She adds, "It's easy to get people to come together for Earth Day because we can all see a strong connection to what we do for the Earth and what we do for ourselves."

Browne and Harper demonstrate that individuals, through advocacy of something they believe in, can make a meaningful contribution in small and large ways. To remain silent, motionless, and effortless gains nothing, eliminating opportunities for rehearsal and recruitment around causes that need to be invented, that can be rewarding, and that constantly need renewal. If these voices disappear the suffering will continue.

Volunteerism

In the United States the proportion of corporations participating in employee volunteer programs (EVPs) has more than doubled over the past seven years. According to the Points of Light Foundation, 81 percent of 248 respondents reported participating in EVP programs, an increase from 31 percent in 1992 (LaGow 1999, 39). People do things as volunteers that they would have been most unlikely to do as paid workers. Shy people become more open and communicative. The person who was a bully on the job is hard to keep out of the hospital because he or she loves to help others. People with skills and talents have the opportunity to use them when what they are good at was taken for granted for years on the job. Volunteers feel needed; they become involved; they find a new meaning in the term "work," while volunteering in something they see as meaningful.

Many people turn to volunteering when no longer in the paid workforce. Arylis Neal, a volunteer in a local hospital, voices the feeling of being appreciated that most volunteers experience. She says, "I would never work for a paycheck after doing this. I get treated so differently here. They never appreciate it on the job like they do when you are volunteering." This is a sad but true commentary about many organizations.

LINKING THE WORKPLACE COMMUNITY
TO THE HOME COMMUNITY

Based on the discussions in this book, are there signals of responsibility and concern made by organizations that can positively impact the home communities around them? Many would answer that question as follows: "The business organizations in my community have demonstrated little or no responsibility to contribute to improving community existence. Some give a little money and encourage their executives to give positive rhetoric about the community. That's about all." Like it or not, a business's existence in a home community suggests responsibility and accountability to the members of that community for activities that affect the welfare of the people who live there. As CFO J. Pedro Reinhard of Dow Chemical says, "You have to look at [performance] from three perspectives." These are economic, environmental, and social. "The public gives us a license to operate" (Birchard 2000, 22). After all, organizations depend on these communities for members and resources.

Most business organizations ground themselves in Milton Friedman's "social responsibility of business," saying that maximization of profit is their only social obligation. The assumption is that by being profitable the organization provides jobs for people, purchases goods and services, pays taxes, and, as an outcome, adequately contributes to the welfare of the home community. Paul Camenisch (1995) states, "Friedman . . . does seem to put undue emphasis on business's profit-making function in answering the question of its social and/or moral responsibility" (p. 254).

But there are many examples in every community of organizations who merge the welfare of the company with the circumstances of the community surrounding the company. There is a well-known story of Aaron Feuerstein, president of Malden Mills in Lawrence, Massachusetts, and his commitment to his workers when three buildings of the 130-year-old company burned just before Christmas in 1995. The next morning, as Feuerstein viewed the mess, he shocked the grieving observers by committing to the task of rebuilding the plant. He also said he would pay the salaries of the workforce and their medical benefits until work could be restored within. Three months later (with $10 million spent on salaries and health benefits) 1,400 of the 3,000 workers whose jobs had been burned out were back to work in a company-owned warehouse on machinery ordered prior to the fire to refurbish the aging plant. Two years later a new plant was finished.

Aaron Feuerstein is at an advantage. He is the owner and can make quick commitments to do whatever he thinks best. He answers to himself, not anonymous shareholders. He could have made a nice profit and taken the plant elsewhere, and it would have not been questioned by today's corporate standards. "What kind of an ethic is it that a CEO is prepared to hurt 3,000 people who are his employees [and] an entire city of many more thousands . . . in order for him to have a short-term gain?" asked Feuerstein. "It's unthinkable" (Coolidge 1996). Even during a disaster, Feuerstein's strong beliefs in social responsibility were grounded in action.

Surely, besides being profitable, one of the most socially responsible things a company can do is to provide jobs at fair wages and to treat organizational members with respect and dignity. Doing so contributes greatly to the prosperity and sustainability of workplace communities as well as the home communities in which the companies operate in. Yet this limited yardstick does not include product pricing, quality, and advertising; workplace health and safety practices; plant openings and closings; the company's record of environmental impact; its role in the community; and its philanthropic practices, all of which have social responsibility elements. Many would say this list goes far beyond the norm of organizational accountability to "social investment." For the naysayers, social investment is the role of governments, nonprofits, and individual philanthropists, not businesses. Feuerstein says, "It speaks poorly for society that standards have decreased to the point that I'm considered a superb example. If the average CED did what he ought to, I . . . wouldn't be receiving such acclaim."

Although these naysayers see social responsibility as disconnected from the "real work," an ever-growing segment of the corporate world is seeing new financial reasons for organizations to be socially responsible. Organizational efforts toward social responsibility increase feelings of hope, pride, and the sense of "workplace community" by internal participants and ultimately impact the organization's reputation with outside observers. Ultimately, it also influences the availability of new workplace members.

Consumers are also developing strong viewpoints about the organizations they frequent. Statistics are backing up the desire of consumers to do business with socially responsible businesses. In 1997, 76 percent of consumers polled said that, assuming no difference in price or quality, they would change brands to align themselves with a good cause. These striking numbers are beginning to get the attention of businesses. In a recent survey conducted by Research and Forecasts for the Chevas Regal Company, more workers desire to have the ability to do some good in the world (15%) than cited earning great wealth (10%). (Having a happy family life was chosen more often than wealth, news Brim (see Chapter 5) will appreciate hearing.

How organizations address social issues, both inside and outside of the workplace, directly impacts survival over the long run. To ignore these issues is irresponsible, even foolish. The following points suggest actions that represent characteristics of the socially responsible workplace:

- Seeks to purposely create an overarching design that includes social responsibility.
- Makes decisions based on the three bottom lines (social, human, financial), as well as the overarching design.
- Bases decisions on the authenticity and integrity of what is being considered.
- Makes "principled profits," not profits just for the sake of profits.
- Willingly commits workplace energies to the external community.
- Focuses on developing and nurturing partnerships, both inside and outside the workplace community.
- If a publicly held organization, has shareholders and board members who value and insist on socially responsible activities.
- Balances the welfare of shareholders, products, workplace members, and the external community.

Of course, social responsibility is a process rather than a program. It requires organizations to constantly strive toward the ideal, even though it may be seen as unattainable. For example, an organization that is seen as having good relations with its members and a history of partnership with their external community, but whose environmental record is less than perfect, can still be described as moving toward social responsibility if they are attempting to make meaningful strides in the offending area. Continuous improvement toward social responsibility by leaders is a factor of organizational achievement.

According to Business for Social Responsibility (http://www.bsr.org), companies focusing on expanding their environmental focus are experiencing benefits. Herman Miller and DuPont are among those who have found that environmental initiatives help attract and retain talented and committed employees. Swiss Bank, as part of its efforts to invest in companies with strong environmental and financial performance, purchased several million shares of stock in Bristol-Myers Squibb, enhancing the company's access to capital. Without increasing costs since 1990, McDonald's has bought $2 billion worth of recycled products. Through the Atlanta Project, many individuals and companies have provided volunteers, resources, and finances toward revitalization of their external community.

Workplace members are not blind to how the activities and environment of their workplaces and home communities interlink. A responsible workplace continually seeks to be aware of and search for ways to improve that link. The leaders are also aware that the membership wants their workplace to appear more responsible and accountable regarding their impact on the external community. Leaders know they can benefit through having a better "fit" with how the members want their workplace community to be seen and experienced, and the members want to be part of the process. The reputation of a company matters to its members.

Aligning the Culture of the Workplace Community

Many informal exchanges are held about whether things are actually as stated in the formal or informal overarching design of an organization. Many organizations represent themselves, for a multitude of reasons, as being member focused. They make statements such as, "we are a family," "teamwork works here," "employer of choice," and the like. Yet in some of these same organizations, if one talks to an employee, his or her "yeah, right" scoff says it all. There are gaps between what is claimed and what is experienced on the job. The goal is to align the stated or hoped for with the experience of the members inside the organization.

On purpose or by accident, organizations develop philosophies as mechanisms for integrating their missions, values, goals, and purposes into the internal community. These overarching designs are usually developed by early founders or leaders and are tested early on to see if they fit the goals of the organization and the way it wants to be seen by those inside the organization, as well as by outside observers. If these philosophies are accepted and open to adjustment, they will provide a stable direction while allowing flexibility enough to adapt to changing conditions (Ouchi and Price 1993, 69–70). As the company matures there may be a need to change the working philosophy. Change agents may bring to attention issues that require a change in direction, or there may be issues around how people are working together.

It is obvious that changing the internal image of a workplace community does not happen through extravagant PR campaigns directed outside the workplace (corporate advocacy). When the leaders remain focused on only one bottom line (financial), nothing changes in the long term. Changing the assumptions and thoughts of the members inside the community requires new initiatives around how leaders lead and clearer understandings by the membership of the worthwhileness of what people do on the job. Jobs and processes may need to be changed. Involving the members in deciding and piloting changes on the job can bring huge insights. The everyday contributions of members should be openly valued and linked to the purpose and accomplishments of the collective organization.

Efforts toward internal congruence are demonstrated in various ways in different organizations. An example would be Hunter Douglas, Inc., the Window Fashions Division (WFD). The WFD innovates and manufactures custom, high-end window-covering products. Having experienced off-the-chart growth during its first ten years of business (27 people in 1985 to nearly 1,000 in 1998), the leadership was seeking ways to reinstill the creativity, flexibility, intimacy, and sense of community which had led to the WFDs original success.

The Hunter Douglas WFD leadership initiated an organizationwide culture-change effort that would support the WFD in rediscovering its roots. The quest was to become, once again, an organization whose sense of humanity, community, and global leadership would permeate all of its decisions and actions. They wanted to create an organization whose vision, strategy, culture, people, communications, customers, and business processes would be aligned and founded upon the best of what might be. This intervention, which was founded on the process known as "appreciative inquiry," engaged nearly 1,000 employees, customers, suppliers, and community members in discovering, dreaming, and designing an organization that combined the best of both "past and possibility."

After the first two years of the culture-change process, Rick Pellett, general manager, and Mike Burns, vice president of human resources, noted several of the more striking changes experienced by the Hunter Douglas WFD. Rick Pellett notes, "Our production and productivity have both improved—largely as a result of people's increased participation in 'problem-solving' and decision-making activities. Turnover is the lowest it has been for six years, despite extremely low unemployment in our local job market. Our operations improvement suggestions are up over 100 percent. This, in turn, has had a big impact on both our quality and our internal customer service."

Burns adds, "Perhaps the most telling change in our division is demonstrated by people's increased involvement in personal and professional development activities—both on and off the job. This includes such things as formal course work, training programs, mentoring, and career development activities, as well as peer support groups." Research performed by WFD conducted in early 1998 statistically confirmed positive changes since commencement of the culture-change effort, including the following:

- Understanding of organizational goals.
- Understanding of how work fits with the organization's goals.

- Commitment to the organization's goals.
- Sense of ownership for work.
- Motivation to be productive, innovative, and creative.

Another example of internal connection is Harley-Davidson Motor Company, Milwaukee, Wisconsin. Employee feelings of belonging and pride in their organization and the product they produce suggest movement toward becoming a workplace community. According to Nola Vander Meulen, communications coordinator at Harley-Davidson, "Pride in our product is demonstrated by the astonishing number of owners and riders of Harleys among our 7,700 employees. Many of them ride their Harleys to and from work as well as for pleasure." It is a breathtaking experience to see the line of gleaming Harleys parked all leaning the same way in special spaces just outside the door of the plant in Milwaukee from April to October.

Experience, Education, and Training Lead to Wisdom and Heightened Personal Responsibility

As noted by Mike Burns, the need for education and training has turned the attention of organizations to how to provide meaningful opportunities to learn. The informal discussions of members are affected by the amount of learning a member experiences both on and off the job. Hopefully, the outcome of constant and consistent learning is "wisdom." Andrew Brown and Ken Starkey (2000) say, "Wisdom, at the individual and organizational levels, is a composite of curiosity, a willingness to learn, and an openness to learn new things about one's environment that challenges the assumption that we know all that we need to know and all that could possibly be relevant to our present situation" (p. 113). Wisdom also includes reflection on what has happened in the past and projection to the potential future consequences of what is being done or is under consideration. Those individuals who are contributors to this process are practicing workplace adulthood. Workplace adulthood does not mean that people are tall; it suggests that they are actively working toward the accomplishment of something seen as worthwhile, and are putting energy into productive activities (a definition of being personally responsible). While doing so, adults are willingly accountable for their own actions (being alert to the outcomes and what needs to be done to get maximum results). Many organizations are in need of members, especially in places of influence, who are practicing adulthood in the workplace.

A responsible adult has a full awareness that relationships, both inside organizations and in their home communities, are interconnected systems. The behaviors and attitudes of one person in a community affect the worldview of others. And the relationships, memories, and hopes—as well as the willingness to let go of those things that are not productive—within groups are what sustain the spirit of a collective group.

Spirituality in the Workplace

What is this "spirit" that so many are writing and talking about as it relates to work? It is belief, the source of what one is dedicated to, the reason one puts so much effort into his or her work. It is also the character of those who believe, their commitment, and their trust, faith, hope, and conviction. Some organizations will frown on verbalizing beliefs that reflect connotations of "spirituality" because of the possibility of the person doing something not seen as part of the way people routinely express themselves or how they work together. These same organizations will praise the member who demonstrates high energy and enthusiasm that is channeled to workplace performance. For sure, the words "advocacy participation" and "spirituality" may be seen as "going over the edge into the weirdo stuff." There is little understanding that both are about connection, belonging, the willing expansion of contribution, and being other-regarding. It is, in essence, having a caring orientation about how you impact others and having a deep involvement in something meaningful. Spirituality in this context may or may not be based on religion, but it certainly is a desire to consider the welfare of others and the workplace community. Spirituality is the sense of connection with something and someone that can be relied on and believed in. It is, as Jack Hawley (1995) states, "belief in one's self and one's company." Also, as Barry Heermann (1997), the originator of *Team Spirit*, says, "It is a building block for creation of solid, connected relationships in teams and groups, as well as full organizations." It is knowing that what we think, say, do, appreciate, and believe in is the bedrock of our existence, both at work and outside of work.

Do I believe in the work I am involved in? This is the basic question members face as they go to work every day. It is an absolute requirement for us to feel justified in putting our energy into an activity and community. Yet belief in the company as an advocate is not blind belief. Belief is the reason why we question and continue to seek improvement in whatever our efforts are put toward at work; we believe in our company and what is being done. It is through belief that people exercise free will. Belief creates a reason to support what is believed in. It also contributes to innovation, reasoned and spontaneous risk taking, and the exercise of high levels of enthusiasm for the people worked with and the company we represent every day, both on the job and off.

The energy we put into our work does wax and wane. Today my energy is high and my commitment to it is charged. Yesterday I felt drained and less than enthusiastic. To think we and others can maintain high levels of energy all the time is to predict failure, even despondency. I am human, so it is impossible to maintain high-energy involvement all the time. It is also beneficial to remember that everything we think is best may not be so. Because of that, the belief we have for something is open to understanding there may be other ways to reach a goal we believe in or are committed to achieving. Listening to understand is vital to successful advocacy participation.

Belief in our organization and its purpose does matter. Without it, the member's work is a mere gesture. Without most members having a spirit of belief in the overarching design of the organization, the company will be less than it can be. Hawley (1995) says, "Apparently some measure of—that is, 'enough' belief—is needed even if it's not 100 percent. Expecting total belief every time would be oppressive" (p. 96).

MY ROLE IN PRODUCING MY OWN STORY

Each person produces his or her own story through what he or she believes in and the outcome of what he or she thinks, says, and does. The story is formed through a history of how he or she is perceived and the experiences of others in working with the person over time. Members make choices about what and who they value and what and who they don't value. They signal whether they are trustworthy or not trustworthy. Their agreement or disagreement on certain issues and how sincere or insincere they appear in their partnering efforts are all part of production of their own story. One should continually ask, what have I done today that impacts the story of my work? Is my story one I can be proud of? Like it or not, seeing and experiencing the stories around us is what constructs our own working world story.

Producing the Organizational Story

The goodwill and reputation of an organization is represented by stories about past actions of the organization that are told by members and customers. Corporate advocacy, as noted earlier, is assigned as an accountability of a specific person to "mold" how the organization or an action of the organization is seen by outsiders. Different than corporate advocacy, organizational advocacy is a spontaneous activity of each and all members that reflects pride or displeasure about their organization. What members say in informal conversations and activities, both on and off the job, contributes to the reputation of the organization. Each person, by his or her stories told to others, impacts in some small (or large) way what is believed about his or her organization.

The storyteller produces the story of his or her organization. And the stories being told are shaped by the attitude and character of the teller. As noted earlier, when organizations hire a person it is assumed that, as a representative of the organization, he or she will share the stories of the organization in ways that will create goodwill and enhancement of the reputation of the organization. Yet goodwill stories may not happen for several reasons: (1) The person hired is not aware of the benefits of being an advocate for the organization, (2) the wrong person was hired, (3) the person may be seen as not fitting in and is ignored or victimized, (4) the physical and/or psychological environment of the organization is so demoralizing that the end of each day feels like an escape, or (5) the character (desire to do right) and competence (the ability to do right) are lacking, impacting the judgment of the member. But even in the best of circumstances, people are not understanding the benefits of producing good stories. It seems some people think others only want the bad news.

People hear and decide whether there is a benefit to repeating the stories they hear. Each person

1. selects what is to get their attention.
2. experiences through what is heard or observed.
3. decides how to interpret what he or she sees and hears.
4. adds or takes away from the story.
5. impacts what others understand through retelling or not retelling the story.

Behind what is said, a story often has a second message the teller may or may not be aware is being told (Kapferer 1990, 145). Does the story demonstrate appreciation or anger? Does it talk about being respectful or disrespectful? Stories can be uplifting, or stories can create victims. Stories can be truth telling, or stories can be fabricated with some basis for truth.

The storyteller feels justified in telling the story. People who are sharing uplifting stories are often sharing enthusiasm and connection to something they feel good about. Those who tell negative, destabilizing stories about their organization may feel threatened, angry, or frustrated. The amount of information reaching members that is experienced as believable impacts the stories being told. If people feel "out of the loop" and they are hungry for information, the void will be filled somehow. They may put less than factual information together to create information to be shared with others.

In the case of someone telling a story or repeating a rumor, a story can serve to rekindle the flames of dampened anger, or it can pour water on the heat and lessen the damage. Those hearing the story decide if it is believable. As a measure of believability, consciously or unconsciously, the person hearing the story may check for the level of the storyteller's anger. Is the way this person is reacting appropriate to what has happened? Allcorn's (1994) "indicators of the maturity with which anger is being dealt with" (p. 45) describes the basis for assumptions about the teller's anger depicted by the storytelling.

1. The [storyteller] and others know the person is angry.
2. Neither the [storyteller] nor others know the person is angry. This form may contribute to physiological symptoms.
3. The [storyteller] knows but others do not. The anger is camouflaged.
4. The [storyteller] does not know but others do. The person is known to be angry but he or she is not aware of the anger they are projecting.

Unfortunately, stories (and rumors) take on their own life. Stories are never fully retrievable. Even if they are proven wrong or the storyteller acknowledges the falsity of the story, the story will still retain life. Somehow a kernel of doubt will be retained in the hearer's mind. He or she will remain alert to information that may rekindle belief in the story. Or someone doesn't get the message of its lack of truth and it is retold and retold as true. The story, unfortunately, remains amazingly alive and growing. Hopefully, the story will take a good shift, but it is unlikely.

Caring Enough

To be involved in community service all day every day, "caring enough" is essential. An example would be Family Advocacy Services, located in Baltimore. Family Advocacy Services serves students and families in a community-based environment, providing community "wraparound" services. Tim Simmons, staff development coordinator, notes, "Those services include individual, group therapy, and multi-family therapy. Making these services available in a caring way can make it possible for our clients to deal with issues and decisions they otherwise may deal with poorly." Family Advocacy Services provides their services in the least restricted environment possible in order to help the kids and families to grow individually as well as together. Simmons adds, "One of our primary or core values is that we believe that healthy relationships are important. Therefore, we look for employees who possess a passion in their caring for families and kids. We believe that passion is the driving force for providing extraordinary service."

Family Advocacy Services has a dedicated membership of 180 staff members. What they do is not always easy—in fact, it is rarely easy. And the members don't always get the results their hearts desire. It is through their passionate advocacy of their work and the passion of Bruce E. Bertell, president/CEO of Family Advocacy Services, that they go on, and because of the exhilaration of the successes that do occur. Thomas Petzinger, Jr. (1999), in his book *The New Pioneers*, says, "Ethics and integrity are about knowing the effects of your actions on a wider circle—and caring about those effects." That is what working passionately is about. But in the case of the work of the caring people at Family Advocacy Services, it is unlikely they will ever really understand the true impact of their efforts. They just keep trying anyway, because they care about the kids and families they serve. My guess is that these workplace members are telling good stories, both on and off the job, about their organization, their colleagues, and the work being done because they care. If there is someone who is not telling good stories, he or she probably lost the passion for the work. If so, it's time to move on.

THE NEXT FOCUS ON COMMUNITY

Small and large companies and individuals have gotten over the shock of becoming "Internet enabled." For many, e-commerce is reshaping how they do business, and reshaping front-office applications and back-office systems. New opportunities and new risks are falling on the shoulders of existing companies and unforeseen competitors are appearing.

Customer-relations management provides quick information availability through software that can provide instant salesforce information, keep track of customer interactions, and view each customer's data as well as making the data available to the customer. Customers want to know that they can order what they want and get it in two days (or less). The next level is to exchange ideas and experiences, learn from one another, merge that information, and then, if it involves a product, get the product that reflects what has been mutually decided. The third level is to make a connection, exchange information, and stay in touch, developing an ongoing online connection.

Early on, it seemed absurd to think that people could become a community on the Internet. It seemed so impersonal. People can say or claim anything and maintain that facade as long as they can "be" the created person on the screen. Or one can disappear with the use of a delete button and end the connection.

When people start interacting regularly on the Internet, the word "community" starts popping up. And yet at this time few people fully understand the concept of community. They are even more confused with how it relates to their interactions on the Internet. Avik Roy, president of Nimbal, a consulting firm in Princeton, New Jersey, notes,

The Internet will change the way business is conducted in the future. Yet, for most people the Internet remains a mystery. They go to work every day to workplaces using the same skills, doing the same jobs, for the same bosses and companies. Computers may be used in their work but they really do not relate that to how computers impact how their work is done and how the new, changed marketplace works. Even with all the hype, it would be easy to ignore the Internet and keep working the same old way. However, business has already changed. Many companies are already feeling pressure on their bottom lines and are struggling to attract and retain the best talent. The way their work is done will continue to change. Many are going to struggle and some will be left behind in the 20th century.

We must be alert to this new frontier and strive to understand and contribute to the new opportunities in the new and different communities we design.

PARTING THOUGHTS

It is no longer possible for members of organizations to be taken for granted. It is also no longer possible for individuals and organizations to take the home communities around their organizations for granted. As community advocates, members want their companies to be involved and valued by the communities in which they are located.

Membership, whether inside organizations or in home communities, is built on relationships and the activities of contributing members and citizens—

people who are personally responsible and willingly accountable for addressing the issues around them. This is also true for changing the complex and even burdensome communities members live in.

To change our communities is to start by changing ourselves. Without doubt we have in some way contributed to how things are around us by our own attitudes and actions (or inaction). We must change our thinking, change our actions, and change how we respond. We must examine what, who, and how we judge others. Not to change ourselves and the way we relate to our communities is to be willing to buy into the silent sabotage that is going on around us, causing what we are concerned about to worsen. This means settling for less.

BIBLIOGRAPHY

Allcorn, Seth. (1994). *Anger in the Workplace: Understanding the Causes of Aggression and Violence*. Westport, Conn.: Quorum Books.

Birchard, Bill. (2000). A Social Report for a Public Audience. *CFO* 16 (2).

Brown, Andrew D., and Ken Starkey. (2000). Organizational Identity and Learning: A Psychodynamic Perspective. *Academy of Management Review* 25 (1): 102–120.

Camenisch, Paul F. (1995). Business Ethics: On Getting to the Heart of the Matter. In *Moral Issues in Business*, edited by William H. Shaw and Vincent Barry. 6th ed. Belmont, Calif.: Wadsworth.

Coolridge, Shelley Donald. (1996). "Corporate Decency" Prevails at Malden Mills. *Christian Science Monitor*, 8 March.

Hawley, Jack. (1995). *Reawakening the Spirit in Work*. New York: Fireside.

Hearman, Barry. (1997). *Building Team Spirit*. New York: McGraw-Hill.

Huy, Quy Nguyen. (1999). Emotional Capability, Emotional Intelligence and Radical Change. *Academy of Management Review* 24 (2): 325–345.

Kapferer, Jean-Noel. (1990). *Rumors: Uses, Interpretations, and Images*. New Brunswick, N.J.: Transaction.

LaGow, Robert. (1999). Employee Volunteer Programs Becoming More Widespread. *HR Magazine*, December, 39.

Nossiter, Bernard D. (1964). *The Mythmakers: An Essay on Power and Wealth*. Boston: Houghton Mifflin.

Ouchi, William G., and Reymond L. Price. (1993). Hierarchies, Clans, and Theory Z: A New Perspective on Organization Development. *Organizational Dynamics* 22 (2): 62–67.

Petzinger, Thomas, Jr. (1999). *The New Pioneers: The Men and Women Who Are Transforming the Workplace and Marketplace*. New York: Simon & Schuster.

Vickers, Geoffrey. (1965). *The Art of Judgment: A Study of Policy Making*. New York: Chapman and Hall.

CONVERSATIONS AND INTERVIEWS

Chester Bowling, Community Development Specialist, Ohio State University Extention.

Bliss Browne, Imagine Chicago.

Mike Burns, VP of Human Resources, Hunter Douglas WFD.
Aaron Feuerstein, President, Malden Mills, conference presentation.
Leatra Harper, Nature Reserve, Bowling Green, Ohio.
Barry Heermann, *Team Spirit*.
Stephanie Hemingway, Hemingway & Co.
Arylis Neal, volunteer.
Rick Pellett, General Manager, Hunter Douglas WFD.
Avik Roy, Nimbal, Princeton, N.J.
Tim Simmons, Family Advocacy Services.
Nola Vander Meulen, Harley-Davidson.

10

Inclusion Advocacy

Written in partnership with Marge Schiller.

Today, the numbers of diverse workers who expect more than tolerance or indifference from their managers and their organizations have reached critical proportions—making "vigorous indifference" far less effective as a strategy for managing America's changing workforce.
Marilyn Loden and Judy B. Rosener (1991)

At Xerox we view diversity as something more than a moral imperative or a business necessity—we see it as a business opportunity.
Paul A. Allaire, chairman, Xerox (1999)

How can you see her as an appropriate presidential candidate when she admires the color of the carpet in a press room?
Reporter regarding the candidacy of Elizabeth Dole,
CSPAN, March 1999

Many people show up for work every day even though there are constant, consistent signals that they aren't wanted—and are definitely not invited into the "in group." They may be seen as undeserving of inclusion because they are, in some way, defined as different. Those seen as undeserving are treated as so.

The "defining dozen" in most organizations are gender, color, age, physical and mental abilities, sexual orientation, geography, culture, religion, personality style, tenure, and organizational position. Sometimes differences are not obvious. The group "senses" there is a difference. It is equally significant when an individual experiences himself or herself as different. He or she may appear the same to others but feel very different internally. When differences are not noted, opportunities to contribute might still be made available, but the person may not be able to take advantage of those opportunities.

Members in an inclusive environment actively and hopefully create and support a cooperative, interactive, and member-oriented community. Common sense tells us that in order to work well together, people must move beyond tolerance. We must live our acceptance of the contributions of others, including their suggestions, statements, concerns, and efforts to influence that may be seen and stated differently. For this reason, "inclusion advocacy" is defined as the responsibility and accountability of the individual, whatever his or her role, and the organization in the quest to include and respect the world-views of all members in the expansion of individual and organizational potential.

Individuals and groups choose who is accepted and who is not, and they act accordingly. Effective members, including formal leaders, know that responsibility for their own and their organization's success starts with the purposeful contributions of each member. Influential people, wherever they are located in the organization, are recognized as leaders. Those who are not accepted potentially have little influence on the work and the people around them. Acceptance and liking are important in interpersonal influence because they identify one as being included in the ongoing organizational dialogue invoking the rule of reciprocity. Moreover, people prefer to agree with and say yes to the requests of people they like and appreciate. Inclusive groups create a history of relationships through appreciation, acceptance, connection, and reciprocity.

DIFFERENCE AND DIVERSITY

Difference and diversity in the United States are facts. This nation was designed to be a "melting pot" from the beginning. For a while we talked about a quilt or a stew, with distinct, separable differences. Demographically, most of us are now a mix of ethnic, racial, religious, and geographic cultures, but the paradox is that we are living in a country where difference and diversity are becoming more pronounced every day, while at the same time public policy is leaning toward removing special access (i.e., affirmative action) to bring us back to the one-standard "melting pot."

At the turn of this century, one-third of America was projected to be black, Latino, or Asian, up from just over one-fifth in 1985. In 1985 the proportion of women and people of color was 57 percent; in 2000, although the census figures are not as yet available, women and people of color are projected to comprise nearly 67 percent. These statistics, when read or heard on television, do not adequately represent the needs of our workplace communities around this changing reality: How will the majority deal with being a minority? The concept of a "majority" population no longer has any reality as the demographics of who lives and works where continue to shift. While the statistics are being rearranged, recognition of the differences within diverse cultures are also being acknowledged. Issues of diversity and difference create opportunities, challenges, and different realities for everyone.

In order for all to take advantage of these new opportunities, the definition of "diversity" must be consciously expanded from race and gender to be replaced by an awareness that diversity and difference are the fabric of life. To do so affects appreciation, acknowledgment, acceptance, and accomplishment. The term "diversity" implicitly suggests everyone who is not white, male, thirty-five to forty-five, Christian, heterosexual, and part of the prevailing cultural norm. Many claim that in their own definition and application diversity does mean all differences. But there are limitations in what some understand when they hear the word diversity. Some are only hearing a reference to color and gender; others will add ethnicity and sexual orientation. The language and framing of a definition drives assumptions and, ultimately, behavior. (Fortunately, many diversity practitioners have expanded their definition.) Past definitions limit what can be accomplished. New definitions are called for or new language designed. John Fernandez (1998) says, "We believe that the first step toward a solution of the race and gender problem is to get rid of the term *diversity*. . . . Like *affirmative action*, the term is nothing if not loaded" (p. 18). Although there are ample reasons to agree with Fernandez about the term "diversity," we will leave it to others to fully address the change in language.

Whether acknowledged or not, there is a "corporate caste system," a way of identifying people to "their place" through inclusion, toleration, or exclusion. This caste system is intensified by tendencies to act out the desire to maintain separateness. As described by Kenneth Gergen, Sheila McNamee, and Frank Barrett (in press) the problem of difference is intensified by (1) the tendency to avoid meetings, conversations, and social gatherings with those who are different; (2) a tendency for accounts of these others to become simplified (leads to few challenges to the descriptions and explanations made through stereotyping); (3) a movement toward extremity, bringing explanations of actions made in a negative way, in turn bringing an accumulation of explanations that eventually shape a sense of inferiority, stupidity, or the villainous. Yet all are expected to be top performers focused on the well-being of the organization. Remaining oblivious and pretending differences are invisible or discountable limits the expansion of the circle of inclusion. Optimization of involvement through valuing and inclusion is the objective.

Every day, outside of work, we read and see the stories of racial, ethnic, and religious intolerance and the inhuman acts people perform to justify a noninclusive, adversarial position. It is time to acknowledge the problems of lack of acceptance and inclusion in our communities and inside our workplaces. Anxiety, passivity, disconnection, hostility—these are not new. What is new is the willingness of many to recognize that vast resources of knowledge, competence, and energy have been wasted. The future depends on successfully working together and connecting to the basic need for acceptance and achievement by all individuals and groups.

The idea that many minds working together are better than one isolated person is also not new. Leaders, researchers, and academics have been saying so for decades. The opportunity is, through deeper levels of inclusion, to cocreate more interconnection at work and to expand the possibilities for significant contribution by all members. Our challenge is to make stronger connections between multiple interpretations, meanings, and assumptions. We need a clearer vision of the benefits and challenges of being together in a workplace where there is no statistical majority.

Although it is still alive and thriving, many have moved beyond the old command-and-control concept of organizational life. Communication and relationships are recognized as necessary for competence and accomplishment. Each of us depends on the partnerships and resources made available by others. Achieving a task cannot be separated from the relationships that make it possible. In our technology-driven and global community, markets are calling organizations to work faster, better, and cheaper while being discerning and thoughtful. This means organizations are even more dependent on broadening communication and the establishment of better relationships.

The future depends on making the expanded meaning of diversity a positive, creative, and contributive advantage. This will not happen by "just following the rules" in doing our work. Influencing, education, awareness, and open discussion develop the individual's internal reasons for inclusion. Inclusion advocacy suggests that diversity starts with the actions of the individual and the formal and informal leaders who acknowledge and openly discuss the value-added impact of diversity, difference, and inclusion. Leaders who care show how the benefits of inclusion far outweigh the benefits of separation and wholesale sameness. To "walk this talk," they live and work accordingly. Expectations based on obvious support of inclusion by those respected as credible is essential. These same formal leaders regularly revisit, revitalize, and reconfirm their beliefs in the potential of all participants. Inclusion advocacy can become a part of the culture of an organization if leaders incorporate inclusion into the strategies, structures, and systems of the organization. If the leadership group continues to reflect sameness, the commitment to difference will be seen as questionable.

New concepts of organizational membership are emerging, confirming Peter Senge's phrase, "thinking partners" (leaders who work for positive change at every level of the enterprise) in all workplace roles and relationships. Thinking partners know that people who think differently add to the workplace equation. Inclusion is advocated by these thinking partners as an open-ended question of how to better work together. A diverse workplace population cannot occur without signals of determination by these thinking partners, leaders, and change agents willing to work at inclusion. Cris Wildermuth, a diversity specialist in Lima, Ohio, cautions "There is a huge amount none of us know about diversity. Our assumptions about the culture and beliefs of others may be faulty. It is essential we continue to find oppportunities to learn."

In 1998, after hosting a number of half-day seminars with Dr. Roosevelt Thomas, Jr., author of *Beyond Race and Gender*, it dawned on Jim Rector that there was a deep desire by the attendees to more deeply understand diversity. They wanted to hear about the problems and solutions of diversity that had been experienced by other practitioners, they wanted to talk about how to get leader support, and they wanted a forum for diversity practitioners to express their concerns, successes, and failures.

Rector decided that a publication would be the most practical way to provide a platform for sharing diversity information. It had to be different. Yet it had to be written by the diversity practitioners themselves. The outcome was *Profiles in Diversity Journal*. In early 1999, there was a great, genuine excitement. Even before the first edition there were subscriptions people waiting to write meaningful articles. The list of articles written by representatives of major companies willing to describe a specific diversity initiative in a "how-to" format continues to grow.

Profiles is still in its early stages, but it is already beyond Rector's imaginings. Companies represented have included Boeing, Ernst & Young, Xerox, Fannie Mae, the National Security Agency, and Hallmark Cards. These are merely a sampling of the contributors. It is almost astonishing what one person can accomplish that is meaningful in a short length of time—when they believe in what they are doing. Jim Rector is a very effective advocate for inclusion.

Dialogues of inclusion require the exploration of alternatives, which always require looking at diversity. Learning and serving organizations are built on the foundation of dialogue. Marge Schiller has been conducting appreciative inquiries into diversity and differences. These dialogues have covered issues of gender plus the wide range of other topics that people in organizations find differentiating. One-on-one conversations around affirming topics, such as inclusion rather than exclusion or respect rather than disrespect, have produced conscious organizational choices about the way people want to be and to behave. (An example woud be Avon Mexico, who won the Catalyst Award for her groundbreaking work in this area.)

Inclusion

Inside the term "inclusion" are various words and activities that suggest connectedness. Partnering and partnerships, diversity, collaboration, participation, teamwork, empowerment, and interdependence all reference the desired behavior of inclusion.

Some of the most penetrating questions around inclusion are coming from people who have in the past been ignored and isolated and have experienced limitations in their own opportunities to contribute. Previously excluded constituencies are forcing the examination of assumptions about inclusion. Erroneous assumptions have been made every day, eliminating talented, thinking people's potential for heightened contribution and connection.

The examination of assumptions is bringing a new emphasis on both mutuality (identifying common interests and values) and inclusiveness (the willingness to include those experiences and ideas that are very different without requiring homogenization) (Lipman-Blumen 1996, 12). To talk about these assumptions is uncomfortable. They perfer "silent diversity"; if you are different, let's not talk about it openly. Instead of seeing inclusion as a problem to be solved, mutuality and inclusiveness bring new, more informed viewpoints that add value. Differences become a mystery to be uncovered or a puzzle to be fit together. The strategic priorities of organizations can be heightened and/or changed through new levels of inclusion. Leaders are learning to listen to ideas coming from new places.

Respectfulness as an Ingredient of Valuing

Civility, a recurring theme in this book, includes respectfulness. Chris Wildermuth notes, "Civility also has cultural norms. In some cultures showing respect requires not looking others in the eye. In others it suggests weakness or deviousness." To be respectful requires us to be open to acceptance of the people around us, as well as their differences, thoughts, and ideas. One of the base points of respect is receptivity: being willing to reflect and ponder, receive and accept, or collaboratively identify new ideas and knowledge. We are better able to consider and use the most beneficial solutions. When we do so, respectfulness becomes a frame for inclusion advocacy, encourages investigative questioning and the offering and reflection on new information. Respect nurtures thinking partnerships and deeper connection in relationships. People more fully hear, learn from, believe in, and serve each other.

Incivility is based on judgments people make about others. Judgments, according to Doug Shadel and Bill Thatcher (1997), are "nothing more than a series of assumptions about who they are, what they mean and how they feel. And if this is true of the judgments I make about others, the judgments others make about me are also assumptions which may or may not be true" (p. 106). Judgments are made very quickly in some instances, based on past assumptions that have not been thought through as reasonable or unreasonable. This is especially true about exclusion. Decisions are made, and once they are made the decisioner usually does not reflect on why they were made and what they were based on. For this reason, inclusion advocacy as a concept is essential to establishing new reasons as to why old assumptions of diversity are no longer reasonable.

A respectful culture advocates inclusion to promote thinking, saying, and doing together. Asking and answering responsible questions about diversity and inclusion starts with personal introspection. In these organizations it is possible to be different and to not be afraid of overreactive repercussions or embarrassment. These organizations know that respect of all members is essential to the coconstruction of first-rate strategies that ensure innovative, creative, and productive opportunities to be involved. Respect is propelled by connection, contribution, and the willingness to learn and serve in ways that are beneficial to everyone's growth. Inclusion advocacy positively impacts the growth of the total organization.

People quickly identify whether the organization has a respectful, valuing culture. Shaming and blaming fosters fear and low self-esteem. In this "gotcha" atmosphere people anticipate being the target of the moment. These organizations ask people to be either less than human—disconnected and fearful—or more than human—perfectionistic and righteous. Those seen as different are constantly striving to fit in, to not make waves. They stay to the background in order to blend in and avoid creating displeasure of the "in" group. Different ways of being and thinking are discouraged. The concern is this: What if something is said or done that causes embarrassment or discomfort to those who really fit here? What if a "different" suggestion or question turns the organization in a direction that may be unknown or fearful?

In these disrespectful cultures people and things are never quite good enough. Disrespectful judgment, a signal of lack of appreciation, becomes internalized and built into the corporate culture. Huge waste occurs when ideas are dismissed or ideas are labeled as poor or lacking without real examination for value. People lose motivation because they know their work will be ignored or sent back. "Getting it right" (if there is a right) is the province of a select few who complain about how hard they work and how others are not stepping up to contribute. Disrespect drains organizational energy.

Respectful cultures are high-energy places to work. Respectful cultures strive to build a climate of responsibility and consturctive accountability for all participants. They seek a community where corporatewide empowerment and individual and group exchanges and partnerships occur. They want to create a community that reflects ongoing efforts to consistently include and seek the talents and input of everyone. The goal is for every member to have an opportunity to develop and reach his or her potential, ultimately making it possible for each to contribute in ways that are most significant to his or her own success and that of the organization. These leaders seek and nurture new performance models, making a learning and serving community possible.

Lipman-Blumen (1996) defines community "simply as an environment in which individuals and groups, representing a broad band of ideas and values, can all hold rewarding membership" (p. 19). A respectful workplace community that makes full, meaningful, and productive membership and inclusion possible for everyone reflects the following characteristics:

- It is inclusive, inviting participation by all who wish to participate in ongoing improvement and accomplishment.
- It encourages people to see diversity and difference as beneficial and necessary to the growth of the organization.
- It empowers all people to seek, see, and consider new opportunities and abilities for themselves.
- It knows that new voices will identify opportunities not previously seen as possible.
- It frees people to be creative and innovative.
- It is a place where people work together to identify new ways of addressing organizational challenges.
- It is a place where people are interested in learning from and serving with one another.

INTEGRATION

The root of the word "integration" is integrity. Integrity has long been recognized as vital to effective leadership. Integration suggests behavior in harmony with the environment; a unified system. In organizations, integration ties various individuals and systems into a more coherent whole. It makes possible shared experiences, which implies the coconstruction of a unified system. Edgar Schein (1992) says, "Once people have a common system of communication and a language, learning can take place at a conceptual level and shared concepts become possible" (p. 11). Integration is not complete unless there are shared learning experiences and an openness to integrating people and ideas for improvement and change. New patterns of functioning are developed in which all can freely participate. Eventually, there is a shared sense of stability and consistency that permits connected daily functioning and the ability to adapt.

In this place, gestures of inclusion advocacy occur, integrating members into the processes, actions, and decisions that promote achievement for all. This cycle of inclusion brings expansion of organizational wisdom and performance. People bounce ideas off of others, mixing information and intuition to the benefit of participants. The cycle of inclusion is an exchange that is self-perpetuating (see Figure 10.1).

A connected community is integrative when, according to a 1996 study, it "involves bringing together people of different cultures, personalities, and stages of development and integrating them into a whole that is greater than the sum of its parts." Integration is important to success and the achievement of community. A community that is not integrative is in grave danger of disintegration. Closedmindedness and compartmentalized thinking are both causes and outcomes of lack of integration.

Where organizations become open to integration and inclusion, responsibility for valuing differences is shared by all. Encouragement and facilitation of conversations about diversity and difference minimize disconnection, iso-

Figure 10.1
The Cycle of Inclusion

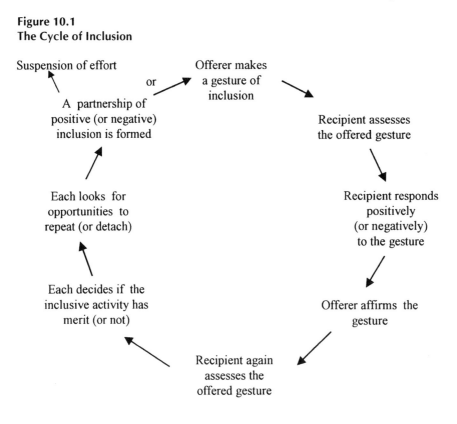

Suspension of effort

A partnership of
positive (or negative)
inclusion is formed

or

Offerer makes
a gesture of
inclusion

Recipient assesses
the offered gesture

Each looks for
opportunities to
repeat (or detach)

Recipient responds
positively
(or negatively)
to the gesture

Each decides if the
inclusive activity has
merit (or not)

Offerer affirms the
gesture

Recipient again
assesses the
offered gesture

lation, and alienation. Patrecia West, working in the area of professional development in one of the largest professional service firms, asks, "When will we learn that diversity, in its broadest sense, is fundamental to our existence? We work hard at it but I continue to ask myself, does anyone have it right? Accepting differences in ourselves and others—freeing our own spirits that lead to more creative innovative ideas—makes us more open to new thinking, the source of which is coming from these different others." West touches the heart of the practice of dialogue; it is interactive and continuing. As soon as things are "right," right has changed.

It is equally important to consider our commonalties. Recent scientific research indicates that human beings are remarkably genetically alike yet different. This has profound implications on our ideas of the differences between people: It should make connection easier. Similarities and commonalties play a significant role in work relationships. While first impressions may be of how different we are, the challenge of conversation is to find those areas of common values, experiences, and interests.

Organizations with a higher focus on valuing all members—those organizations that do it, not just say it—recognize that living values that incorporate promoting diversity and difference enhances corporate growth and survival. Valuing means that the people and the organization have the desire to appreciate, to include, and to use the multitude of knowledge resources, experiences, and talents that are brought to the organization by a diverse workforce. Valuing requires an expanded mind-set that calls for the conscious design of a culture open to recruiting, hiring, supporting, and training nontraditional members at all levels. This culture encourages self-acceptance and recognizes difference and uniqueness as enhancing organizational success. This mind-set requires not just telling nontraditional members they are valued, but providing authentic opportunities for them to feel and experience that they are being valued.

Organizations are seeing the need to openly express their cultural stance around respect, and are including the valuing of all members in vision and culture statements. One example is AT&T's values code, entitled Our Common Bond (Morin 1995, 115). Within this statement, which is meant "to guide our decisions and behavior," is a segment labeled, "Respect for Individuals":

We treat each with respect and dignity, valuing individual and cultural differences. We communicate frequently and with candor, listening to each other regardless of level or position. Recognizing that exceptional quality begins with people, we give individuals the authority to use their capabilities to the fullest to satisfy the customer. Our environment supports personal growth and continuous learning for all AT&T people.

It is not for the authors to judge whether AT&T's people live up to this standard, or if the collective organization believes in dignity and respect and valuing diversity and uniqueness. We applaud the intent. The true evaluators work at AT&T. Everyday workplace routines tell the workplace members if what is claimed as a common bond is really happening. Once out the door at the end of the day, minds and memories do not go blank. The home community also knows if the claims are genuine. Members carry the true messages with them. Efforts activated by many companies around this new realization are initiating change, offering new opportunities and new learnings—and more profits.

Definitive actions encouraging inclusion are processes of legitimization. Education, training, and dialogue are required. Holding back, pushing for political correctness, and sublimating ideas and feelings puts a stop on the output of positive energy that is the fuel for inclusive organizations.

Sameness

In thinking about diversity, it is equally important to consider commonalties. Recent scientific research indicates that we human beings are remarkably genetically alike. This has profound implications on our ideas of the differences between us. Similarities and commonalties also play a significant role in work relationships. While first impressions may be of how different we are, the challenge of conversation is to find those areas of common values, experiences and interests.

People are attracted to "similar others" and are prone to behave like these others. Research is also telling us there are situations in which people want to appear and feel different (Snyder and Fromkin 1980, xiii). They want to see themselves as unique, important, and meaningful forces in making a difference at home, in their communities, and on the job. Yet they sense that to be highly unique may bring problems or discomfort. Their discomfort is based on a fear of disapproval and exclusion with the possibility of mistreatment or the potential withholding of rewards. They know that rewards often are given for normalcy (doing as others do) and conformity (doing as others say).

The need to be alike continues to be emphasized at all levels in many organizations. Those doing the hiring want to hire and promote people just like themselves and expect them to remain the same. Unfortunately, being the same emphasizes dependency and the need to walk together in unison. Difference causes people to be out of step and brings criticism, possibly even the threat of disagreement, something many are willing to experience to have the chance to contribute meaningfully. It is the challenge of the new workplace to embrace difference and sameness.

The Theory of Uniqueness

The theory of uniqueness is explained as seeking to be just enough alike and just enough dissimilar to achieve a level of comfort. People are most uncomfortable when they are assumed to be a lot different or a lot alike. "Emotionally . . . our pursuit of difference," according to Snyder and Fromkin, "may be best conceptualized as a pursuit of some degree of dissimilarity relative to other people" (p. 50). Reaction usually happens when people are highly similar or highly different from others.

The suggestion that "birds of a feather flock together" may be contradicted in the human world. Individuals want to be like their peers, but not too like them. When pushed toward similarity, people often seek ways of appearing unique or different. According to Patrecia West, "The pressure to assimilate, to become what some embrace as a 'true American' has been tremendous. To be American, their values, norms, practices have to become 'the same.' In response this pushes some to become even *more different*, to the consternation of the In Group." It is, for many, uncomfortable to be a clone of others. People want to be somewhat unique, and they take steps to be so. People become very sensitive to the need to redefine themselves. They may do things differently or do things that have not been done before in order to maintain some sense of uniqueness.

New Members Are Different

Even new members who appear the same may be automatically suspected as "different" when joining a long-established group. A highly connected group may be suspicious of new members and may not appreciate the contribution of new ideas and talents. Instead of supporting and encouraging the new member upon arrival, current members may seek to emphasize how the new person does not fit in. By signaling the new member's lack of fit, the membership is signaling to the new member to "do things our way or you will pay a high price." Until the new member proves him or herself as belonging, taking on the group's norms and acting as the group does, he or she will not be "legitimate" group members. A new nontraditional member has a higher, potentially insurmountable barrier to legitimacy in the long-established group suspicious of any degree of difference. Acceptance will be a long journey. In too many groups it may not be fully attainable. Some groups treat diverse members as "curiosities," deepening their sense of disconnection.

Formal leaders may not appear to be aware of problems of acceptance, ignore the problems, or feel powerless to support the acceptance of new members. "It will work itself out," they tell themselves. Or "I learned the hard way; they can too." The leader is either not aware of his or her role in sponsoring the member for membership, he or she may see the new member as a threat to his or her own membership in the group, or just disinterested in doing so. The outcome: The leader goes on about his or her business. The excluded member is left to survive on his or her own. The skills of the new member go unknown or unused until legitimacy in the group occurs—if it ever does.

Being a curiosity is even stronger when one is highly different from those already settled into the group. Since this group has already decided who or what is acceptable, anyone newly hired who doesn't fit the accepted criteria may not achieve inclusion. This may be coupled with signals of being less than (inferior). An example is the story of the first woman of color hired in the accounting department of a large corporation. People walked to her door and occasionally into her personal office to openly stare and "get a look at her." The story of the man who came into her office, sat down, and told her she had his job—that the only reason she was there was because of her race and gender—expanded further her feelings of humiliation. Eventually she was a participant in a discrimination lawsuit. The class action suit cost the organization dearly, both in money and reputation. The costs to the woman accountant are harder to calculate.

A Response to Being Treated as Less Than

A role of the inclusion advocate is to provide support and sponsorship for new and current members who are not seen as fitting in. As noted in Chapter 7, when management is not willing to sponsor these members, competition, hostility, isolation, and disruption by other members are also often ignored—signaling approval and toleration of the demeaning activities tied to the lack of acceptance and inclusion. The responses of members not feeling included or accepted—those getting the "you-are-less-than-I-am" message—may include frustration. Frustration, according to McKay, Rogers, and McKay (1989, 49–50), may result from the following:

- Blocked needs or desires. A member may see the struggle to get what he or she feels is deserved (promotion, recognition, acceptance) as hopeless.
- Seeing that things are not as they should be. A sense of order (how things "ought" to be; a need for fairness and correctness) is violated by the messages being generated.
- A sense of being forced. Not only is he or she not getting his or her way, but there is a feeling of being forced to do things that are opposed to his or her needs and values by someone that is signaling superiority. The unsung signal is I am more than you are.

Feelings of frustration may result in lowered productivity, confrontational situations, dissatisfaction, and eventual resignation—and potentially to negative advocacy. It is important for leaders to recognize the atmosphere where a member, for some reason, is feeling discounted and undervalued. This atmosphere is not conducive to the establishment of trust and commitment, cooperation, risk taking, or creative decision making. A negative impact could also occur in the work of those around them. Management's lack of effort to deal with this situation does not go unnoticed.

CONDITIONS CONTRIBUTING TO MEMBER DEVELOPMENT

People want to work with those who are both willing partners and competent workers. Opportunities to participate in challenging projects are heightened by development of diverse group members. Development can extend the desire to contribute to the welfare of the group. Michael Maccoby (1988), in his first edition of *Why Work,* notes there are five conditions to be met for individual development in the workplace as well as in other areas of life: care, freedom, discipline, balance, and commitment. "Each condition implies both good human relationships and conscious individual decision-making. Family, school, and work organizations either succeed or fail in satisfying each of these conditions," says Maccoby (p. 200). These conditions are especially important in an inclusive environment. Maccoby's conditions (pp. 200–207) that encourage individual and group development, as adapted to inclusion advocacy, include the following.

More Care and Less Neglect

Most of us want to have a life, both at home and on the job, that contributes to the welfare of ourselves and others. To do so, feeling connected to those around us is essential. Caring makes it possible that others will be available when support is needed. An empathetic attitude by participants is reflected through intentional and unintentional actions. "Sensitivity to other people's feelings is essential for understanding diversity in the workplace and may form the foundation for organizational change," say Putnam and Mumby (1993, 55). In an inclusive environment, caring attitudes tend to include sincerity, empathy, humility, optimism, and the demonstration of caring concern about the feelings of others. These attitudes deepen relationships and encourage spontaneous sharing of learnings without hidden agendas. Caring in a multicultural environment makes it possible to recognize and respect the perspectives of others in nonjudgmental ways.

Neglect causes disconnection and lack of a sense of security. A predictable outcome of neglect will be anger, frustration, and conflict. The sense that one is not needed or valued is depersonalizing and degrading.

More Freedom and Less Oppression

Freedom expands personal responsibility and accountability. Responsibility and freedom are two sides of the same coin. To take advantage of the benefits of freedom requires personal responsibility. Release from unreasonable, nonproductive control opens opportunities to be free to make choices for being responsible. Members are encouraged to make decisions. It is a mind-set that says, "Go ahead." You are able to do what you think is right, without being fearful of retribution if wrong. The freedom to take responsibility for your own ideas, decisions, and actions requires information. Freedom is the impetus for information. Withholding information negates inclusion.

Yet the demand for constant inclusiveness may take away valued freedoms. To be able to close the doors to others, to exclude others temporarily, is a freedom we all value. Examples would include networks of women who meet regularly in the workplace to mentor and support career growth; Hispanic Americans who meet to exchange information; or professionals, such as nurses, who meet to highlight happenings in their professions. These meetings call for exclusion. Patrecia West says,

Separation leads to oppression. We cannot have the rewards of diversity without addressing the issues around inclusivity and exclusivity. It is a paradox and a both/and place. You have to have both—yet, most people do not want to hear that there is no one answer. There are times when members need to be inclusive (open the circle) and there are times when the group must be exclusive (close the circle) to some degree, honoring individual and job needs for exclusivity, when needed. Giving people permission to do so is important to maintaining and valuing their many identities. Focusing on one of the defining dozen to the neglect of the others maintains isolationism. An example would be what happens when too many issues signifcant to the different identities are being heard at the same time. Some issues get lost. You have to focus on one issue, sometimes, and let others temporarily remain in the "background" and concentrate on what needs attention now, allowing exclusivity-for-the-moment. For some, closing the circle, even exclusion, will be hard to accept.

These are hard messages to make understandable to the membership.

More Accountability and Less Indulgence

True discipline starts with making choices of self-management and self-regulation while balancing the need to question, seek information, and seek action on the things they believe are right: to be an ethical advocate. When there are reasonable standards that place a frame around how people work together, it creates a baseline against which to measure behavior. To reject workplace rules is to reject the system. To not follow rules brings a response either from above, from below, or from one's peer group (Katz and Kahn 1967, 309–310). For this reason, diverse members may receive unexpected penalties for seeking group membership.

In effective groups, abusive, uncivil behaviors to new and/or diverse members are not ignored. Effectively addressing these activities early on can make clear there is a norm of courtesy, manners, and openness imperative to effectiveness *and* inclusion.

More Balance and Less Excessiveness

Inclusion advocacy suggests that all members have the opportunity to contribute, to learn, and to serve. The existence of integrity and trust balances self-interest with meeting the needs and providing opportunities for active development of individual interests and abilities. Excessiveness is reflected in overdoing and getting out of balance. The workplace of the last century exemplified excessiveness through its valuing of sameness and uniformity in the workplace. Certain jobs were stereotyped as most suitable for specific genders, ethnic groups, or races.

Workaholism is an example of an excess that can jeopardize other areas in our lives. Kim Bachmann (1998), coauthor of a Conference Board of Canada study (Is Work–Life Balance Still an Issue for Canadians and Their Employers? You Bet It IS!) notes that when work and life are out of kilter, workers say they look after their family and work responsibilities, and give up time for themselves. She adds, "What suffers are the things we do to recharge our batteries—rest, self-development and fun. The net result is greater stress and health-related problems."

More Commitment and Less Diffusion

In reference to the workplace, "commitment" refers to a bond or attachment to the organization. Commitment to their employer encourages members to be change agents. They notice the lack of inclusive practices and bring these issues into the light. Or they may choose diffusion: denial and the choice to ignore issues around the lack of inclusive practices. Commitment to self, group, and organizational well-being supports the willingness for ongoing learning and serving, the basis for the advocacy of inclusion.

More Learning and Serving and Less Stagnation

We include this addition to the list. Learning and serving, as discussed in previous chapters, happens through the energies of individuals and the groups they belong to. The largest responsibility for learning is with the person, the one seeking to grow. Effective leaders listen to people's needs and support them in gaining opportunities to expand their current skills and to prepare for future workplace changes. Employability is expanded through the energy and efforts of the individual member.

Expanded awareness regarding inclusion advocacy (1) depends on the attitudes and willingness to learn on the part of each member, (2) emphasizes the need to serve and partner with all members at all levels, (3) includes the understanding that past experiences and learnings may cause some to struggle especially in actively seeking the ideas and innovations of others not previously included, and (4) is influenced by the messages of formal and informal leaders.

Stagnation may have its roots in laziness, lack of interest, extreme selfishness, and/or isolation. Stagnation interferes with the willingness to invite others inside the circle. People who want to keep things the same feel threatened by new people, new ideas, and new approaches. Keeping things the same helps them feel temporary security.

The Buzz Word: Teamwork

There are different perspectives on what "teamwork" looks like in organizations. These perspectives are constructed through the culture of the organization. For some, teamwork is a behavioral tool or a technique for effectively meeting goals regarding quality, service, and productivity, carrying a meaning of how people work together in informal and formal relationships. For others, it includes empowerment and the opportunity to influence decisions, processes, and change efforts. Some organizations incorporate teams in the conventional structure. Others introduce teams as part of a restructuring and redesign of the whole organization. For all, the effective group or team decides early on that (1) the success of the group depends on each person and the group being highly responsible and accountable for achievement of goals, and (2) the quality of the outcome is dependent on each person's and the collective group's contributions toward those goals.

Inclusive teamwork is best shown by members paying attention to four major activities of group membership. These activities provide opportunities for all to learn and serve together over time. On occasion, everyone contributes through one or more of these roles.

Teaching and Coaching

Each member shares his or her experience, expertise, and learnings and strives to learn from others. Teaching and learning from and with others is an inclusive activity. Supporting other members in their learning and serving efforts while coaching them in application of new knowledge, behaviors, and effectiveness is an ongoing role. In organizations where inclusionary behaviors are high, everyone serves as both teachers and coaches.

Leading

Although teams may have assigned leaders, the actions and activities of all members include being leaders of the moment. Inclusive leadership includes actions that inspire, focus, motivate, facilitate, and sponsor and advocate the performance of all members.

Sponsorship

As discussed in Chapter 6, sponsorship is a specific role for leaders. "*Sponsorship (advocacy) is an important determinant of promotions to senior levels*" (Thomas 1991, 78, italics orig.). Leaders should be attuned to whether they are adequately promoting the welfare of diverse members. According to Thomas's research, there is a dissatisfaction in training and development efforts and a lack of sponsorship for advancement of women and minorities. Inclusion advocacy specifically requires *all* members to be provided opportunities to learn and serve. Inclusion in promotional opportunities may need extra effort to support and sponsor those diverse members who have routinely been overlooked in the past.

It is highly beneficial for teams and team members to learn and understand the concepts of advocacy participation as related to inclusion. Inclusionary behaviors are significant to the willingness of members to be responsible and accountable to their groups. Inclusion also stimulates the willingness to participate in deep discussions. West notes, "There must be constant expansion of communication so conversations include undiscussable issues. Teams and individuals are less successful, even at times nonfunctional, when what is being addressed has fences around it—places in conversation where people do not want to go." Conflict festers and grows within the individual and expands into the group when discussions are limited by avoidance. Avoidance makes it potentially impossible to address the issues that provide the way to better, more long-lasting solutions.

Partnering

Inclusion advocacy suggests the importance of every member being a willing partner in personal, group, and organizational growth and achievement. This includes, even mandates, that organizational leaders initiate and sponsor partnerships across the organizational circle as examples of connected partnerships.

Inclusive Decisioning

Controlling, bureaucratic organizations are mouthing the words of inclusion while their actions still reflect the old paradigm of "I'll listen but I still know better." Leaders still aren't listening with the intention of learning. Those being pseudo-included still stand at the side and watch foolish decisions being implemented. In decisioning, controlling leaders are still giving out the same exclusive signals, especially with the diverse and different populations in their organizations. The message is that only leaders have the right answers. These signals include the following:

- Treating members like children instead of adults.
- Practicing high levels of narcissism (high selfishness and control, even incivility).
- Disregarding the learnings and experience of others.
- Ignoring the human and social bottom lines in decisioning.
- The invitation to participate really means to comply.
- Thinking that only the leaders at the top matter.

It doesn't make much sense that our companies are hiring the best available people and then treating them like children—signaling that they don't know enough or that they don't need to know. Most members want to contribute to the best of their abilities; they want to feel that what they do is valued every day and is significant to the accomplishments of the company they work for. They want to be in connected partnerships that use their expertise. They want to be leaders of the moment, making decisions they know how to make. And if members do not know how to make decisions in their own areas, they want to learn to do so.

Moral Imagination

From the framework of organizational advocacy, envisioning what real inclusion could mean is vital to challenging the actions that hamper inclusion. Inclusion for many is a step of faith. No one who has not been part of the minority population can fully understand that experience. No one who has not been part of the majority can appreciate the implications of that condition.

Patricia C. Werhane (1999, 5), in her book *Moral Imagination and Management Decision Making*, suggests that those in leadership roles should practice "moral imagination." Moral imagination includes, according to Werhane, the ability to understand from a number of different perspectives. It is to be able to "step away" from our own narrow view and see what is being looked at through the eyes of someone else or from a different viewpoint. Furthermore, it means understanding what *is,* but, more important, also envisioning *what could be.*

Real inclusion requires the integration of business reasoning and ethical responsibility. The integration of business and ethics, according to Werhane (1999, 117), requires the merging of moral imagination and moral reasoning. To do so is significant to inclusion advocacy in that inclusion is reasonable and requires us to attach this reasonableness to an imagined and hopeful future and then to identify and implement the tools to get to that imagined future. The alternative to moral imagination is less beneficial to anyone but those using self-interest and personal gain as the only goal of their activities: Limitations for their actions are based simply on whether they might be caught. These people, in making conscious or unconscious decisions to be inclusive, have a narrow view of their situation and what the outcomes might be if they take a less desirable but beneficial route of inclusion. Their viewpoints do not include moral imagination and moral reasoning because their decisioning processes do not take into account moral concerns (p. 11). Unfortunately, their limited ability to see things through the eyes and experiences of others can lead to little consideration of alternatives.

INCLUSION AS AN ONGOING PROCESS

Ground zero for inclusion advocacy is to seek the benefits of identifying and utilizing diversity and inclusion specialists. We must use knowledgeable, well-trained, responsible, and accountable diversity professionals who seek to address the fears and concerns of the attendees. To not do so may reinforce barriers already in place and jeopardizes accomplishment. Actions that are well intended may otherwise be seen as disrespectful. Making statements without action is to further jeopardize understanding. This is an ongoing process of expecting and encouraging changes in behaviors and attitudes. Starting from a place of knowledge will maximize the outcomes.

First, the announcement of a formal organization policy defines the organizational position on the issues of diversity and inclusion. (It is understood that at this point there is a clear understanding of the state, federal, and local laws and policies on this subject.) Of course, the actual practices of support, discipline, and tolerance will display the real views of the leadership. Nemetz and Christensen (1996) state, "As a consequence of the mismatch between formal and informal organization practices and values, individuals may become cynical about formal diversity programs. Little behavior and attitude change is likely to occur when the organization's diversity goals are not perceived as serious" (p. 451).

Second, formal, organizationally sanctioned education and training regarding diversity, difference, and inclusion is part of the process of influencing individual acceptance and contribution in the workplace. In formal training, the view of the training program and/or the trainer is important to the process. Well-defined organizational goals and the trainer's view of what is to be accomplished of necessity coincide. The training is based and focused on using the different skills, talents, and experiences of the attendees. Shame-based "bad dog" training is counterproductive. It is also important to recognize that attendees may be somewhat uncomfortable and uncertain. Until they have become comfortable with what is happening there will likely be barriers to the exchange of information and the reality of inclusion.

Third, informal influence reinforces or trivializes the new information. Again, informal leaders as thought leaders and thinking partners are significant to the opportunity for inclusion to be seen as important to individual and organizational success. Informal influence by these informal leaders includes casual and serendipitous incidences of conversation. They will share and examine the information received in formal learning sessions with others. It is again significant that what is thought, said, and done matters during these learning moments. These conversations take on heightened significance after the training is experienced. These thought leaders will be listened to. As thinking partners, their agreement and disagreement reinforces or takes away from the new information. They may also bring heightened curiosity and justify changed behaviors and attitudes.

Fourth, regular reinforcement of *belief in inclusion and diversity* and its benefits is important. Daniel Goleman (1995), in *Emotional Intelligence*, discusses fear conditioning as "the name psychologists use for the process whereby something [or someone] that is associated in someone's mind with something frightening" is never responded to with a "feeling of calm" (p. 309). Replacing fear conditioning with feelings of acceptance and actual inclusion will take time and patience on the part of all involved. As noted previously, a history of positive experiences of integration contributes to this occurring. A historical reference of positive inclusion takes consistent reeducation and reinforcement over time. We are creating memories that will redesign the future.

The motivation to become inclusive may be spiritual, ethical, moral, or monetary (or maybe a bit of all four), but ultimately the successful productive organizations of this century will be the ones that practice inclusion while advocating for the benefits of valuing all members. Sharif Abdullah (1999) in his book *Creating a World That Works for All*, says, "All of us in this society form one community. The fact that most of us deny it or are ignorant of it doesn't mean the community doesn't exist. It just means the community is highly dysfunctional" (p. 80).

PARTING THOUGHTS

The definition of inclusion advocacy notes that both the individual members and the collective organization are accountable for activating and sustaining activities that reflect real inclusion. For an organization to make statements regarding valuing its members and to not be an inclusive workplace community is to shine a spotlight on cynicism and dysfunction. If organizations don't strive for high levels of inclusion at all levels, they will get the defense mechanisms they deserve. An individual is part of the problem if not willing to accept personal responsibility for inviting and including others. Energies that could have been constructive and productive instead may be reinforcing maladaptive and destructive.

We are committed to dialogue about differences. Using an appreciative inquiry (or another preferred process) into topics such as inclusion, advocacy, membership, participation, and communication brings forward the opportunity for moral reasoning and moral imagination by the individuals and the group. We also favor a diversity process that acknowledges the importance of talking about the "hard stuff" within work teams or groups, organizations, and families. An inquiry that frames conversation with "half-full, not half-empty" assumptions is beneficial. Change happens when people care and build on their mental models for success. In the past the phrase, "Some of my best friends are (Black or Italian or Jewish or southern or hourly workers or whatever)," was code for "I'm prejudiced, but I make exceptions." The response might be, "That's very interesting. What is it that you value in this other person and yourself? How do you maintain the relationship? Tell me the story." It is in the seeds of stories that we will find the model of the mind and the spirit of the heart that expands and extends inclusion. The expansion will not be just for the individual but for the attending work group, the team, and, ultimately, the organization.

In the past, some assumed that if we looked alike, acted alike, and believed alike everything would go well. We now see that among the richest contributions made to organizations are the gifts of "novel thinking": ideas or approaches that are different, progressive, or even out of the lines previously drawn. It is obvious that in many organizations leaders must become sponsors of all members—not only those demonstrating sameness, but also those who have messages not completely agreed with or understood by the rest of the group.

A workplace community emphasizes the need to help each other, blurring the lines of status, title, difference, and sameness. "At the heart of community," says Pinchot and Pellman (1999), "are people caring for the whole and for fellow members" (p. 131). There are fundamental questions that strike even deeper than the heart of the community to the heart of the individual. Asking and answering responsible questions around inclusion and diversity starts with personal introspection. Introspection begins with looking at our "best selves": When have we been most inclusive? Whether the question addresses inclusion, effective contribution, partnering, responsibility, accountability, or a long list of other relationship issues, we ask ourselves, Where am I on these issues? When have I been most effective in demonstrating my own appreciation of differences? And know that where we are impacts what we think, say, do, and who and what we appreciate at work and at home. If we are going to address people where they are, we first start with knowing where we, as individuals, are.

"Where I am" may be in a place of fear. Dealing with inclusion includes the awareness that the "normal person" at work in the past—the white male— is feeling threatened and endangered. He is feeling that "there is not enough for all of us." Somehow, it must also be acknowledged that there are those feeling endangered by real inclusion. To not do so will only move the arrogance of exclusion to another more hidden place. There will only be actions of separation, abuse, and disrespect in less obvious ways.

American corporations, when nondiscriminatory, are uniquely positioned among international firms to gain competitive advantage because of the diversity of their workforce. European and Japanese businesses have fewer opportunities to do so (Wright et al. 1995, 284) because of the homogeneity of their workforce.

Real inclusion is unachievable without first seeing the benefits for doing so. Taking out the threat and providing opportunities for heightened awareness and a deeper understanding of inclusion is a significant step. It encourages the movement of both organization and member choices toward appreciation, acceptance, and inclusion. For members moving toward inclusion is to have added opportunities to participate effectively, even exceptionally, in today's and tomorrow's organizations. For organizations the discontinuation of the waste of talents, skills, and energies of those who desire to contribute will bring new exciting ideas and unanticipated profits.

NOTE

This chapter was written in partnership with Marge Schiller, Ph.D., a consultant and writer based in Hingham, Massachusetts. There have also been many learning discussions with Patrecia West, a learning and education specialist.

BIBLIOGRAPHY

Abdullah, Sharif. (1999). *Creating a World that Works for All.* San Francisco: Berrett-Koehler.

Allaire, Paul A. (1999). Diversity: Building on Our Heritage, edited by James R. Rector. *Profiles in Diversity Journal* 1 (3): 16–17.

Bachman, Kim. (1998). Study: Is Work–Life Balance Still an Issue for Canadians and Their Employers? You Bet It IS! News Release. Conference Board of Canada, Toronto.

Fernandez, John P. (1999). *Race, Gender and Rhetoric.* New York: McGraw-Hill.

Gergen, K. J., S. McNamee, and F. J. Barrett. (In Press). Toward Transformative Dialogue. *International Journal of Public Administration.*

Goleman, Daniel. (1995). *Emotional Intelligence: Why It Can Matter More Than IQ.* New York: Bantum Books.

Katz, Daniel, and Robert L. Kahn. (1978). *The Social Psychology of Organizations.* 2d ed. New York: John Wiley & Sons.

Lipman-Blumen, Jean. (1996). *The Connective Edge.* San Francisco: Jossey-Bass.

Loden, Marilyn, and Judy B. Rosener. (1991). *Workforce America.* Homewood, Ill.: Business One Irwin.

Maccoby, Michael. (1988). *Why Work: Leading the New Generation.* New York: Simon & Schuster.

McKay, Mathew, Peter Rogers, and Judith McKay. (1989). *When Anger Hurts: How to Change Painful Feelings Into Positive Action.* New York: MJF Books.

Morin, William J. (1995). *Silent Sabotage: Rescuing Our Careers, Our Companies, and Our Lives from the Creeping Paralysis of Anger and Bitterness.* New York: AMACOM.

Nemetz, Patricia, and Sandra L. Christensen. (1996). The Challenge of Cultural Diversity: Harnessing a Diversity of Views to Understand Multiculturalism. *Academy of Management Review* 21 (2): 434–462.

Pinchot, Gifford, and Ron Pellman. (1999). *Intrapreneuring in Action: A Handbook for Business Innovation.* San Francisco: Berrett-Koehler.

Putnam, Linda L., and Dennis K. Mumby. (1993). Organizations and the Myth of Rationality. In *Emotions in Organizations*, edited by Stephen Fineman, 36–57. London: Sage.

Schein, Edgar. (1992). *Organizational Culture and Leadership.* 2d ed. San Francisco: Jossey-Bass.

Shadel, Doug, and Bill Thatcher. (1997). *The Power of Acceptance.* Van Nuys, Calif: Newcastle.

Snyder, C. R., and Howard L. Fromkin. (1980). *Uniqueness: The Human Pursuit of Difference.* New York: Plenum.

Thomas, R. Roosevelt Jr. (1991). *Beyond Race and Gender: Unleashing the Power of Your Total Workforce by Managing Diversity.* New York: AMACOM.

Werhane, Patricia C. (1999). *Moral Imagination and Management Decision Making.* New York: Oxford University Press.

Wright, Peter, Stephen P. Ferris, Janine S. Hiller, and Mark Kroll. (1995). Competitiveness Through Management of Diversity: Effects on Stock Price Evaluation. *Academy of Management Journal* 38 (1): 272–287.

CONVERSATIONS AND INTERVIEWS

Jim Rector, *Profiles in Diversity.*

Patrecia West, learning and education specialist.

Part III

ORGANIZATIONAL ADVOCACY AS A MOVEMENT

People and organizations are so poised for change that only a slight but crucial shift in confidence and courage is needed to transform the workplace to a new reality.

Craig Neal, Vision Holder, Heartland Institute

11

Movement Toward Change

It is about a search, too, for daily meaning as well as daily bread, for recognition as well as cash, for astonishment rather than torpor; in short, for a sort of life rather than a Monday through Friday sort of dying.

Studs Terkel (1974)

People will hurt others, double-deal, cheat, or do worse, if the company ethos supports such behavior, *and* the cost of not doing so seems too great. Some will act with a cynical shrug; others will feel ashamed, but still conform. We also know that many corporate actors will do things at work that they would not contemplate doing outside of the organizational setting.

Stephen Fineman (1993)

Every organization is experiencing planned and unplanned change. Because of the turmoil, change is becoming a desperate response instead of an enlivening process. Despite outward signs of successful, flourishing businesses, many are running on a treadmill of anxiety about the future. Members know they have much to offer to lessen the pain and anxiety. They no longer want to be detached from their workplace world. They want to become advocates for the future of their organizations through deeper participation. If not, they sense that the charade will soon be over. They sense that it is time for an ongoing process that includes the aliveness of a movement that includes everyone instead of a change program designed by only the formal leaders in the organization.

What does it require to personally and as an organization move to where advocacy participation is possible? For some, thoughts about this new way to work together will be "reaching afar." For others, it suggests a way of working that is especially reasonable, appropriate, even achievable.

Max DePree (1997), chairman emeritus of Herman Miller, suggests much change is a "movement" toward a more meaningful way of working. He says, "A movement is a collective state of mind, a public and common understanding that the future can be created, not simply experienced or endured" (p. 22). The opportunity to be a part of a 'movement' to a more inclusive, integrative, and flexible community does not come easily. It happens through individual and collective effort and high levels of participation—sweat equity, if you will. DePree describes a movement as

- a collective state of mind that the future can be created;
- having a harmony in relationships and a constructive conflict of ideas;
- demonstrating a palpable unity as the people implement their vision;
- a high level of trust;
- a sense of urgency;
- competence and a sense of creativity;
- a clear commitment to substance over bureaucracy;
- including a spirit-lifting leadership that enables, enriches, holds the organization accountable and then *lets go*. (pp. 22–23)

Another interpretation of a movement is described by Parker J. Palmer. Palmer distinguishes between organizational change and a movement approach. He describes organizational change as a top-down, mandated, mechanical, bureaucratic approach that defines the limits around the change that is to occur. It also controls the direction of the organization it is meant to change. Power in the organization is rearranged and resistance is overcome (resistors are punished for resisting). The "change" usually means a redesign of the old way of doing things. It is not new, it is just different.

Palmer identifies four overlapping stages in the unfolding of a movement. The stages shift back and forth with people who are part of the movement in different stages of the unfolding.

Stage One: Isolated People Choose Authenticity

Individuals awaken to a new view of how things should be. Each one is experiencing limitations that previously were not seen. There has been a blindness, making it impossible to see. A new authenticity is experienced, which strengthens the resolve of the individual. It is impossible to ignore the "correctness" of the past that has demanded compliance. It becomes suddenly intolerable to remain controlled by the intolerable.

Stage Two: People Sharing New Beliefs Discover
Each Other and Connect for Mutual Support

The individual who feels isolated, even disconnected and/or crazy, finds others who share his or her beliefs. Shared beliefs bring energy that heightens opportunities and determination to provide mutual support in order to strengthen the resolve of each other. "What is common in these groups and discussions," says Tom Heuerman and Diane Olson, consultants with amorenaturalway, "is the energy, the honesty, the mutual support, the feelings of community, and an emerging worldview that feels real" (http://www.amore naturalway.com). Of course, there are those who choose to avoid the movement (see "Incompetence," Appendix B).

Stage Three: Empowered by Their Collective Energy,
They Learn to Translate Private Dilemmas into Public Issues

The movement is now picking up energy. New language is designed in order to interpret the meanings, emotions, and learnings that are now being openly discussed with others who can influence issues and circumstances. In organizations, a difference begins to be made through one-on-one conversations and stories that are repeated over and over. As noted previously, each conversation has impact, whether to move the hearer forward or backward in the understanding of what is occurring. The conversations continue. Eventually a small movement permeates the social, cultural, and philosophical systems of the organization it is reconstructing.

Stage Four: New Reward Systems Emerge
to Sustain the Movement's Vision

Movement members are enlivened by the excitement of being part of something they believe is greater than the way things have been in the past, both for themselves and their organization. Their rewards come with the emotional satisfaction of living and seeing their beliefs "become." Support and affirmation are now coming from others. They are rewarded by seeing the movement enlivened and sustained by new movement members.

Some will be offended by the suggestion that change management can be compared to a movement. The difference is in the two words "program" and "process." Often change is a program disguised as a process. It is a short-term, planned, scheduled activity that claims success whether it succeeds or not. Eventually, it slowly disappears without a murmur. It is done. It is over. That was last year. A movement is a process, a series of actions directed to some purpose, a series of progressive and interdependent steps that become part of the way things happen. It is ongoing. It is never over. It continues on toward an ever-emerging goal that is known and yet allows for the unknown.

"Some major changes," according to Bryson and Crosby (1992, with reference to Trist 1983), "do require paradigm shifts—that is, they seek new patterns of social relations wherein values that were secondary or latent will be articulated and elevated to primacy" (p. 22). It is also noted that in movements the challenges are likely to be great, over a long haul, and "visionary leadership is more critical" (p. 23). People learn new behaviors. It is an ongoing conversation of coconstruction. When people coconstruct, they create different images than in the past. It always takes longer than is envisioned; people become impatient, even discouraged. Appreciation of what is being accomplished waxes and wanes. But at any given moment there will be strong advocates, leaders of the moment, and organizational advocates who believe in what is happening and insisting on continuation of the movement.

Stage Five: Revitalization of the Movement

Stage Five is an addition to Palmer's overlapping stages. Revisiting and revitalization are essential to continuation of the movement. Revitalization reignites the movement, bringing renewed energy and legitimacy to the acknowledged vision of the future. Energy flares and members feel renewed by the accomplishments of the past and the possibilities of the future. People who were doubters are now seeing the possibilities as well as offering new ideas and new acceptance. The movement connects previously disconnected groups. The movement continues.

Grassroots Leaders

A movement toward a workplace where the six issues of organizational advocacy (self advocacy, member advocacy, leader advocacy, customer advocacy, community advocacy, and inclusion advocacy) become evident requires an ongoing dialogue of members at all levels about being trusted and trustworthy and being personally responsible and accountable. These conversations are relevant to heightened achievement for individuals, groups, and the whole workplace community. Successful and respected leaders, it is suggested, listen to the people who know what is needed, wherever they are, and give up some of their power to those who know what would be beneficial to address what is happening. Christian Crews, a long-range planner at Toshiba International Corporation, suggests, "In many organizations, giving up control of the present adds value. Maybe it's time for companies to give up some control of the future, by using the established machinery of grassroots leadership."

Grassroots-movement members are willing to participate in meaningful ways while doing quality work with others at all levels. Working together toward understood and valued goals makes it possible to connect to the coconstructed overarching design. Each member looks for and acts on purposely creating a place he or she values, a place where many can at the grassroots level shape a "new way to do business as usual." The result can be a new collective energy that revitalizes a previously destablized workplace commitment and concerns.

A movement toward this new environment and advocacy participation starts with leaders who want a working environment that is believed in, an environment that positively affects thoughts, judgments, and how the work is done. Instead of having to make bleak circumstances survivable by looking for hidden opportunities for action that are possible within the limitations of a controversial workplace, new possibilities become obvious. Instead of small things being done through compulsion, larger things begin to happen with new excitement. Heightened connection stimulates greater involvement, energy increases levels of responsibility, and a sense of significance—feelings of being valued and that "what I do matters"—increases exchanges of constructive accountability. When members know they can influence how and why things get done, things change.

"The only way we really know that the organization has changed is when people's behaviors change," says Edward Marshall (1995, 134). He adds, "Leaders usually do not implement change. The workforce does." A "change management program" does not work unless the members decide it needs to be done and that it is a workable and beneficial process they can be part of. This is where a movement thrives: There are signals in the culture as to whether something definitive has occurred.

The Ups and Downs

When there are slumps in the movement toward change achievement, people get discouraged. Edward Marshall (1995), in his book *Transforming the Way We Work*, addresses the psychology of change, indicating that ups and downs are inevitable (see Figure 11.1). Although Marshall's model is designed for the organizational change process, the model can be translated to the individual's journey as an organizational advocate participating in a movement. Disappointments and failures are normal occurrences in personal change and organizational change. The advocate must remain aware of his or her level of energy and commitment to being an advocate. Advocacy participation is not a constant line of upward involvement, achievement, and commitment. There are dips, when the inevitable concerns and fears of being on the wrong path occur. In order for personal appreciation of deeper participation to grow and for others to see the benefits of advocacy participation, the advocate seeks to see these dips (potential personal disconnection and disbelief) as natural phenomena of the movement toward deeper involvement.

Level 1: Excitement

A member becomes excited about what the outcome could be when he or she is "engaged, facilitated, educated, incented, and coaxed out of their . . .

Figure 11.1
The Psychology of the Change Process

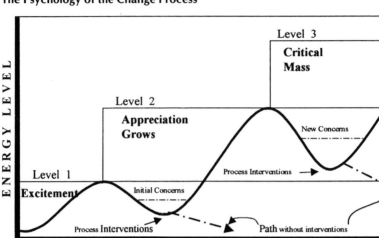

Source: Edward M. Marshall, *Transforming the Way We Work: The Power of the Collaborative Workplace* (New York: AMACOM, 1995). Used with permission.

paradigms" (Marshall 1995, 155). When excited about advocacy participation, members care, seeing opportunities to become more involved and more connected to their work and their organization. It sounds right, yet there is a long way to go. It is important at this point to not have high expectations. Ups and downs will happen. New behaviors may not be understood or appreciated by others. High expectations create the possibility of strong defensive responses and/or disappointments. The new advocate, as a change agent (and participant in the movement):

- Knows that it will not be easy. Comembers may discourage personal change and advocacy participation. They are comfortable with the old way of working—or at least they know it. They may not automatically be understanding or welcoming of new behaviors and expectations. Expect bumpy roads.
- Knows why personal change and advocacy participation are important so he or she explains, explains, explains—and then reexplains "why it is important."
- Actively rehearses, recruits, and reinvents while standing his or her ground appropriately.
- Forgives himself or herself and others when incidents occur.
- Reaches deep inside for the motivation to continue. This is a personal journey, a movement that hopefully others will join. The advocate designs what will happen by his or her attitudes and activities of learning and serving.

Initial Concerns. During the early learning process, concerns will arise regarding the benefits and outcomes of the new behaviors, of being an organizational advocate. Concern brings logical and illogical questions requiring answers, support, and, possibly, intervention by credible others who understand the meaning of sponsorship and what it means to support the process of positive personal change. Asking questions is safe and encouraged in inclusive organizations, but may feel perilous in noninclusive organizations. Without answers and sponsors, staying the course over time is more difficult—but it can happen. Determination is important to accomplishment.

Level 2: Appreciation Grows

Appreciation of possibilities expands with pleasant surprises of success. Previously unsuspected potential for how relationships and processes can work—and how individuals affect what is going on—also creates new growth. This releases new energies and new understanding of what is real and valued. Experimentation and testing will be done using these new energies. As new successes occur, appreciation of the outcomes of these new behaviors continues to grow.

Appreciation of new relationships and expanded potential supports "personal alignment." Alignments are orientations a person develops through considering what is the best way to get things done (making appreciative judgments). How one is "personally aligned" decides whether one is—according to one's own perceptions—using strategies that will achieve personal effectiveness. When someone changes what is personally appreciated, it signals to others something has changed. In the ideal workplace environment, it is possible to be personally aligned and attuned with the organization's needs, and to be personally responsible and accountable at the same time. As noted, working in compromising, self-defeating ways causes high levels of stress. Appreciation of the organization and organizational advocacy participation will be difficult to maintain in a highly stressful environment. When alignment is impossible, many consider the consequences of moving to a work environment where alignment is possible.

New Concerns. New applications of partnering and participation will bring new concerns and questions. The opportunity to become more involved is not without issues and problems. New competencies, skills, and processes are learned and rewarded in an atmosphere that encourages expansion of personal responsibility and accountability. Some will be disturbed by the need to make changes: After all, working together in the old way has worked in the past. Why will it not work in the future?

Level 3: Critical Mass

Deeper involvement in the system a member works in brings opportunities to contribute in new ways; the member learns to understand previously misunderstood things about the system. He or she appreciates his or her own contributions and feels more significant to achieving goals that previously held little interest. Energy and enrollment expand and others notice. The member is seen as being more trusting, trustworthy, and contributive. Other people respond to the new way of working and, once accepted as real, see the benefits. The member's influence on others expands, and potentially the behaviors are "caught" by others, increasing the number of people performing as organizational advocates to a critical mass. At what number is critical mass? Sometimes it is only one—the right one.

Judgment Based on Trust and Wisdom

An organizational movement starts with individual choices to make things different. Like it or not, it becomes an emotional journey. And when emotions get involved, sometimes the journey is unpredictable, even unpleasant. As long as the person wanting the change remains firm in his or her desire— and personal change remains the goal—the movement stays alive. With a focus on a goal, people become leaders of their own processes, motivated to make it happen. This is where a "personal critical mass" occurs. The member is doing what he or she believes. He or she has become a "self-leader." This is where Covey's trustworthiness fostered by good judgment occurs. "Trust is the highest form of human motivation," notes Covey. "It brings out the very best in people" (p. 178). To indicate that one is being trusted enlivens the mature member to make the best possible judgments, and to perform at his or her best.

The two ingredients of judgment based on wisdom, according to Covey, are character and competence. Inside good character is integrity, maturity, and an abundance mentality, all discussed in preceding chapters. Significant to character is that all three ingredients are necessary to the reality of good character; one does not happen without the others. To be immature is to demonstrate that there is less than enough to go around, to believe that one must "take as much as you can" before others do (scarcity mentality®), and to seek to succeed alone instead of with others. The final ingredient of integrity is impossible when maturity and the abundance mentality® are in question. All three ingredients of character, coupled with the ingredients of competence and appreciative judgment, can result in personal contributions to the trustworthiness of the collective organization the member represents on and off the job every day.

Also according to Covey, competence is technical, conceptual, and includes interdependency. Competence includes the ability to perform the technical activities necessary to top performance, an understanding of the concepts as essential to achievement by the individual and the organization, and the willingness to work interdependently—to work with others as partners in accomplishment (see Figure 11.2).

Figure 11.2
Trustworthiness

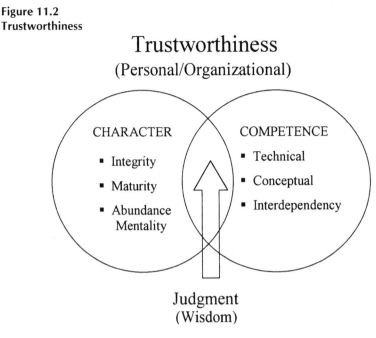

Trustworthiness
(Personal/Organizational)

CHARACTER

- Integrity
- Maturity
- Abundance Mentality

COMPETENCE

- Technical
- Conceptual
- Interdependency

Judgment
(Wisdom)

Source: ©1999 Franklin Covey Co. Used with permission. All rights reserved.

Total Behavior

William Glasser (1984) notes there are *"four separate components of what is always a total behavior."* The four behaviors are (1) doing (active behaviors), (2) thinking (voluntary generation of thoughts), (3) feeling (such as anger and joy), and (4) physiology (body mechanisms involved in all we do, think, and feel) (pp. 46–47). These are powerful components of how we control our lives and how we function on a day-to-day basis. We all make choices, both on and off the job, in how we are going to invest our energy in these four components. The outcome is a total behavior. If I am feeling tired, I do, think, and act like I'm tired. If I dislike someone, it is most likely I think certain thoughts, do certain things, and respond in certain ways.

According to Glasser (1984), "Unless I choose to change what I do, think, or both—and almost always I can—I will not change what I feel, because the total behavior of [what I am doing] makes good sense to me right now" (p. 49). Whatever we do in some way makes good sense at the time we do it, or we wouldn't make the choice to do it. When a person is getting signals that how he or she is behaving isn't working, there is more likely to be a motivation to change. When one ignores the signals of needed change, it is a choice to continue to think and do even though it may be uncomfortable to do so.

Organizations are seeking ways to start positive movements within individuals and groups. Barry Heermann, author and designer of *Building Team Spirit* (1997), is an example of efforts toward creating connected workplace relationships where partnering and teaming become highly productive and contributive, places where thinking, saying, doing, and appreciating happens in ways that make top performance possible. Healthy organizations, with the involvement of their members, address the need for continuous movement toward and maintenance of a more beneficial and desirable workplace. To do so calls for addressing needed changes in individual and group behavior, making it possible for whole system movements to occur.

MEMBER WORKPLACE DESIRES

Three things are common desires of people in the workplace, whatever their status or title. To work in an atmosphere that does not address these desires contributes to the expression and growth of cynicism and feelings of being captive in our jobs—or serves as a catalyst for taking personal learnings to another organization. The common desires of members in the workplace are as follows:

- To be treated with respect and dignity.
- To have their work acknowledged and appreciated.
- To know their work is important to accomplishment for their comembers, their organization, and themselves.

The last two desires are more likely to happen when the first desire occurs consistently. Sometimes it is hard to describe dignity and respect in words, but if it is not happening, we know it. There are messages—explicit or implicit—that occur, creating a sense as to whether respect and dignity are part of the culture of our workplace. Although many management groups may act so, expectations of being treated with respect and dignity are not located solely at the top of our organizations. Nor is the offering and exchange of acknowledgment and appreciation limited to certain levels.

Meeting the desires of members makes it possible for each to experience connection to comembers and the organization. Without addressing these desires, disconnection is inevitable. The top four reasons why members quit either directly or indirectly verify the importance of acknowledging the three desires:

1. Career path is cut off or there is no career development. Future career possibilities give members hope and a sense that striving to do their best may result in future benefits. Formally organized learning creates a sense of being valued by the organization.

2. Lack of respect and support from management and comembers. People do not leave companies, they leave the people in it. Gestures of respect and dignity are

the outcome of active, ongoing support and encouragement being provided by leaders and peers. Effective, respectful partnerships are possible when people are responsive to the needs of others and value those they work with. It is common sense to provide respect and support: No one succeeds alone.

3. Lack of nonmonetary employee acknowledgment, recognition, and awards. Organizations are finding out that appreciation and acknowledgment of the contributions of members are important to individual and organizational achievement. Compensation continues to be low on the list of rewards people seek in the workplace.

4. Inadequate compensation. The provision of fair and equitable pay minimizes feelings of being taken advantage of. Secrecy of compensation levels is not beneficial and creates issues that can be avoided if compensatory policies are discussed openly. Keeping all members informed of financial issues and sharing the benefits of growth and achievement is also a compensation issue that must be visited regularly.

When the three workplace desires are successfully met, people at all levels of the organization are more willing to be alert to issues which may impact the success of their organization (and, ultimately, their own opportunities). The successful company has participants everywhere in the organization who are anticipating the future needs of the organization: They are seeking and creating new markets and meeting the needs of the company's current markets, they are actively developing new services or products, and they are concerned with the treatment of their internal and external customers. By doing so, they contribute to the organizations positioning for future success.

Experiencing the three desires impacts choices being made toward being willing, trusting members who are positive organizational advocates instead of captive, mediocre performers. A sense of connection and ownership becomes possible when members feel they are working in a respectful workplace, an organization in tune with the three desires of members.

Yet it is still essential for members to see their role in activating the three workplace desires. For these desires to become part of organizational culture, members at all levels must participate in the exchange of respect, dignity, and so on. It is essential. Each one is a leader of the moment in establishing and experiencing the reality of the desires in the culture of his or her organization.

The Reasons for New Approaches

There is evidence that new kinds of leaders are looking beyond profit management. They are recognizing that despite belt tightening and downsizing, there are new reasons why ways of leading must change. New approaches to leadership are being called for. There are strong indications that

- A new kind of leadership is needed that recognizes all members contribute to and are essential to organizational success.
- There is a growing emphasis on members inside the organization replacing the traditional focus on shareholders and customers.

- A new recognition is being placed on member knowledge, capability, spirituality, freedom to choose, and deeper participation.
- Decisioning is being moved to the members who more clearly understand how the work is to be done.
- A new consciousness of the exaggerated compensation for those "at the top." There is an expectation of equitable rewards and treatment for all individuals and groups.
- The global reality is expanding our local communities.
- An interest is awakening to the long-term consequences when the organization's mission, customer focus, and human and social bottom lines are ignored.
- Renewed relational and ethnic pride is impacting expectations.
- Issues around community and social responsibility, both in the workplace and in the home community, are becoming more fully discussed.

Integration of these concerns into the workplace reality and the need to stay profitable requires leaders all through the organization to seek new ways to lead. Changes in systems supportive of the new way to work together are essential while at the same time supporting innovative contributions of individuals. As noted by Frohman, "Most organizations today do not foster conditions in which personal initiative can ignite change. While the leaders may defend themselves as wanting, valuing, and rewarding initiative, their behavior actually suggests the opposite" (1997, 47).

It is unfortunate that in the United States we have long been confused by leaders who seek to bring others into the decisioning circle, wondering how it can possibly work. Surely, we think, individualism is the only way to achieve, thus stubbornly sticking to what "I" want and continuing the drive forward on our own. We question whether people who achieve by contributing to another's task, or simply by encouraging others, could make it on their own (Lipman-Blumen 1996, 52). Yet it happens every day, and we don't take note of it.

A well-designed organizational structure has blurred lines, making it possible to get the services and/or products of the company to the customer. There is a hum and flow to how work is accomplished. The formal structure of the company is aligned around the purpose, goals, values, and vision of being an inclusive organization. The structure also sustains the desires of members by contributing to performance and efficiency, eliminating excessive controls and limiting bureaucracy, and actively encouraging partnering across blurred lines of status and title. This calls for utilizing a systems approach that is alert to the proliferation of respect and dignity for all members. The informal structure of the organization also sustains these messages. These messages are initiated because

- At all levels, people know what is expected (and have reasonable, respectful expectations of others).
- People experience the three workplace desires expanding their willingness to coconstruct a beneficial organization.

- A sense of being a member (willing participant) instead of an employee (captive) prevails.
- Members are selected against valid criteria.
- "Different" is not automatically seen as "difficult."
- Everyone is highly trained, capable, and has the opportunity to become experienced.
- Quality products and services are produced.
- People choose personal responsibility and demonstrate performance-based philosophies.
- There is a sense of purpose as well as commitment and ownership of the organizational purpose.
- Empowerment and accountability are spread across the organization and members choose to be empowered and accountable.
- Members are fairly and equitably compensated.
- There is a learning and serving orientation to how work gets done.

Inside the formal structure, the informal structure is made up of the casual and purposeful activities of individuals and groups. This is where an organization is strengthened and sustained. It is the informal structure that responds to leadership by designing and sustaining beneficial interpersonal relationships that grease the wheels of heightened advocacy participation. It is where innovation and creativity reside, merged with yet outside the formal structure that seeks order and the status quo. In many cases the formal structure gets in the way of the informal structure, slowing the intuition and energy of informal networks. When the formal structure attempts to stifle and/or destroy the informal structure, messages of disrespect, lack of appreciation, and lowered motivation are heard. Informal structures are dependent on the consistency and predictability of how systems of the formal structures work. It is the optimal combination of and tension between the formal and informal structures that make it possible for organizations to be at their best.

An example of a long-term, caring organization that seeks the optimal combination is Sauder Woodworking of Archbold, Ohio. Sauder was established in 1934 on the premise that individual creativity and contribution matters. Long before the recent emphasis on workplace spirituality became a focus of consultants and writers, Erie Sauder, grandfather of the current president, Kevin Sauder, started his own business. He was propelled by a vision of two important principles: stewardship and servanthood. His thinking, talking, and doing early on demonstrated the concepts of membership and organizational advocacy. Erie believed in serving God and his fellow man through his work. His service started with building chicken crates for local farmers, moved to building church furniture and eventually to using the scraps from the church furniture to build the occasional table-in-a-box to be assembled in the customer's home. Erie called it "knockdown furniture" (today's "ready to assemble").

In 1975 Maynard and Myrl, Erie's sons, became the president and vice president, respectively, of engineering and research and development. Maynard and Myrl surrounded themselves with a team of people who would carry Erie Sauder's beliefs forward while holding their leaders accountable for the decisions that needed to be made. With the help of this group, the company grew over 4,000 percent in the next twenty-four years, still using the principles of stewardship and servanthood.

In 1999 Kevin Sauder became the president of Sauder Woodworking. He is determined to continue to lead the organization according to promises he made to his grandfather, a story he uses often in advocating the vision and purpose of Sauder. According to Kevin, he promised his grandfather to continue to lead the company with the concepts of stewardship and servanthood and to practice integrity in all business dealings. He feels that a continuously learning environment makes this possible.

The team members at Sauder Woodworking acknowledge that these philosophies are not always easily translated into action. They also know these principles may not be directly traceable to the financial bottom line. Yet they continue to intentionally build a culture of teamwork and service that does impact the human and social bottom lines of the company. A "Team College" is attended by all employees after sixty days with the company, and the company culture emphasizes the need to build its workforce through individual character development and collective vision. Kevin Sauder continues to implement the beliefs of the founder and attributes much of its success to operationalizing Sauder's guiding principles. The business is built on everyone sharing core values that promote the following:

- Respect for all people.
- The right and need of each person to grow and learn.
- Serving the well-being of others.
- Fairness, integrity, and openness in all we do.
- Stewardship and development of human and material resources.
- Work as an important component of a balanced quality of life.
- A community that seeks to include rather than exclude.

Team members will remind one another of what the company represents and how to apply it to their everyday lives, not just at work. Sauder Woodworking members know the company is not perfect; however, everyone is continually working to improve and, as one member said, "at the end of the day, be able to say: 'We did the best job we could today.'"

Although changing or sustaining the culture of an organization requires time and commitment, consistent observable determination can move a company from disrespect to respect and move dignity deficiency to appreciation and respect on the job. Changing the culture of the organization requires the change of meanings and a full understanding of those meanings by everyone. The culture of a respectful organization, sustained through actions that demonstrate the meaningfulness of willing contribution, ownership, and loyalty, activates internal drivers vital to relationships that work within the workplace community. To do so, the individual and the collective organization works together to

- reach a clear understanding of how to work well together.
- construct a performance-based (doing and serving) and purpose-driven (thinking and learning) organization with appropriate goals.
- focus on actively seeking input from all members and know that different viewpoints and different "voices" contribute to coconstructed achievement.
- encourage and sustain learning while serving both the internal and external customer.
- eliminate barriers to performance and achievement.
- construct and take action through a philosophy of partnering.
- work well in informal partnerships that are respectful, no matter your status or title.
- forgive, because "perfect" is understood to be impossible.
- constantly be aware that asking and answering questions are important parts of the process.

The practice of internally marketing what is to be valued is essential. It is necessary to state what is expected and the values that will produce what is expected and then to reward, support, and expect activities and behaviors that will consistently deliver new behaviors. This requires someone (preferably many) be deeply committed to spreading a broad interpretation of what is required. There must be advocates for excellence. These persons need not be located at the top, but lack of top support may increase the frustrations that occur with the slow pace at which a movement or change may occur. The pace increases when the new behaviors are consistently—even automatically—happening in the workplace exchanges of the critical mass.

By design or accident, people every day come to work without making a meaningful contribution. Some will make their workplace worse than when they came to work. For this reason, organizational advocacy includes constructive exchanges of accountability as a vital ingredient to sustaining positive contributions inside organizations over time. Member advocacy by leaders includes the willingness to let go those who are not willing to learn and serve and be responsible and accountable in the changing organization. A leader's positive actions of member advocacy also include making it possible and probable that members

- Carry advocacy messages of what is needed to do their work well to those who can do something about it.
- Make the urgent decisions and carry them through.
- Listen and ask for reasons instead of assuming the worst.
- Do what is beneficial after thinking things through and practicing consultancy.
- Assume justice instead of injustice.

- Influence others without criticism and condemnation.
- Have partnerships that are contributive and valued.
- Recognize that participation at the deepest level is personally rewarding.

The positive actions of organizational advocacy help people to align *for* instead of rebelling *against* a movement through contributing to its design. A contributing advocate has the opportunity to bring his or her beliefs to the table. Proactive organizational advocacy includes actions taken toward the accomplishment of strategic priorities around change.

Organizational members—no matter their level—at the beginning of the new century do not want to work on mindless, unnecessary projects. They want meaningful work with short-term and long-term goals. They want to be able to challenge (question) the status quo and be listened to when they make suggestions. They want on-the-job learning and growth. They want to know they are producing a product or service they can be proud of in an organization they can be proud of. They do not want accountability from people who, for the most part, don't have a clear understanding of what they do, what works, or what matters. They want to work in an environment that is open, integrative, flexible, supportive, and productive. They want to know that they can change their minds and change directions if things aren't working. And they want to do it without having to gain permission to do work in their areas of expertise.

Free to Choose Captivity

Americans are verbal and political about freedom. Yet at the same time, most go to work in controlling, punishing organizations. Every day these participants hang their brains at the door, willingly or unwillingly forfeiting responsibility for how work gets done to those in control for the next eight to ten hours of their day. How can we claim to be free when we are willing captives working in organizations that require dependence and servitude?

Some would struggle with the word "willingly." In some cases, when it is "the only job," or when we have made choices based on the needs of others, we do feel captive. Captivity can be an outcome of things people see as important and not replaceable—and these irreplaceable things are not always the same for different people. For some, it is the salary ("I'm used to this lifestyle"). For others, it is the location ("It is near good fishing," or "The mountains are nearby"), the nature of the work (profession), retirement and its compensation from the company, someone they honor and care about works there, or the like. Something "forces" the choice to remain captive.

Unfortunately, the same people who originally made this choice often are making those around them miserable based on their own choice for captivity. Their attitude reflects entitlement and their energy reflects their feelings of being captive. Even though "forced" to be where they are, they could have chosen to be an organizational advocate instead of a captive. They were free to choose captivity.

Reinventing Organizations

Many organizations will have to reinvent (a pseudonym for reconstruct) themselves in order to even approach becoming a more inclusive, flexible, and integrated organization where learning and serving is possible; that is, a place where members can risk being organizational advocates. The collective organization changes with guidance and stimulation from leaders and grass-roots organizational advocates who are willing and able to promote and support authentic change over the long term, while changing themselves. This may require new members in the leadership group, and most definitely requires leaders to be advocates for the movement and change they are promoting. In doing so, the leader–change agents do several things.

First, they hook everything to an overarching design that is understood by all. An overarching design makes it possible to align the movement, initiatives, systems, and human resource development of the organization to identified outcomes. This overarching design connects all actions and activities of the individual and collective organizational membership, spreading understanding of "why our organization is doing this."

Second, they rethink the role of the core group. Rethinking where knowledge is and how it is used as well as where decisions are routinely made requires organizations to reexamine core-group activities. Could it be the formal and informal leaders are not modeling what is expected of members?

Third, leaders build and maintain a membership with strong, learning members, who include same, diverse, and different people who are fully included and who bring new ideas, talents, skills, and energies into the organization. This is reasonable thinking, yet leaders are still only hiring those just like themselves and doing it without including in the process those the hirees will be working with regularly. It is still common to hire in HR and then send the new employee to the area where he or she will be working. Even in times when the member candidate pool is limited, raise your required qualifications, pay competitively, and wait until you find the right person. It is, in the end, less costly.

Fourth, they make it possible for everyone to learn and apply effective skills while ensuring value-added opportunities to perform. It is a myth that the only meaningful knowledge is located at the leadership level. Members want to learn and share their knowledge, talents, and skills. Instead of going outside to recruit unknown strangers for growth and expansion, the first place to look is inside. Otherwise, what are we telling the people who have vast historical knowledge and experience in our organizations?

Fifth, leaders, together with the membership, coconstruct an organization and a product or service that everyone can trust and be proud of.

Ken Blanchard (1999) says, "Front line people are always honest." Although this may be stretching it a bit, he is right. If you listen and care, you are hearing the truth even though it may be delivered rather crudely. In the preferred workplace, in some cases you hear and see spontaneity and naturalness, hear caring and respectful accountability statements, feel these front line members look you in the eye when they have questions, and initiate "checking" statements. They tell you their concerns, wants, and needs with openness and an expectation that their needs will be met or they will be given an explanation for why those needs can't be met (that is believable and authentic). They perform with integrity because it is reflected from the leadership circle. And they sound and act as if they have a role in making the workplace work well. There is a sense of relaxed urgency. They are willingly and freely involved. They speak the truth with compassion and claim their right to contribute—and they know that personal responsibility is a partner with accountability for everyone. They consciously and consistently measure their work and level of effort against their own standards of involved high performance, instead of comparing themselves to others. In doing so, they create a capacity to accept the uniqueness and offerings of others. They are learning and serving authentically in partnerships and relationships with others, making a difference in both personal and organizational achievement. Both the collective organization and the members have the potential of being at "optimal flow." Organizational advocacy is the way to work here.

Every day when members come to work they are met with a puzzle, one that constantly gets remixed before it is finished and one they want to believe in. Their question: How can we be really a part of constructing an organization of value? Ultimately, things will change when people—one at a time, forming partnerships with others—are participating in meaningful movements toward change. And when things change at work, everything gets better.

Barriers to Organizational Advocacy

Obstacles do exist, explaining why organizational advocacy does not become a total behavior in many organizations. First, people want guarantees that it will bring benefits, and that it will happen immediately. There are no guarantees, because our organizations are "human." Personal responsibility for performance is something people have been denied in the past. Will members choose personal responsibility when those who have told them what to do in the past are now insisting on them making decisions and being accountable for those decisions?

Second, change is often spouted, yet things stay the same. The Insanity Principal says, "I want different results but I keep doing it the same way." Organizational advocacy actions and behaviors will not happen until the holding environment people work in makes them possible. The environment must make the following possible:

1. People feel like members, not employees.
2. People know their work is important and that they are contributing in a meaningful way.
3. People are committed to the success of their organization and value its potential.
4. People are open to and expected to participate in creative partnerships that are valued by the participants.

Third, our organizations are full of people not being held accountable for their lack of contribution and how they treat others. Mediocrity and bullying must stop for advocacy participation to thrive. One cannot take their work to the fullest when positive regard does not—even cannot—exist between members. If only a few members are willing to be organizational advocates, how can the organization itself be seen as having a total behavior of learning and serving?

Fourth, members are often willing but have not been asked to provide what they owe their organization around the theme of learning and serving with integrity. Working with integrity would include (but is certainly not limited to) the following:

- Energy around the purpose of the organization.
- Concern for the reputation of the organization.
- A willingness to nurture strong relationships that are based on maturity, civility, and caring partnerships that are intertwined across every level.
- A desire to serve internal and external customers like they matter.

Fifth, some leaders see their people as expenses instead of assets. When turnover is high and the atmosphere is toxic, they are most likely being treated like expenses. The message is: People are expendable, replaceable, and insignificant. Competition, bullying, blaming, and my-way-or-the-highway thinking prevails. The leaders don't always say it out loud, but people know when they are valued—and when they are not. I don't believe that loyalty is dead. The companies with high turnover are driving people away. Those with skills, knowledge, commitment, abilities, and talents won't stay long under these circumstances. These trusting, energetic, responsible, and accountable people decide early on how long they have to suffer to keep a good resumé and move on. Without members who stick around and value their jobs and the companies they work in, these organizations will struggle. For workplaces that are great to work in, there never will be a shortage of talented, contributing people.

Sixth, they just don't get it. Some companies do not have leader groups who see the linkage between the consideration of all three bottom lines (human, social, and financial) and the successful organization. The financial bottom line is all they consider. This affects how people contribute and how they work together. Any movement that is going on in such an organization is a member movement toward uniting to be safe against the company. This suggests a subversive, get-all-you-can-get, sabotaging movement that is not contributive to the success of the organization or the people working there.

Without an ongoing movement toward conditions where advocacy participation can flourish, a movement toward what Bedeian and Armenakis (1998) call "The Cesspool Syndrome" may occur. This is the organization where the knowledge and talent has fled and all that is left are the "dreck that rises to the top and the sludge that forms below them" (p. 59). This includes organizations that are purposely laying off, cutting to the bone, and causing those they want to keep to flee.

LePine and Van Dyne (1998) verified through their research that being highly satisfied and working where there are favorable group conditions has a strong influence on the involvement and performance of the members. It was also noted that, "When individuals feel their work situation has meaningfulness (perceiving positive return on their physical, cognitive, or emotional energy), they tend to become personally engaged in their work. That is, they more fully employ themselves . . . during task performance" (p. 11). People make choices about how responsible they are going to be in their work. Those choices are an outcome of the environment they work in and their personal perceptions of whether it is beneficial to work hard in the environment where they work. This again verifies that the holding environment of an organization is significant to the amount of effort and engagement members decide to put into their work. This environment is not constructed by a solitary person, it is coconstructed. What each member thinks, says, and does is contributing to the improvement or deterioration of the holding environment. How can it be decided if a movement toward a more inclusive, flexible, efficient, and rewarding environment is needed? Look around... listen around, walk around, ask around, be around, but not in people's faces—let them do their work. You may get a nice surprise. Or you may not.

CLOSING THOUGHTS

The quality of our choices (appreciative judgments) results in what we experience. Our experiences either stimulate or detract from the willingness to participate in the design, construction, and sustainability of the place where we spend most of our energy each day. Over time, those choices and experiences in the workplace provide and shape most memories, thoughts, and feelings about the benefits of contribution and connection, and continue to design our future choices and experiences. This calls for the need to recognize and activate personal activities of organizational advocacy and its practices of personal responsibility, exchanges of accountability, and the willingness to lead in the moment. This is how meaningful contribution happens in successful organizations. A movement starts with one.

Contemplative boundaries have here been designed around the term "organizational advocacy" and what it means to be an advocate in the workplace. Movements of change in our organizations and associations are stimulated by the determination of individuals who hear of and learn new meanings, who rehearse, recruit, and reinvent what is possible and then persuade others of new workplace possibilities.

Learning and serving are not new terms. In recent years, both have been discussed regularly by scholars and leaders. As with all change efforts, organizational advocacy cannot happen without new behaviors (serving), new competencies (learning), and having hope that a new, more appreciative, genuinely accepting and accountable workplace is possible.

The advocacy issues discussed here are also not new, but they have been "borderless" and have not been connected together as the contributive, merging behaviors they are. Previously, names had not been assigned to their existence. For advocacy participation to become part of the way people work together, these behaviors must be noted and rewarded or they will not become part of how work is accomplished. They will remain extra-role behaviors. Self advocacy is a recognition of the need to tell others of our abilities and interests and to promote the abilities and needs of those around us. Leader advocacy, the recognition that supporting our leaders is important, is a much needed member role. Member advocacy, the leader's role of promoting the capabilities of members as an obligation of leadership may be a struggle for many who choose to assume and promote deficiency. Customer advocacy is a role of all members who serve others inside and outside the workplace circle while representing their customers to the company and the company to their customers. Community advocacy and its two communities (workplace and home) expands what community means in organizations. Inclusion advocacy moves beyond diversity to include the understanding that all people are different—some differences are just more obvious. Acceptance and appreciation of difference is beneficial. Inclusion is a choice that must be made. Within these meanings of organizational advocacy are the realization that membership and community are part of the successful workplace of the future.

In the book *Servant Leadership*, published originally in 1977, Robert Greenleaf (1991), in talking about responsibility, says, "At the heart of every constructive action are responsible persons, those who reach out to engage with real life issues where the going may be rough, lay out alternatives (invent some if necessary), assess their relative merits, choose one that accords with virtue and justice—with their own hearts—make the choice knowing they may be wrong and suffer for it, *and bear the risk bravely*" (p. 304, italics orig.). Greenleaf is saying, It starts with me. There is no doubt that to be an organizational advocate in some organizations may be tough—and our jobs are already tough. And it does require more energy because more involvement creates more knowledge and more opportunities. It also brings more risk and more potential for disappointment. Standing firm in the belief in your organization's potential and contributing accordingly means not settling for the ordinary. As noted earlier, organizational advocacy (including advocacy participation) is now seen as an extra-role behavior, going beyond the ordinary performance in our work. Unfortunately, this is an excuse for mediocrity. Eventually, when others also take on these total behaviors, advocacy participation will become the ordinary. It will become the normal way to work. The work being done by organizational advocates will open opportunities for times of invigorating flow—interrupted with times of chaos. Being willing to accept moments of leadership will contribute to designing flow: times that make a difference. Our organizations will remain imperfect and even, at times, ponderous, and the challenges to become better will still necessarily be called for, because their members are human.

In reality, it is all about personal responsibility, distributed leadership, and constructive accountability. What we think, what we say, what we do, and what we appreciate, wherever we are in the workplace, really does matter. As members and organizational advocates, the outcome is we are more able to leave an organization, but we are more willing to stay.

> What I do, how I act;
> what I praise, and what we ridicule;
> what I see as consequential and what I see as inconsequential;
> what I appreciate and what I do not appreciate; and how
> I support the appropriateness of the actions of my
> comembers and our collective organization
> demonstrate our message of encouragement or our "wish" for failure
> of my comembers, customers, and my organization.
> It starts with me.

BIBLIOGRAPHY

Bedeian, Arthur, and Achilles A. Armenakis. (1998). The Cesspool Syndrome: How Dreck Floats to the Top of Declining Organizations. *Academy of Management Executive* 12 (1): 58–67.

Blanchard, Ken. (1999). Presentation given at Lessons in Leadership: Leadership from the Ground Up: Teaming Up for the Year 2000. 17 November, Dallas, Texas.

Bryson, John M., and Barbara C. Crosby. (1992). *Leadership for the Common Good: Tackling Public Problems in a Shared-Power World.* San Francisco: Jossey-Bass.

Covey, Stephen R. (1999). Presentation given at Lessons in Leadership: Leadership from the Ground Up: Teaming Up for the Year 2000. 17 November, Dallas, Texas.

Covey, Stephen R. (1989). *The 7 Habits of Highly Successful People: Powerful Lessons in Pesonal Change.* New York: Simon & Schuster.

DePree, Max. (1997). *Leading Without Power: Finding Hope in Serving Community.* San Francisco: Jossey-Bass.

Fineman, Stephen. (1993). Introduction. *Emotion in Organizations*, edited by Stephen Fineman. Thousand Oaks, Calif.: Sage.

Frohman, Alan L. (1997). Igniting Organizational Change from Below: The Power of Personal Initiative. *Organizational Dynamics* 25 (3): 39–53.

Gibb, Jack R. (1978). *Trust: A New View of Personal and Organizational Development.* Los Angeles: Guild of Tutors Press.

Glasser, William. (1984). *Contrōl Theory: A New Explanation of How We Control Our Lives.* Grand Rapids, Mich.: Harper & Row.

Greenleaf, Robert K. (1991). *Servant Leadership: A Journey into the Nature of Legitimate Power and Greatness.* New York: Paulist Press.

Heermann, Barry. (1997). *Building Team Spirit.* New York: McGraw-Hill.

Heuerman, Tom, and Diane Olson. (1999). Pamphlet 28: Movements. Available <http://www.amorenaturalway.com>.

Kolb, David A. (1988). Integrity, Advanced Professional Development and Learning. In *Executive Integrity: The Search for High Human Values in Organizational Life*, edited by Suresh Srivastra. San Francisco: Jossey-Bass.

LePine, Jeffrey, and Linn Van Dyne. (1998). Predicting Voice Behavior in Work Groups. *Journal of Applied Psychology* 83 (6): 1–15.

Lipman-Blumen, Jean. (1996). *The Connective Edge.* San Francisco: Jossey-Bass.

Marshall, Edward M. (1995). *Transforming the Way We Work: The Power of the Collaborative Workplace.* New York: AMACOM.

McKnight, D. Harrison, Larry L. Cummings, and Norman L. Chervany. (1998). Initial Trust Formation in New Organizational Relationships. *Academy of Management Review* 23 (3): 473–490.

Palmer, Parker J. (1992). Divided No More: A Movement Approach to Educational Reform. *Change Magazine*, March/April.

Schenkel, Susan. (1991). *Giving Away Success: Why Women Get Stuck and What To Do About It.* Rev. ed. New York: Random House.

Spencer, Lyle M., Jr., and Signe M. Spencer. (1993). *Competence at Work: Models for Superior Performance.* New York: John Wiley.

Terkel, Studs. (1974). *Working People Talk about What They Do All Day and How They Feel about What They Do.* New York: Pantheon Books.

Trist, E. (1983). Referent Organizations and the Development of Inter-Organizational Domains. *Human Relations* 36 (3): 269–284.

Urdang, Joan. (2000). *Money Isn't Everything.* Boston: CFO Publishing.

Whitener, Ellen M., Susan E. Brodt, M. Audrey Korsgaard, and Jon M. Werner. (1998). Manager As Initiators of Trust: An Exchange Relationship Framework for Understanding Managerial Trustworthy Behavior. *Academy of Management Review* 23 (3): 513–530.

CONVERSATIONS AND INTERVIEWS

Christian Crews, Toshiba International Corporation.
Jeff Smith, Sauder Furniture.

APPENDIXES

U.S. Environmental Protection Agency— Region 10, Seattle, Washington

LEADERSHIP PHILOSOPHY

We expect all Region 10 employees to be leaders as a vital part of their work performance. Leadership is not a position that someone occupies; it is how we all strive to behave. Leadership is the art of inspiring and motivating ourselves and others to realize our personal and collective best.

ALL EMPLOYEES ARE LEADERS

A leader inspires, prepares, and mobilizes self and others to accomplish organizational goals consistent with Region 10's Vision and Mission. A leader embodies and displays tolerance and respect. A leader values diversity, allows and encourages others to lead, perseveres in the face of adversity and stress, and remains accessible and approachable. A leader has compassion and empathy for others. A leader is dedicated to making personal accountability a reality. A leader is able to appropriately acknowledge and share in the learning from accomplishments and mistakes. A leader is committed to personal and professional growth for both self and others. A leader is self-confident, but appropriately humble.

IN REGION 10, WE WILL STRIVE TO BE:

Committed to the Organization:

Participating in the development and communication of a shared vision. Being dedicated to making the Vision, Mission, and Goals of Region 10 a reality.

Representing the organization in a positive light in external and internal contacts. Constantly seeking ways to improve the organization and build the organization's capacity by challenging conventional wisdom and the status.

Clearly understanding, championing, and employing diversity in all its forms, while being aware of own personal biases.

Leading and/or actively participating in designing and managing change projects (a change/new-idea champion).

Acting on the understanding that we are here to serve, not to be served.

Able to Translate the Vision and Mission into Action:

Integrating a variety of related and competing information to arrive at a path which will achieve Region 10's Vision, Mission, and Goals.

Ensuring that short term actions are consistent with the long term Vision and Mission.

Fitting current tasks into the "Big Picture."

Considering the impact of decisions on all related issues before taking action.

A Learning Advocate for Self and Others:

Constantly engaging in both the giving and receiving of information with the common goal of increasing our overall effectiveness.

Actively listening and using constructive questions to promote mutual learning.

Utilizing mentoring and coaching techniques to help others learn and grow.

Seeking ongoing, continuous learning opportunities and realizing that learning occurs through both education and action.

Knowing the limits of own knowledge, understanding own biases and asking for help when necessary.

A Decision Maker:

Collecting, organizing, analyzing, and synthesizing data to reach sound conclusions based on less-than-complete information and data.

Making principled, timely decisions—even when unpopular.

Assuming accountability for own actions and decisions.

Exhibiting sound judgment.

Promoting debate, actively questioning, and listening in order to learn about the issues.

Anticipating the consequences and effects of decisions and actions.

Taking reasonable, well-thought-out (wise) risks when necessary.

An Effective Communicator:

Respecting the ideas and contributions of others, seeking to understand and clearly acknowledge such information.

Assessing the impact of communications and matching the impact with the intent.

Asking for feedback.

Clearly, frequently, honestly, effectively, and openly communicating Region 10's Vision, Mission, and Goals.

Preparing and delivering organized and coherent written and oral communications. Using the techniques of active listening and questioning in order to understand others' perspectives and to promote dialog.

Knowing and being aware of our own strengths, weaknesses, and biases.

Addressing conflicts through effective diagnosis and resolution.

Being forthright, sincere, and authentic in all situations.

A Relationship Builder:

Communicating effectively and resolving conflicts.

Looking for commonalities in purpose by actively seeking and sharing information.

Building and maintaining strong internal and external working relationships.

Allowing self and others to develop a good balance between personal life and work life.

Being accessible and fair in all dealings.

Treating others with respect, trust, sincerity, and empathy.

Not gossiping.

Dealing directly and openly with others in all situations.

Trusting self and others.

Avoiding stereotyping.

Seeking interactions with diverse groups within and outside the organization.

A Model for Others:

Exemplifying the skills, knowledge, behaviors and leadership qualities expected of all Region 10 employees.

Exemplifying integrity and maintaining high ethical standards.

Being enthusiastic about the work.

Maintaining awareness of our own behavior and its impact on others.

Acting in a forthright, sincere, and authentic manner during all interactions.

Being personally accountable for and following through on all personal actions, words, commitments, and decisions.

Having the courage and commitment to take wise risks.

A Problem Solver:

Understanding how a current issue fits into the larger organizational whole, and how problems affect the larger system.

Seeking practical, environmentally effective solutions within the constraints of the law.

Actively seeking and sharing information to effectively and quickly solve the current issue in accordance with Region 10's stated vision, mission and goals.

Looking for win–win solutions.

Using creativity to solve problems and understanding how creativity enhances problem solving abilities.

Respecting diverse opinions and using all points of view to resolve issues.

Using a full range of problem solving tools and techniques.

A Motivator:

Recognizing the contributions of others with respect to the success of the project and the organization.

Understanding motivation and using it to maximize personal and group task performance and problem solving.

Recognizing and rewarding desirable behavior, particularly intangible behaviors such as perseverance, enthusiasm, integrity, and honesty.

Empowering self and others to make and be accountable for decisions, actions, and ideas.

Defining issues and the associated work in order to enable focused progress.

A Collaborator:

Understanding and practicing the principles of high performance teaming.

Developing, negotiating, and evaluating working relationship agreements between team members, individuals, and regional partners.

Empowering self and others to make and be accountable for decisions, actions, and ideas.

Recognizing that each team member is a vital part of the working whole and that no staff person can do it alone.

Working effectively across organizational and programmatic boundaries.

Articulating how involved parties relate to each other, to tasks, and to issues.

Supporting designated decision makers.

Utilizing performance planning and assessment principles for performance evaluations of all team members.

Encouraging others to contribute while listening with an open mind.

Clearly understanding, championing, and employing diversity in all its forms.

Designing and conducting meetings which encourage participation and which achieve stated objectives efficiently.

Setting up projects by clearly identifying issue statements, practical outcome statements, key deliverables, role definitions, evaluation processes, design constraints, work plans, and time lines.

In addition, individuals in positions of authority must show leadership by:

Creating an organizational climate and culture in which employees realize their potential while contributing to the organization's Vision and Mission.

Understanding that the people of Region 10 are their most valuable resource/asset and acting accordingly.

Having a strong commitment to diversity by designing a relevant recruiting process, maintaining a network of resources, and developing and using culturally neutral hiring criteria.

Understanding motivation and using it to maximize personal and group task performance and problem solving.

Promoting and providing support for organizational learning, individual learning, growth, and risk taking.

Intentionally negotiating and agreeing upon levels of empowerment, and delegating the appropriate amounts of authority.

Providing an organizational structure that supports the goals and objectives of Region 10.

Appropriately exercising the appropriate balance of formal and informal authority when making decisions.

Providing and actively seeking direct, timely, and non-judgmental feedback.

Objectively assessing organizational strengths and opportunities for improvement through the use of organizational health assessment tools, and actively involving others in the organization in the assessment.

Designing and implementing communication systems that insure that diverse viewpoints are represented.

Using priority setting processes and appropriate criteria to balance competing organizational interests.

Being aware of the changing organizational environment, and developing strategies accordingly.

Evaluating and diagnosing external conditions and designing organizational responses appropriately.

Re-directing the organization when necessary to adapt to the changing environment.

————————————— B

Incompetence
http://amorenaturalway.com

Pamphlet 32

Tom Heuerman with Diane Olson

On the surface the senior vice president was a nice man, as many incompetent people are. He took secretaries to lunch. He even took retired secretaries to lunch. He strove to please his bosses over the years. He complied his way up the organization's chain of command for 30 years and reaped the rewards of his inauthentic behavior. He spoke often of his entitlement to his position and the rewards the job title bestowed upon him.

He was politically correct and said the right things. He had the modal personality of the industrial era: docile and subdued in the presence of the powerful but aggressive and even abusive toward competitors and subordinates. He pursued his agenda with little regard for good judgment, common sense, or long term benefit to the organization. This modal personality is familiar to anyone who works in an organization: the mindless, oblivious, and obedient bureaucrats and technicians who do what they are told and refuse to think for themselves.

The senior vice president didn't work hard. He never came in early or stayed late. He left early on Fridays and came in late on Mondays. He went to all the industry conferences and mingled with others like himself. He assigned all meaningful work to others, and he reacted to their efforts by playing the devil's advocate, as he called his hostile challenges. The people who worked for him considered his devil's advocacy a defense that masked his ignorance of the particular project.

Good people labored to correct the errors of the senior vice president and accomplished the real work of the division. The company president nominated the senior vice president for an industry award. Division managers got a copy of the letter. Page after page extolled the achievements of the senior vice president. When the managers read the letter of recommendation aloud, their laughter reverberated off the walls. The senior vice president had no involvement with any of the accomplishments. If anything his arrogance combined with his ignorance were obstacles. He went off and accepted his award and hung it on his office wall. He never said a word to his colleagues about the event or the award.

He made bad choices and poor decisions and didn't deal with the real problems around him. He denied them, ignored them, and blamed them on others. Denial allowed him to become indifferent, to ignore what happened right in front of him, and to create and sustain a false version of reality. As a result, small issues became big ones. On several occasions unions tried to organize groups of employees under his direction. Others were blamed and lost their jobs or were transferred to other positions in the company. No one ever held the senior vice president accountable for his many failures.

On occasion the helpless senior vice president brought a smart, talented, and aggressive manager into the division to deal with problems he had created. Inevitably the capable manager solved the problems and began to gain broader acknowledgment. This recognition foreshadowed trouble for the successful manager. With appreciation came betrayal by the senior vice president and ultimate demotion, transfer, or departure from the organization. The senior vice president was not as nice as he appeared to be.

The senior vice president didn't want to deal with human emotions. The Cartesian split worked well for him, at least in the short term. He separated his mind from his body and drove his emotions underground and denied the feelings of others. He once said, in a panic, that he did not want to deal with emotions. Those who expressed themselves authentically were punished, neutralized, marginalized, or driven from the enterprise. Often this scapegoating took the form of fabricated personality conflicts that allowed the truth put forth by the courageous truth teller to be discounted.

The senior vice president had no idea of how others felt about him or the humiliation he caused scores of other people. He was unaware of how his poor decisions hurt the larger organization. As a result, he never apologized for his many mistakes. He was unable to say the simple words: I'm sorry, let's fix it. The refusal to apologize was a denial of his impact on others. His bosses colluded with him in this mindlessness. They knew for a dozen years that he was incompetent. Then reorganized around him, shifted him from one executive to another, and made excuses for him. After all, they had promoted him.

Finally after many good people left the organization the senior vice president was removed from his position. By then most departments had been assigned to other divisions. He was kept on the payroll for a couple of years and contributed nothing. He was then given a lucrative early retirement package.

Through the years the senior vice president seemed so confident. Often people wondered aloud if he had any clue as to how incompetent he really was. New research suggests he probably didn't.

Psychologists David Dunning and Justin Kruger reported that the incompetent lack metacognition: the ability to judge their own judgments. They found in a series of studies that incompetence often accompanies overconfidence. Asked to rate their skill on tests of logic, humor, and grammar, subjects who scored lowest were also the most likely to grossly overestimate their performance. The incompetent need much help just to realize they are incompetent.

Becoming competent is another matter entirely.

Organizational dynamics collude with the incompetence that pervades many organizations. Nice people don't want to hurt others or deal with embarrassment or emotional issues. So important issues, like incompetence, don't get talked about. Every senior and middle manager in the company knew the senior vice president was inept. But his ineptitude was not talked about except between trusted colleagues over lunch.

Research by the Gallup organization found that people don't quit companies; they quit their manager or supervisor. How many talented people quit the company because of this senior vice president? How much discretionary energy was withheld by employees because of this person? How many talented people have left your organization (or checked out mentally) because of incompetent managers and supervisors? What are the systemic, long term impacts of these departures? Can any organization afford to lose good people today because of the incompetence of others? Good leaders know the answers to these questions and, as good leaders do, they take appropriate action.

NOTE

From the Internet newsletter by Tom Heuerman, Ph.D., and Diane Olson, Ph.D., located at http://amorenaturalway.com. Reprinted with permission. All rights reserved.

Recommended Reading

Carr-Ruffino, Norma. (1999). *Diversity Success Strategies*. Boston: Butterworth-Heinemann.

DePree, Max. (1997). *Leading Without Power: Finding Hope in Serving Community*. San Francisco: Jossey-Bass.

Dixon, Nancy M. (2000). *Common Knowledge: How Companies Thrive by Sharing What They Know*. Boston: Harvard Business School Press.

Graham, Pauline, ed. (1995). *Mary Parker Follett—Prophet of Management: A Celebration of Writings from the 1920s*. Boston: Harvard Business School Press.

Hawley, Jack. (1993). *Reawakening the Spirit in Work*. New York: Simon & Schuster.

Jaworski, Joseph. (1996). *Synchronicity: The Inner Path of Leadership*. San Francisco: Berrett-Koehler.

Lewin, Roger, and Birute Regine. (1999). *The Soul at Work: Listen . . . Respond . . . Let Go*. New York: Simon & Schuster.

Namie, Gary, and Ruth Namie. (1999). *BullyProof Yourself at Work!* Benicia, Calif.: DoubleDoc Press.

Oakley, Ed, and Doug Krug. (1991). *Enlightened Leadership: Getting to the Heart of Change*. New York: Simon & Schuster.

Pinchot, Gifford, and Ron Pellman. (1999). *Intrapreneuring in Action: A Handbook for Business Innovation*. San Francisco: Berrett Kohler.

Ryback, David. (1998). *Putting Emotional Intelligence to Work: Successful Leadership Is More Than IQ*. Boston: Butterworth-Heinemann.

Scott, Gini Graham. (2000). *Work With Me! Resolving Everyday Conflict in Your Organization.* Palo Alto, Calif.: Davies-Black.

Terey, Tom. (2000). *22 Keys to Creating a Meaningful Workplace.* Holbrook, Mass.: Adams Media Corporation.

Index

ABOUT THE AUTHOR

Jane Galloway Seiling is founder of Business Performance Group, Lima, Ohio. An associate of the Taos Institute, Cleveland, she holds an advanced degree in organizational development, has taught at the college level, authored an award-winning book on membership organizations, and is in wide demand as a speaker and lecturer. Her current research interest is focused on constructive accountability™.